100 Hikes / Travel Guide

Oregon Coast
& Coast Range

William L. Sullivan

Navillus Press
Eugene

Seaside's Promenade (Hike #6).

Published by the Navillus Press
1958 Onyx Street
Eugene, Oregon 97403

Printed in USA

Cover: Boardman State Park (Hike #89). Inset: *Kalmiopsis leachiana* (Hike #94). Spine: North Head Lighthouse (Hike #2). Back cover: Stout Grove (Hike #96). Frontispiece: Dead Man's Cove in Fort Canby State Park (Hike #3).

SAFETY CONSIDERATIONS: Many of the trails in this book pass through Wilderness and remote country where hikers are exposed to unavoidable risks. On any hike, the weather may change suddenly. The fact that a hike is included in this book, or that it may be rated as easy, does not necessarily mean it will be safe or easy for you. Prepare yourself with proper equipment and outdoor skills, and you will be able to enjoy these hikes with confidence.

Every effort has been made to assure the accuracy of the information in this book. Local agencies have reviewed the Travel Guide sections. The author has hiked all 100 of the featured trails, and the trails' administrative agencies have reviewed the maps and text. Nonetheless, construction, logging, and storm damage may cause changes. Corrections and updates are welcome, and may be sent in care of the publisher.

KEY:

Great for kids
Near campground
Lighthouse
Tidepools
Birdwatching
Old-growth forest
Backpackable
Closed seasonally

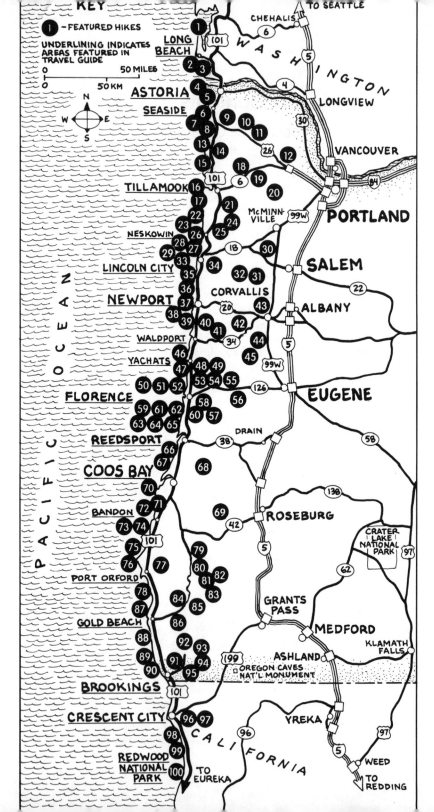

KEY:

🛶 Great for kids   📷 Lighthouse   🌲 Old-growth forest
🏕 Near campground   ☆ Tidepools   🎒 Backpackable
   🐦 Birdwatching   ❄ Closed seasonally

5

Introduction

Welcome to Oregon's Coast—363 miles of cliff-edged capes, public beaches, wild rivers, sand dunes, rainforest, and coastal mountains. Many of the top attractions are within easy reach of Highway 101, but others are accessible only by trail. To help you explore both the civilized and the wild parts of Oregon's spectacular shore, this book blends 2 kinds of guides— a detailed Travel Guide for touring by car and a complete Trail Guide for planning adventures on foot.

HOW TO USE THIS BOOK

The Travel Guide

The book is divided into 18 sections from Washington's Long Beach south to California's Redwood National Park. Each section begins with a Travel Guide that includes an overview map and a description of the area's car-accessible attractions. Both the map and the text are annotated with symbols (described below), identifying campgrounds, lighthouses, museums, and other popular destinations. Here too are tips for bicycling, birdwatching, kayaking, canoeing, and horseback riding.

The overview maps show major Highway 101 mileposts, so it's easy to use the Travel Guide as a highway logbook. As you drive from one area to the next, simply flip forward or backward through the book to the next Travel Guide map.

The Trail Guide

Following each Travel Guide section are descriptions of that area's hiking trails. To help you choose a hike, symbols in the upper right-hand corner of each hike's heading identify trail features. For example, 64 of the hikes have symbols recommending them as best trails for hikers with children, 36 hikes begin near campgrounds, and 44 pass through old-growth forest. Travelers with limited physical abilities need not miss the fun, because a list at the back of the book describes 42 paved, planked, or graveled trails accessible to everyone.

A hike's difficulty is rated in the boldface listing at the start of each entry. **Easy** hikes are generally less than 3 miles round-trip and gain less than 500 feet of elevation. These short hikes usually only require a couple of hours to complete.

Trips rated as **Moderate** range from about 3 to 5 miles round-trip and may gain 1000 feet of elevation. Some moderate hikes require a bit of route-finding —for example, following posts through sand dunes.

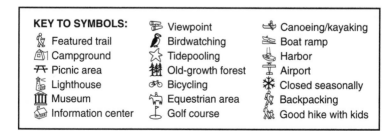

KEY TO SYMBOLS:		
Featured trail	Viewpoint	Canoeing/kayaking
Campground	Birdwatching	Boat ramp
Picnic area	Tidepooling	Harbor
Lighthouse	Old-growth forest	Airport
Museum	Bicycling	Closed seasonally
Information center	Equestrian area	Backpacking
	Golf course	Good hike with kids

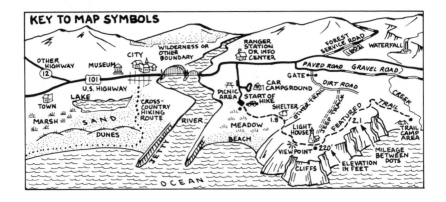

Difficult hikes vary from 4 to 8 miles round-trip and may gain 2000 feet of elevation. Hikers need to be in good condition and will need to take several rest stops. **Very Difficult** hikes demand top physical condition, with a strong heart and strong knees. These challenging hikes are 8 to 15 miles round-trip and may gain 3000 feet or more. Backpackers can break these hikes into easier 2- or 3-day trips.

In general, the trails of the Oregon's Coast and Coast Range are less demanding than trails in more mountainous parts of the state. As a result, this book uses a slightly easier rating scale than other volumes of the Oregon 100 Hikes series.

Distances are given in round-trip mileage, except for those trails where a car shuttle is recommended. Then the hike's mileage is listed as one-way only.

Elevation gains tell much about the difficulty of a hike. Those who puff climbing a few flights of stairs may consider even 500 feet of elevation a strenuous climb, and should watch this listing carefully. Note that the figures are for each hike's *cumulative* elevation gain, adding all the uphill portions, even those on the return trip.

Only a few trails are **closed seasonally** by snow or to protect wildlife. Identified by a snowflake symbol, these hikes include a boldface listing with the approximate dates the trail remains open. Note, however, that winter storms may temporarily close any of the trails in this book, or may cause icy or muddy conditions that make trails unsafe even when they are technically open. Hikers must rely on their own caution and good judgment.

TIPS FOR TRAVELERS

Climate

Marine air keeps Oregon's coastal climate mild, with generally snowless winters and cool summers. Summertime visitors are often puzzled to find a strip of **fog** hugging the beach while skies are sunny just a few miles inland. As a rule, expect fog on the Coast when high temperatures in Portland and Eugene hit the 90s. One way to avoid the problem is to visit the beach in spring or fall. The crowds are thinner then and there are a surprising number of warm, sunny days—especially in March, April, and May.

Summers also bring **north winds**, which is why cagey hikers and bicyclists trek from north to south, keeping the wind at their backs. Even if you're just planning a picnic on the beach, it's often wise to choose a spot on the south side of a headland's cliff, where you'll be sheltered from the north wind. In summer, north winds generally bring good weather while south winds presage a storm.

Winters are less predictable. Storms come from all angles, pounding 20- and 30-foot waves against the shore. Snow is truly rare, but much of the Coast's 60 to 100 inches of annual rainfall hit in winter—at times, almost horizontally. High surf strips the beaches of most of their sand. The sand is then washed offshore by wave action and returned neatly in the spring like a batch of fresh laundry. Despite winter's wet and wild ways, the season has its charms. Beachcombing and wave watching, for example, are at their peak after a winter storm.

Beach Rules

Oregon's 260 miles of beaches are entirely open to the public. Visitors should keep in mind a number of rules, some of which are simply good advice:

- Never turn your back on the ocean. Unusually large "sneaker waves" can sweep up the beach at any time.
- Don't swim. The Alaska Current chills the water year-round to a numbing, goosebump-and-blue-fingernail temperature. The more serious hazard, however, is the undertow—the pull of withdrawing waves. Only wade on shallow beaches, and only then if the tide is coming in. Never wade on the north side of headlands, where the southbound current is deflected to sea.
- Pick up a free tide table at a local store or visitor center. Oregon's share of the Pacific Ocean rises and falls about 8 feet twice a day, so high and low tides are about 6 hours apart.

Several other beach rules have the force of law:

- Fires are banned in driftwood piles or against large logs.
- Climbing on most offshore rocks is banned to protect sea birds.
- Harassing seals, sea lions, and other marine mammals is forbidden. Do not approach a cute, "abandoned" seal pup. It is resting while its mother hunts for food, and human contact may simply scare the mother away.
- Collecting tidepool life is banned in most places, even for educational or food purposes. Do not pry starfish or other living animals from the rocks. Do not poke sea anemones or walk on top of living mussel beds. Do not leave rocks overturned, because the animals on both the top and the bottom are adapted to their positions and will die if left in a new habitat.
- Cars are banned on 67% of the state's beaches and are restricted seasonally on another 7%. Where driving is allowed, the speed limit is 30 miles per hour and all the usual highway regulations apply.
- Shooting firearms on the beach is illegal.

Campgrounds on the Oregon Coast

More than 70 public campgrounds along the Coast and in the Coast Range make camping an attractive option. In general, the 19 state park campgrounds here are somewhat larger, more popular, and more expensive, but they offer hot showers when other public camps generally do not. Some of the smaller public campgrounds do not even have running water, and in this case are usually free.

While most coastal county parks are also fairly primitive, 3 exceptions are not only large but have hot showers: Barview (north of Tillamook), Windy Cove (at Winchester Bay, south of Reedsport), and Bastendorff Beach (west of Coos Bay). All 3 are near major river mouths.

Virtually all Forest Service, county, BLM, and state forest campgrounds are open only in summer. By contrast, state park campgrounds stay open from April through October, and a few stay open year-round (Fort Stevens, Nehalem Bay, Cape Lookout, Devils Lake, Beverly Beach, Beachside, Washburne, Honeyman, Bullards Beach, Harris Beach, and Loeb). At many of these state parks, tenters can escape rain by renting a yurt, a circular, framed tent with a plywood floor.

State park campsite reservations for the summer season from the Memorial Day weekend to the Labor Day weekend are accepted for 10 of the most popular parks (Fort Canby, Fort Stevens, Cape Lookout, Devils Lake, Beverly Beach, South Beach, Beachside, Honeyman, Sunset Bay, and Harris Beach). To place a state park reservation, call 800-452-5687 during business hours at least 3 days in advance, but not more than 11 months in advance. Expect a nonrefundable $6 service charge in addition to the campsite fee (about $17 for a tent, $22 for a full RV hook-up, and $27 for a yurt). For instant confirmation, pay by VISA or Mastercard. When paying by check, book at least 21 days in advance.

The Coast's many private campgrounds cater primarily to RVs and typically offer less secluded sites. However, private campgrounds provide hot showers and other services.

Bicycling the Oregon Coast

The 367-mile Oregon Coast Bike Route from the Washington border to California is one of the most scenic bicycling tours anywhere. Although most of the route follows Highway 101, where car and truck traffic is a serious distraction, the highway shoulder has been widened to 3 feet in most places. Detours on backroads avoid 6 of the least scenic parts of Highway 101. The route is not flat, gaining a cumulative total of 16,000 feet—mostly in climbs across coastal headlands. Bicyclists typically complete the tour in 6 to 8 days. Virtually all pedalers travel from north to south, both to catch the prevailing north winds of summer and to see the much better views on the ocean side of the road.

Hiker/biker campsites are available at major state parks (Fort Stevens, Nehalem Bay, Cape Lookout, Devils Lake, Beverly Beach, South Beach, Washburne, Honeyman, Tugman, Sunset Bay, Bullards each, Cape Blanco, Humbug Mountain, and Harris Beach). For a couple of dollars a night, these grassy, shared areas are a great way to meet other non-motorized travelers and get hot showers. For a free Oregon Coast Bike Route map with touring tips, write the Oregon Dept. of Transportation, Transportation Bldg., Salem, OR 97310, or call 503-378-3432.

TIPS FOR HIKERS

Safety on the Trail

Hikers on the Oregon Coast are rarely more than an hour's walk from civilization. On these trails you're more likely to worry about running out of film than running into wilderness hazards. In fact, the biggest danger is leaving the trail to explore coastal cliffs. Each year slippery rocks and unpredictable waves claim an amateur rock scrambler or two.

Drinking Water. Day hikers should bring all the water they will need— roughly a quart per person. A microscopic paramecium, *Giardia*, has forever

Foredune at South Beach State Park.

changed the old custom of dipping a drink from every brook. The symptoms of "beaver fever," debilitating nausea and diarrhea, commence a week or 2 after ingesting *Giardia*. If you're backpacking, bring an approved water filtration pump or boil your water 5 minutes.

Proper Equipment. Even on the tamest hike a surprise storm or a wrong turn can suddenly make the gear you carry very important. Bring a pack with the 10 essentials: a warm, water-repellent coat, drinking water, extra food, a knife, sun screen, a fire starter, a first aid kit, a flashlight, a map, and a compass.

Parking Permits

Hikers should expect to pay a day-use parking fee of about $3 per car at 31 of the featured trails in this book, including every trail in the Siskiyou National Forest (Hikes #79-81, 83-86, and 92-95) and every trail in the Oregon Dunes National Recreation Area (Hikes#60-67). Details are in the text or at the trailhead.

Rules on the Trail

As our trails become more heavily used, rules of trail etiquette become stricter. Please pick no flowers, leave no litter, and do not shortcut switchbacks.

For backpackers, low-impact camping was once merely a courtesy, but is on the verge of becoming a requirement, both to protect the landscape and to preserve a sense of solitude for others. The most important rules:

- Camp out of sight of trails, at least 100 feet from lakes or streams.
- Build no campfire. Cook on a backpacking stove.
- Wash 100 feet from any lake or stream.
- Camp on duff, rock, or sand—never on meadow vegetation.
- Pack out garbage—don't burn or bury it.

Eight of the featured hikes pass through designated Wilderness Areas. Additional restrictions apply only to these areas, with violations subject to fines:

- Mechanized equipment (including bicycles) is prohibited.
- Groups in Wilderness Areas must be no larger than 12.

Astoria's 1885 Flavel House.

The Oregon Coast Trail

The Coast's ultimate hiking challenge, the Oregon Coast Trail (OCT) follows beaches, trails, and highways for over 360 miles from the Washington border to California. Bits and pieces of this ambitious route have been constructed since work began in 1972, but large gaps remain. Only about 70 miles of the route consist of actual trail. Scattered up and down the Coast, these completed trail segments are popular for day hikes, and are all described in detail in this book. Another 200 miles of the OCT simply follows public beaches. About 90 miles still follows the shoulder of Highway 101 and other roads.

The northernmost portion of the OCT is the most popular, stretching 61.6 miles from the Columbia River to Tillamook Bay. This segment is interrupted by roads 5 times, for a total of 8.9 miles. To take this trek, connect hikes #4, 6, 7, 8, 13, 14, and 15, following the beach or Highway 101 between featured hikes. To arrange for a skiff to ferry you across Nehalem Bay, call Jetty Fisheries at 503-368-5746..

Many long-range OCT hikers simply stop for the night in motels. Others tent in campgrounds. Camping on the beach itself is banned in state parks and within most city limits, but it's an acceptable option elsewhere, as long as you pitch your tent out of sight of houses, and well above the flotsam that marks the night's high tide limit. Bring a good pad, because sand is rock hard.

A free OCT map with detailed descriptions of the entire 360-mile route is available by writing to the Trails Coordinator, Oregon State Parks, 1115 Commercial St. NE, Salem, OR 97310.

FOR MORE INFORMATION

Visitor Bureaus

Many of the best things to do and see on the Oregon Coast are free—or nearly free—so this book focuses on noncommercial tourist destinations. Local visitor bureaus are glad to provide information about restaurants, motels, and commercial attractions. Here are the telephone numbers to call for this free service.

Astoria, 503-325-6311	Long Beach, 800-451-2542
Bandon, 541-347-9616	Nehalem Bay, 503-368-5100
Brookings, 541-46-3181	Newport, 800-262-7844
Cannon Beach, 503-436-2623	Pacific City, 503-965-6161
Coos Bay, 800-824-8486	Port Orford, 541-332-8055
Crescent City, 707-464-3174	Reedsport, 800-247-2155
Depoe Bay, 541-765-2889	Rockaway Beach, 503-355-8108
Florence, 541-997-3128	Seaside, 800-444-6740
Garibaldi, 503-322-0301	Tillamook, 503-842-7525
Gold Beach, 800-525-2334	Waldport, 541-563-2133
Lincoln City, 800-452-2151	Yachats, 541-547-3530

Trail Management Agencies

If you'd like to check trail conditions, call directly to the trails' administrative agencies, listed below along with the hikes for which they manage trails.

Hike	Managing Agency
42	Alsea Ranger District—541-487-5811
96-98, 100	California State Parks—707-445-6547
92-95	Chetco Ranger District—541-469-2196
69	Coos Bay District BLM—541-756-0100
56	Eugene District BLM—541-683-6600
30, 44	Finley Wildlife Refuge—541-757-7236
83-86	Gold Beach Ranger District—541-247-6651
24, 25, 27, 28, 34	Hebo Ranger District—503-392-3161
51-55, 57, 58	Mapleton Ranger District—541-902-8526
29	The Nature Conservancy—503-228-9561
60-65, 67	Oregon Dunes Nat'l Recreation Area—541-271-3611
50, 59, 66, 68, 70, 72-76, 78, 87, 88-91	OR State Parks (Coos Bay Region)—541-269-9410
4-9, 12-17, 22, 23, 26, 33, 35-39, 46	OR State Parks (Tillamook Region)—503-842--5501
43	Oregon State University Forest—541-737-4434
77, 79-82	Powers Ranger District—541-439-3011
99	Redwood Na'l Park—707-464-6101 (voice or TDD)
31, 32, 37, 45	Salem District BLM—503-375-5646
71	South Slough Estuarine Reserve—541-888-5558
21	Tillamook County Parks—503-965-5001
10,11, 18, 19	Tillamook State Forest—503-357-2191
40, 41, 47-49	Waldport Ranger District—541-563-3211
20	Washington County Parks—503-648-8715
1-3	Washington State Parks—206-753-5755

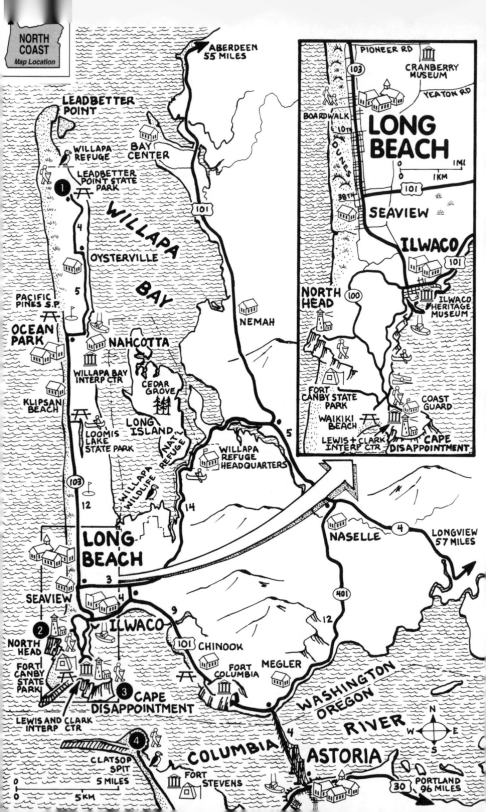

Cape Disappointment.

LONG BEACH

One of the world's longest beaches—a 28-mile strip of wave-packed sand—lines Southern Washington's Long Beach peninsula. Since the 1880s the broad beach backed with low, grassy dunes has drawn summer visitors, largely from Portland. But the beach is just one of the area's charms. Inland is vast Willapa Bay, teeming with bird life. To the south are the rugged headlands of Fort Canby State Park, with two scenic lighthouses guarding the Columbia River bar. And the peninsula is dotted with quaint villages of Victorian vintage.

Boardwalk

The city of Long Beach bustles with a carnival atmosphere in summer. The best place to see and be seen is on the Boardwalk, a half-mile raised promenade meandering along the grassy beachfront dunes from the Bolstad Street beach access (two blocks west from the town's only traffic light on Highway 101) to the 10th Street beach access. The beach itself is tops for kite-flying, volleyball, and sand castling. Cars are allowed on most of the area beaches (with a 25 mph limit), but are banned April 15 to Labor Day from the Boardwalk south to the 38th Street beach access in Seaview.

Fort Canby State Park

At the mouth of the Columbia River, this erstwhile artillery base has become one of Washington's most popular state parks. Short trails lead to picturesque lighthouses on the headlands at North Head (Hike #2) and Cape Disappointment (Hike #3). The park's campground has 250 sites, open year-round. For a picnic, try Waikiki Beach, set in a scenic cove beside Cape Disappointment's cliffs. Or drive 1.5 miles past the picnic area to the North Jetty's viewing platform and watch waves roll through the Columbia River bar.

Lewis and Clark Interpretive Center

Also in Fort Canby State Park, this museum is perched atop the bluff where Lewis and Clark first saw the Pacific Ocean. Exhibits feature the explorers' two-and-a-half-year trek across the continent, as well as the history of Cape Disappointment's lighthouse, artillery bunkers, and Coast Guard station. Free admission includes a 15-minute slide show. The center is open daily 10-5.

Ilwaco

When fishing cutbacks staggered this port's fishing and charter boat industry, the town began capitalizing on its rich history, touting its Victorian houses and historical murals on downtown buildings. The Ilwaco Heritage Museum, a block off Highway 101 on 115 SE Lake Street, features displays of Native American culture, a pioneer village complete with trading post, and a restored railway depot housing a 50-foot model of the Long Beach peninsula's "Clamshell Railroad" as it looked in 1920. The museum's winter hours are Mon-Sat 10-4; summer hours are Mon-Sat 9-5 and Sun 12-4.

Nahcotta and Oysterville

Discovery of rich oyster beds in the bay made Oysterville a boomtown in 1854 and county seat from 1855 to 1893. Today the community is on the National Register of Historic Places, with a schoolhouse, cemetery, and restored church worth a visit. The Long Beach peninsula's "Clamshell Railroad" never reached Oysterville, instead stopping at Nahcotta, 4 miles to the south. Nahcotta is a livelier burg, and a good place to buy oysters or stroll the harbor's dock. A replica oysterhouse on Nahcotta's bayfront houses the Willapa Bay Interpretive Center, with exhibits of the bay's historic oyster industry. Admission is free to the museum, open 10-3 Fri-Sun from May 1 to October 30.

Cranberry Museum 🏛

By a cranberry bog, this museum features the history, machinery, and products of the local cranberry industry. At the north end of Long Beach turn right on Pioneer Road. Open daily in summer, and weekends in winter.

Fort Columbia State Park

This restored 1903 fort overlooking the Columbia River has been converted to a picnic area, museum, and youth hostel. An interpretive center in the former officers' barracks (open Wed-Sun 9-5 May through October) features exhibits on the area's early exploration, coastal artillery, and Chinook tribal culture. The former commander's house (open summer weekends 10-5) is a museum of early military life. Artillery bunkers are also open for exploration.

Willapa National Wildlife Refuge

The huge shallow estuaries of Willapa Bay draw tens of thousands of geese, ducks, and shorebirds during the fall and spring migrations. The wildlife refuge protects several areas of the bay, open to hikers and birdwatchers. The Leadbetter Point area is described in Hike #1. Long Island, with its old-growth cedar grove, is accessible only by boat; launch at the refuge headquarters on Highway 101. The freshwater marshes at the southern end of the bay have some of the best birding. Parking areas are located at the end of Yeaton Road (east from Long Beach) and Jeldness Road (off Highway 101, 6 miles south of the refuge headquarters). Unleashed dogs are banned, hunting and clamming are restricted, and camping and fires are only permitted in 5 primitive campgrounds on Long Island.

1   Leadbetter Point

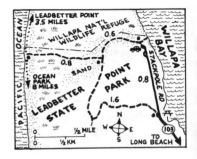

Easy
3.8-mile loop
No elevation gain

At Leadbetter Point State Park, near the sandy tip of the Long Beach Peninsula, a short hike leads from the vast tidal mudflats of Willapa Bay to a rarely visited stretch of ocean beach. Visit in fall, winter, or spring for the best chance at spotting some of the 202 bird species of the Willapa Wildlife Refuge.

To find the park from Long Beach, drive 12 miles north on Highway 103 to Ocean Park. Turn right at a blinking light and follow "Highway 103 North" signs for 9 more miles, zigzagging through Nahcotta and Oysterville to Stackpole Road. Continue to a parking area at road's end.

The sandy trail at the tip of the parking area heads both left and right. The right fork leads 100 yards to Willapa Bay's beach—worth a visit. Then take the trail's other fork toward the ocean. As you hike west the forest downshifts from spruce and alders to shore pines. After 0.6 mile, turn right at a brown post in the sand and continue 0.8 mile to the windswept strand. As far as the eye can see, nothing disturbs the minimalist setting of sand, surf, and grassy foredune.

To make a loop on your return, hike back 0.8 mile and turn right at the brown post in the sand. This path heads south amid sparse pines 0.7 mile, then turns left at a "Loop" sign through shadier spruce woods nearly a mile to Stackpole Road. Walk left along the road 0.8 mile to your car.

Other Hiking Options

For a difficult hike in the wildlife refuge, walk to the ocean and go north 3.5 miles to Leadbetter Point's tip. At low tide you can continue 3 miles south along the bayshore beach to your car. Camping, fires, and unleashed dogs are taboo.

Ocean shore at Leadbetter Point State Park.

Easy (to North Head)
0.6 mile round-trip
No elevation gain

Easy (to McKenzie Head))
3.4 miles round-trip
400 feet elevation gain

The first of these two easy trails ambles 0.3 mile to a picturesque lighthouse above the surf-pounded cliffs of North Head. The second, longer option traverses a dramatic clifftop forest through Fort Canby State Park to an abandoned gun battery and bunker atop McKenzie Head. Since both paths begin at the same trailhead, it's only a 4-mile hike to do both.

From Astoria, take the bridge to Washington and follow Highway 101 west 11 miles to Ilwaco. In the center of town continue straight toward Fort Canby on Loop 100. After 2.2 miles turn right on North Head Lighthouse Road for 0.6 mile. At the sign "Park Hours 6:30am to Dusk" pull into a gravel lot on the left.

The lighthouse trail is the leftmost road, closed by a chain. (The road to the right leads to the light keeper's house, now state park residences closed to visitors.) The lighthouse trail soon emerges from spruce woods to a headland meadow of big white cow parsnip blooms, pink wild roses, curly wild cucumber vines, and blue salal berries. At the short trail's end, views extend from the Columbia River jetties to Long Beach.

The white-towered lighthouse was built in 1898 when the nearby Cape Disappointment lighthouse proved insufficient to prevent a rash of shipwrecks near the hazardous Columbia River mouth. Since 1937 the tower's light comes from an electric beacon. Mounted 192 feet above sea level, the light is visible 20 miles to sea.

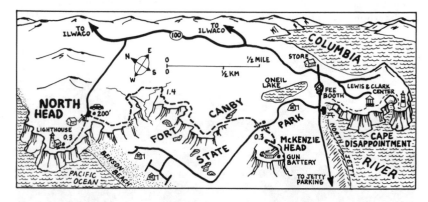

North Head lighthouse.   Opposite: McKenzie Head gun mount.

To try the trail to McKenzie Head, return to the parking lot where you left your car. Notice a brown hiker-symbol sign beside a set of wooden steps leading downhill. Follow this path across a meadow and into a stand of old-growth Sitka spruce, some 6 feet thick. A clifftop viewpoint overlooks the state park campground on the forested plain below. Incredibly, the entire plain did not exist in Lewis and Clark's day; their 1805 sketches show the ocean extending all the way to this cliff and McKenzie Head. Construction of the Columbia River North Jetty backed up a square mile of sand flats that have since sprouted forest.

The trail has a few muddy spots where it dips through a rainforest glen. After 1.4 miles the path drops to an alder forest on the flatlands and reaches the paved entrance road to the campground. Across the road and 50 yards to the left is a big gravel pullout marking the trail up McKenzie Head itself. This broad path climbs 0.3 mile to a huge concrete terrace with a circular pit—all that remains of the artillery that once kept watch over the mouth of the Columbia until after World War II. Today the view still extends south as far as Tillamook Head.

Follow a tunnel-like hallway 100 yards through a monstrous concrete bunker to find a second, matching artillery terrace on the other side of McKenzie Head. Then return as you came.

Other Hiking Options

If you're camped at Fort Canby State Park—or if you want a shortcut to McKenzie Head—you can start this hike from the campground entrance road. Look for a brown hiker-symbol sign by the roadside 0.5 mile past the park's entrance booth.

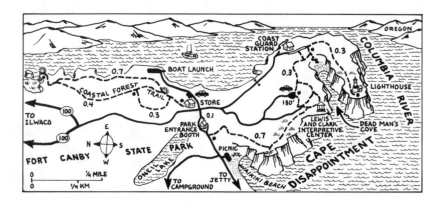

3 Cape Disappointment 🚶📷🗼🏠🌲

Easy (to lighthouse)
1.2 miles round-trip
200 feet elevation gain

Easy (Coastal Forest Trail)
1.4-mile loop
100 feet elevation gain

Lewis and Clark first sighted the Pacific Ocean from this dramatic headland after trekking nearly 4000 miles. Today the hike is shorter and features a number of relatively recent attractions—a lighthouse, an artillery bunker, and a museum.

For the easiest route to the major attractions of "Cape D" (as the locals call this headland), start at the Lewis and Clark Interpretive Center. To get there from Astoria, take Highway 101 across the bridge and north 11 miles to Ilwaco. In the center of town go straight on Loop 100, following signs for Fort Canby State Park for 3.3 miles. At the crossroads for the park's boat launch go straight another half mile to the Interpretive Center's parking turnaround.

At the far right end of the parking lot, climb the broad trail 300 yards to the Interpretive Center. On the way you'll pass the concrete ruins of Battery Harvey Allen, a bunker that housed three 6-inch guns from 1906 until after World War II. Explorable passageways and storage rooms remain. The Interpretive Center itself features walk-through exhibits of photographs, artifacts, and journal entries from the Lewis and Clark expedition. Admission is free. Museum hours are 10am to 5pm daily.

When you leave the museum, turn right and keep to the right to find the trail to the Cape Disappointment lighthouse. After 0.3 mile there's a confusion of trails above Dead Man's Cove, a picturesque chasm in the cape's cliffs. Keep right and go down the stairs to visit the cove's hidden beach, where a shipwreck casualty once washed ashore. Then reclimb the stairs and turn right on a concrete pathway that skirts the cove's clifftops for 0.3 mile to the lighthouse.

Oldest lighthouse still in use on the West Coast, this 53-foot brick tower was built in 1856 to cut the appalling frequency of shipwrecks on the Columbia River bar, the "Graveyard of the Pacific." In fact, the ship that originally tried to bring materials for a lighthouse here in 1853 sank with its cargo 2 miles offshore.

When you return to your car you'll only have logged 1.2 miles. If this sounds short for a day's outing, you might prefer starting the hike at a trailhead that's slightly farther away, where you'll also be able to add a loop through old-growth woods on the Coastal Forest Trail.

To find this alternate trailhead, drive as to the Lewis and Clark Interpretive Center, but when you reach the crossroads in Fort Canby State Park turn left toward the boat launch and immediately park beside a bait and tackle shop. From here the lighthouse is a 1.4-mile hike away. Simply cross the road, walk along the campground entrance road past the fee booth, and turn left at a sign marking the "Discovery Trail." This path climbs steeply to fabulous headland meadows full of browsing deer and viewpoints before delivering you to the Lewis and Clark Interpretive Center and the usual route to the lighthouse.

If you still have energy after your lighthouse hike, spend it on a 1.4-mile loop along the Coastal Forest Trail. This path begins behind the phone booth outside the little bait and tackle shop where you parked the car. Keep right at all junctions to explore this jungly rainforest's trail network. Along the way, 10-foot-thick spruces twist contorted branches above a carpet of wild lily-of-the-valley. Viewpoints overlook tidal flats, sea stacks, and the Ilwaco boat channel.

View from Coastal Forest Trail.   Opposite: Deer on Cape Disappointment.

The lightship Columbia *on Astoria's waterfront.*

ASTORIA

Astoria clings like a barnacle to the Oregon shore of the Columbia River. Wars, boomtimes, and countless winter storms have overswept this tenacious town since 1811, when fur traders built it as the first permanent American settlement west of the Mississippi.

Today the Astoria area not only has its share of beach diversions, but it's also rich with historic forts, Victorian mansions, and the lore of seafarers.

Columbia River Maritime Museum

In this first-rate interpretive center on Astoria's waterfront at 18th Street you can spin the wheel of a replica steamboat pilothouse, walk the bridge of a World War II destroyer, or watch the rotating prisms of a lighthouse's lens. Other exhibits feature shipwrecks, fishing, and early exploration. Hours are 9:30-5 daily. Admission includes a boarding pass to the adjacent lightship *Columbia*, which served as a floating lighthouse at the river's entrance until 1979.

Fort Clatsop National Memorial

The log stockade where explorers Lewis and Clark spent the rainy winter of 1805-06 is gone, but this replica on the original site captures the spirit of those early years. Admission includes a slide show in an extensive interpretive center. In summer, rangers in frontier garb demonstrate sewing moccasins, splitting shakes, dipping candles, and carving dugout canoes. Take Highway 101 south of Astoria 4 miles and follow signs. Open 8-5 daily; in summer, 8-6.

Fort Stevens State Park

This former military reservation at the mouth of the Columbia River is home to the largest campground in the Oregon park system, with 605 sites (summer reservations accepted). There's lots to do for day visitors too: hike or swim at

Coffenbury Lake, explore the 9-mile network of flat, paved bike paths, lounge on a broad beach beside the rusting remains of the 1906 *Peter Iredale* shipwreck, watch for birds on Clatsop Spit, or climb on the Columbia River's south jetty. See hikes #4 and #5 for details.

Military Museum

Also in Fort Stevens State Park, a historic area includes concrete bunkers and gun batteries dating to the Civil War. A Japanese submarine shelled this installation in World War II. Today a military museum displays uniforms, armaments, and photos of the fort's history. Hours are 10-6 daily from June through September and 10-4 Wed-Sun the rest of the year. Civil War reenactments, blacksmithing demonstrations, walking tours of underground bunkers, and tours of the park from the back of a 1950s Army truck are available in summer. Drive Highway 101 south of Astoria 6 miles and follow signs to Fort Stevens Historic Area.

Oregon Coast Trail

The Columbia River's South Jetty marks the start of a 360-mile hiking route along beaches, footpaths, and highway shoulders to California. The 61.6-mile section from the Columbia to Tillamook Bay is the most popular, because it has the fewest interruptions. For details see page 12.

Flavel House

Captain George Flavel built this turreted, Queen Anne-style Astoria mansion in 1885, having profited handsomely from the dangers of river navigation as a Columbia River bar pilot. Elegantly restored and furnished with period antiques, the house at 441 8th Street is open daily 11-5 from May 1 to September 30, and 11-4 the rest of the year.

Uppertown Firefighters' Museum

Built in 1896 for a brewery, this brick building near Astoria's waterfront at 30th and Highway 30 served as a firehouse for 32 years. Now it's an entertaining museum with fire equipment dating to the 1870s and photos of Astoria's most devastating fires. Only open Fri-Sun. Hours are 10-5 from May through September; otherwise 11-4.

Astoria Column

The best viewpoint of Astoria is atop this 125-foot tower on Astoria's Coxcomb Hill. Also look for Mt. St. Helens to the east and Saddle Mountain (Hike #9) to the south. Built by the Great Northern Railroad in 1926 as part of a series of monuments to promote travel, the tower is patterned after Trajan's Column in Rome, but is painted with scenes from Astoria's history. Turn off Highway 30 at 16th Street and follow signs.

Astoria Waterfront

Ocean freighters, tugboats, and yachts tie up along Astoria's busy deepwater docks. Park at the public dock at 6th Street and walk a mile east along the railroad tracks to the Columbia River Maritime Museum at 18th Street. Or walk the other direction and end up at the old-timey Union Steam Baths at 285 W. Marine Drive (almost under the bridge) for a sauna in the tradition of Astoria's Finnish immigrants.

Fort Astoria

Astoria's original 1811 trading outpost, built by order of fur tycoon John Jacob Astor, has been partially restored and is open free at 15th and Exchange. In summer from 11-3:30, volunteers give talks describing the fort's checkered past.

Clatsop County Heritage Museum

A block east of Fort Astoria, the restored 1910 former Astoria City Hall houses exhibits of Astoria's native tribal culture, ethnic immigrants, shipwrecks, and art. The museum at 1618 Exchange is open daily 10-5 from May through September and 11-4 the rest of the year.

Youngs River Falls

A short trail in a woodsy county park leads to the base of the Youngs River's 50-foot cascade. Drive 8 miles south of Astoria on Highway 202 toward Jewell and turn right at a sign for Youngs River Falls for 3.7 miles to a large, unmarked parking area at a hairpin curve.

Cullaby Lake

Two county parks offer boating and picnicking at this long lake off Highway 101 north of Seaside 8 miles. Cullaby Park is a waterskiing center with a huge picnic area. Waterskiers are banned from the northern end of the lake, where little Carnahan Park offers a less hectic dock and a woodsy lakeside path.

Replica of Lewis and Clark's Fort Clatsop.

Cape Disappointment from Clatsop Spit. *Opposite:* Peter Iredale *shipwreck.*

4   Clatsop Spit

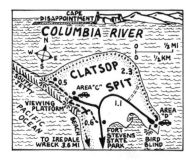

Easy (jetty exploration)
2 miles round-trip
No elevation gain

Moderate (around Clatsop Spit)
4.5-mile loop
No elevation gain

Huge waves explode against the boulders of the South Jetty, where the Columbia River meets the ocean. Freighters steam nearby. Brown pelicans circle offshore, then suddenly dive beak-first in the hopes of spearing fish.

To find the jetty, drive Highway 101 south of Astoria 4 miles (or north of Seaside 9 miles), and turn west at a sign for Fort Stevens State Park. Follow park signs 4.9 miles, turn left at the day-use entrance (just past the camping entrance), and drive past Battery Russell a total of 3.9 miles to a fork. To the left is parking area C at the jetty. To the right the road continues to parking area D.

For a quick hike, keep left to area C and walk to a 20-foot viewing platform overlooking the South Jetty. From here you can either explore left along the jetty a few hundred yards to the broad ocean beach, or hike right 0.5 mile along the sandy margin of the jetty to the Columbia River's calmer beach. On the way watch for the tracks of large brown California ground squirrels.

For a more strenuous 4.5-mile loop—and the best birdwatching—it's best to park at area D instead. A short boardwalk here leads to a bird blind overlooking the tidal flats of Trestle Bay.

Start the loop at the far left corner of parking area D, where a trail leads through the dunes to the Columbia River beach. Walk left along the beach 2.3 miles to the jetty, turn left along the jetty's sandy margin half a mile to the viewing platform, and continue 0.3 mile along the jetty's top to an X-crossing of abandoned roads—now big, sandy trails. Turn left 0.3 mile to the paved road. Then follow the road's shoulder left 1.1 miles back to parking area D.

5 Fort Stevens

Easy (around Coffenbury Lake)
2.4-mile loop
No elevation gain

Moderate (from Battery Russell)
5.3-mile loop
100 feet elevation gain

This 11-square-mile state park between the Columbia River and the Pacific has lots of attractions: the largest campground in Oregon, a popular picnic area at swimmable Coffenbury Lake, a collection of old artillery bunkers, and a broad beach with the rusting remains of the *Peter Iredale* shipwreck.

All of these features are connected by a well-maintained trail network through the flat coastal forest. About half the paths are paved for cyclists. Described here are two hiking loops on quieter footpaths.

If you're bringing kids, head for the 2.4-mile loop around Coffenbury Lake. Drive Highway 101 south of Astoria 4 miles (or north of Seaside 9 miles), turn west at a sign for Fort Stevens State Park, follow park signs 4.6 miles, and turn left into the campground entrance. Stop at the fee booth to buy a parking permit, then continue straight 0.3 mile and park at picnic area A on the left.

There's a dock and boat launch here (no motors allowed). There's also a sandy beach where the swimming is much less cold and windy than in the ocean.

Cross the beach to find the lakeshore trail, a path lined with alder, spruce, sword ferns, and elderberry. After 1.2 miles, turn left for 150 yards on an old road that dikes the marshy end of the lake. Then keep left again on the continuation of the trail around the lake to your car.

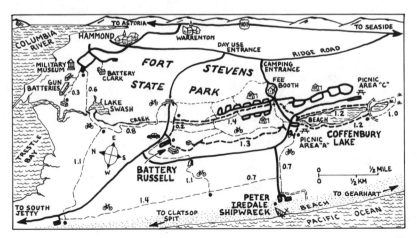

If you wish the hike were a little longer—or if you want to avoid Coffenbury Lake's parking fee—start at historic Battery Russell instead. To find this trail-head, drive straight past the park's campground entrance 0.3 mile to the day use entrance and turn left for a mile to a big parking loop on the left.

Drive around the loop to an exhibit board describing the history of Battery Russell, which guarded the Columbia River entrance from 1904 to 1944. Climb a staircase and walk the length of the enormous concrete bunker to a wide sandy trail. Then keep right at all junctions. The trail follows the crest of an ancient sand dune overgrown with a forest of spruce, shore pines, Scotch broom, and wild lily-of-the-valley.

When you reach a paved bike path, duck right through a tunnel under a road and turn left to picnic area A at the start of the Coffenbury Lake loop trail. After hiking around the lake, you could return the way you came, but why not try a different route through the campground? Walk along the road or one of several trails 0.3 mile from picnic area A to the start of the campground's nature trail. You'll find it behind campsite B5T, a stone's throw from the fee booth. Then go straight at all junctions for a mile, following a sluggish creek. You'll have joined a paved bike path by the time you reach a sign pointing left to Battery Russell and the final 0.2 mile to your car.

Other Hiking Options

Paved paths extend to the *Iredale* wreck and the Military Museum (see map), but these are more fun on a bike than on foot. For a bit of adventure, explore the 1-mile loop trail around a marsh at the far south end of Coffenbury Lake.

Coffenbury Lake.

Nehalem Bay from Neahkahnie Mountain.

SEASIDE

Founded as a tourist goal in 1873 by railroad king Ben Holladay, Seaside today revels in its carnival mood. Arcades and snack shops line the "Million-Dollar Walk," the section of Broadway between Highway 101 and the beach.

But this part of the Oregon Coast is not all glitz. Just south of Seaside lies the upscale village of Cannon Beach and some of the state's most beautiful natural scenery—cliff-edged islands and quiet, forest-draped capes.

Estuary Park

The lazy Necanicum River meanders the length of Seaside, from grassy-banked urban picnic areas to pristine tide flats. For an introduction to this river, visit Estuary Park at 1900 N. Holladay St., where an observation platform with interpretive signs overlooks the estuary. Open daily, dawn to dusk.

Quatat Marine Park

A good place to launch a canoe exploration of the Necanicum River, this downtown Seaside park encompasses four blocks of riverfront between First and A Avenues, with picnic tables, paved paths, and a boat dock. Canoe, kayak, paddleboat, and "bumper boat" rentals are nearby.

Seaside Museum and Historical Society

Indian artifacts, antique firefighting equipment, and the history of Seaside's beach tourism are featured in this museum at 570 Necanicum Drive. Hours are 10:30-4:30 weekends and 9-4:30 weekdays. Admission includes a visit next door to one of Seaside's original beach cottages, fully restored.

Klootchy Creek County Park

The world's biggest Sitka spruce, a 216-foot-tall, 18-foot-thick giant perhaps 700 years old, stands in this 25-acre day-use forest park, 2 miles west of Highway 101 on Highway 26.

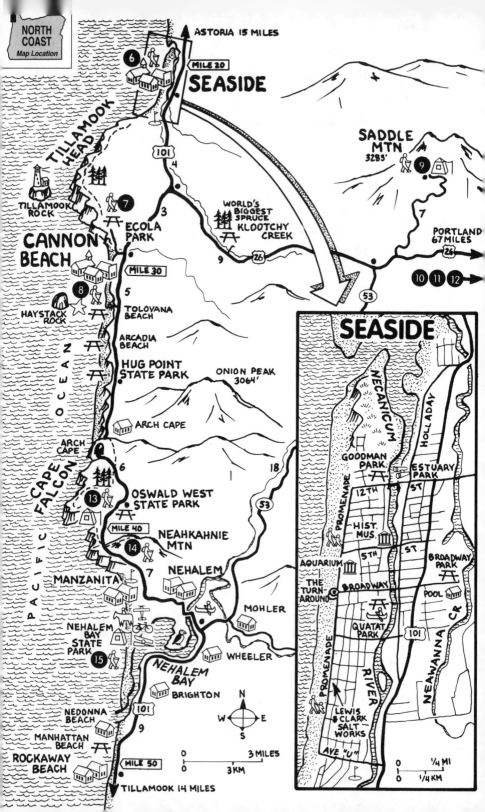

Ecola State Park

Postcards of the Oregon Coast often wear photos of this park on the cliffy capes of Tillamook Head, where waves roll in against craggy islands and secluded beaches. An 8-mile trail extends the length of the park (see Hike #7), but some of the best viewpoints are accessible by car at the Ecola and Indian Beach picnic areas. A day-use fee is charged May through September. Take Highway 101 to the north exit for Cannon Beach and follow signs.

Cannon Beach

Seaside's sophisticated cousin, this coastal village has an artistic flair. The area was named for a cannon that washed ashore from a shipwrecked war sloop. Now the town is packed with coffee houses, bungalows, art galleries, and shops. The community Coaster Theater, downtown on Hemlock Street, stages plays Fri-Sat at 8pm from February to December. Haystack Rock, a massive 235-foot island in Cannon Beach's surf, is off-limits as a refuge for seabirds, but the tidepools at its base are fun to explore. See Hike #8.

Hug Point State Park

A short path descends from this picnic area south of Cannon Beach to 3 scenic sandy coves protected from the wind. A lacy 12-foot waterfall spills into the northernmost cove beside 2 explorable caves. Nearby, an early 20th-century wagon road chipped out around the cliffs is accessible at low tide. See Hike #8.

Oswald West State Park

Wheelbarrows are provided at Highway 101 for campers to wheel their tents a quarter mile to 36 campsites in an old-growth rainforest beside Short Sand Beach's dramatic cove, a spot also popular with surfers and picnickers. Trails from here lead to the tip of Cape Falcon and the viewpoint atop Neahkahnie Mountain (Hikes #13 and #14). The park is named for the clever Oregon governor who, in 1913, had the state's beaches declared public highways to help assure that the beaches would never fall into private developers' hands.

Nehalem Bay State Park

On the sandy peninsula below Neahkahnie Mountain's rugged shoulder, this park has a 291-site campground (summer reservations accepted), a separate 17-site equestrian camp with corrals and horse trails, a 2400-foot airstrip, and a 1.5-mile paved bike loop. HIke #15 describes a walking tour of the sand spit's beaches.

Nehalem Bay Estuary

Kayaking and birdwatching are popular on this sheltered, forest-rimmed estuary. Wheeler and Nehalem Bay State Park have boat ramps, but the most popular put-in is beside Highway 101, just across the Nehalem River bridge from the quaint old town of Nehalem.

Excursion Train

If you'd rather see Nehalem Bay by rail, the Fun Run excursion train departs Garibaldi (9 miles north of Tillamook) weekends at 10 and 1:30 from late May to early October. The 3-hour round-trip tour stops at Rockaway Beach and Wheeler en route to the Nehalem Bay Winery's tasting rooms in Mohler.

6   Seaside Promenade

Easy
3.5-mile loop
No elevation gain

As a beach resort, Seaside might be said to date to the winter of 1805-06, when explorers Lewis and Clark established a salt-making camp on the beach here, perhaps partly to escape the inland gloom of Fort Clatsop, where it rained all but 12 days of their 106-day stay.

Later Seaside became known as the end of the railroad. In the 1920s Portland families would board at 6:30am, bring breakfast to eat on the train, pile out for a few hours on the beach, and return in the evening—all for a 25-cent fare.

Today tourists crowd the "Million-Dollar Walk," a strip of arcades, fast-food joints, and gift shops lining Broadway.

Away from the neon lights, however, Seaside's old-fashioned charm and picturesque natural setting have survived. The 3.5-mile walking loop described here visits the best of old Seaside: the beachfront Promenade, the Necanicum River estuary, and the cottage-lined back streets.

From Highway 101, follow "City Center" signs to Broadway and turn west 6 crowded blocks to the Turnaround, a small circular plaza overlooking the beach. Pull into the city parking lot on the left .

In the middle of the Turnaround a statue of Lewis and Clark portrays Lewis solemnly surveying the volleyball courts, kites, and lifeguard chairs on the busy beach. Clark looks aside to the 1000-foot cliffs of Tillamook Head (Hike #7), at the southern end of the beach.

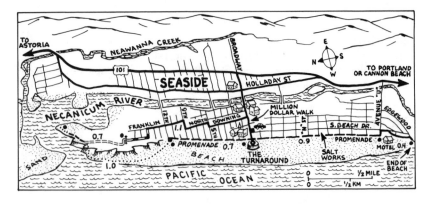

Tillamook Head from Seaside. Opposite: Lewis and Clark statue at the Turnaround.

Turn right at the statue and head north along the Promenade, a 15-foot-wide paved walkway between the grassy foredunes and downtown's hotels. After 2 blocks you'll pass the Seaside Aquarium, a vintage 1937 tourist draw boasting a "hideous octopus." Soon after, the hotels give way to rustic cottages from the 1910s and 20s.

When the Promenade ends at 12th Avenue, walk left through the dunes and continue north along an increasingly quiet stretch of beach. From here you can see the lighthouse on Tillamook Rock, an island off the tip of Tillamook Head. After 0.6 mile the beach peters out beside the mouth of the Necanicum River. Scramble up a 20-foot bluff and continue along its grassy crest 0.4 mile north to the rock-strewn tip of a peninsula in the Necanicum estuary—a surprisingly wild, unspoiled spot so close to town.

To return by a different route, follow the top of the grassy bluff back into town. The path, lined with wild strawberries, becomes a sandy road and then a gravel street that turns left to meet paved Franklin Avenue. Turn right on Franklin and follow it past cute beach bungalows toward town. On the way you'll have to jog half a block to the right at Ninth and Fifth Streets, so you'll end up on North Downing when you reach the Million-Dollar Walk. On your left at Broadway is Seaside Town Center, an indoor collection of 20 shops with a carousel. On your right is the route back to your car.

Other Hiking Options

The Promenade also extends south of the Turnaround 0.9 mile to a blocky motel just a few blocks from the Necanicum riverbank site of railroad czar Ben Holladay's original Seaside House (1873-1882). On this part of the Promenade you'll pass a sign pointing half a block left to a miniature park with a replica of the stone oven Lewis and Clark built in 1806 to boil buckets of seawater for salt.

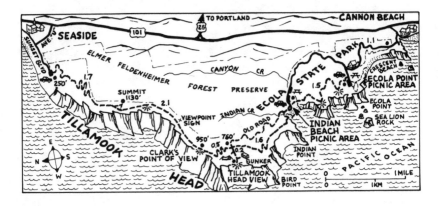

7   Tillamook Head   

Easy (to Indian Beach)
3 miles round-trip
400 feet elevation gain

Moderate (to WW II bunker)
3.9-mile loop
900 feet elevation gain

Difficult (shuttle across headland)
6.1 miles one-way
1350 feet elevation gain

Tillamook Head rises 1000 feet from the ocean, with jagged capes and rocky islands. The Lewis and Clark expedition crossed this formidable headland in 1806 to buy the blubber of a stranded whale from Indians at Cannon Beach. At a viewpoint along the way Clark marveled, "I behold the grandest and most pleasing prospect which my eyes ever surveyed."

The headland itself is a tilted remnant of a massive, 15-million-year-old Columbia River basalt flow. Incredibly, the lava welled up near Idaho, flooded down the Columbia Gorge, and spread along the seashore to this point.

From Highway 101, take the north exit for Cannon Beach and follow Ecola State Park signs, keeping right for 2 miles to the park's entrance booth. A day-use parking fee is collected here.

For an easy 3-mile hike suitable for hikers with children, turn left at the booth and head for the Ecola Point picnic area. As you enter the parking lot, look for a trail sign on the right. The path that starts here climbs around scenic bluffs past 3 of the best viewpoints in the park. After 1.5 miles a left-hand spur drops to Indian Beach, a good turnaround point. Ahead, the main trail bridges Canyon Creek to the Indian Beach picnic area parking lot.

For the longer hikes at Tillamook Head it's best to start at the Indian Beach picnic area. Drive there by turning right at the park's fee booth for 1.5 miles.

This trail starts as an old gated road on the right-hand side of the Indian Beach parking turnaround. After 100 yards keep left at a fork and climb, steeply at times, through old-growth spruce and alder woods. Wear boots, as there are a few slippery spots. After 1.6 miles turn left at a trail crossing near a primitive camping area for backpackers. In another 0.2 mile you'll find the dark, 6-room concrete bunker, which housed a radar installation in World War II. Just beyond is a cliff-edge viewpoint, breathtakingly high above a rugged rock beach.

A mile to sea is Tillamook Rock, a bleak island with a lighthouse that operated from 1881 to 1957. Nicknamed "Terrible Tilly," the light was repeatedly over-swept by winter storms that dashed water, rocks, and fish into the lantern room 150 feet above normal sea level. The island was finally bought by funereal entrepreneurs who bring in urns of cremated remains by helicopter.

If you're ready to return on the loop to your car, simply walk back from the viewpoint to the trail crossing and go straight on a well-graded abandoned road 1.6 miles downhill to the Indian Beach parking lot.

If you'd prefer to continue across Tillamook Head, turn left at the trail crossing. The trail climbs and dips for 2.6 miles, passing some excellent views north (including the one Clark liked), before switchbacking down through the forest 1.7 miles to a parking area at the end of Sunset Boulevard.

To find this northern trailhead, drive Highway 101 to Seaside's southernmost traffic signal, turn west on Avenue U for two blocks and turn left on Edgewood (which becomes Sunset) for 1.2 miles to road's end.

Other Hiking Options

You can skip Ecola State Park's day-use fee by starting at the Sunset Boulevard trailhead and hiking the other way across Tillamook Head. Another free option is to park in Cannon Beach. Simply walk north along the park's entrance road 0.9 mile, and take a well-marked but little-used 1.1-mile trail to the entrance booth. This path often parallels the road, but passes 2 nice viewpoints.

Clark's view from Tillamook Head.   Opposite: Tillamook Rock lighthouse.

8 Cannon Beach

Easy (to Haystack Rock)
2.2-mile loop
No elevation gain

Moderate (shuttle to Hug Point)
5.1 miles one-way
No elevation gain
Open except at high tide

This tidy, arts-oriented village on one of Oregon's most beautiful beaches is grappling with its own popularity—and seems to be winning. Clusters of tasteful shops and boutiques fill the small, busy downtown. Strolling lovers, sandcastling kids, and kite fliers dot the white sand beach. Puffins, cormorants, and murres watch from scenic, protected islands.

When William Clark, Sacajawea, and others from the Lewis and Clark expedition hiked here in 1806 they found Indians using hot stones in wooden troughs to render blubber from a 105-foot beached whale. Clark bought as much blubber as the tribe would sell—300 pounds—to supplement the expedition's lean diet, and named nearby Ecola Creek after the Indians' word for whale, *ekoli.*

The name Cannon Beach dates to 1846, when the Navy schooner *Shark* broke up while crossing the Columbia River bar. A chunk of the deck, complete with capstain and cannon, washed ashore south of Hug Point.

If you're coming from the north on Highway 101, take the first Cannon Beach exit (also signed for Ecola State Park) and keep left for 0.7 mile to a city parking lot by the information center on 2nd Street. (If this lot's full, you may have to drive another 11 blocks to the Haystack Rock parking area on Hemlock Street.)

If you're coming from the south on Highway 101, take the Sunset St. exit and drive 0.8 mile north through town to the information center.

From the info center, walk down 2nd Street to the beach and head left for 1.1 mile to Haystack Rock, a massive, 235-foot-tall sea stack dominating the beachscape. The spires of the Needles rise from the surf nearby. Low tides reveal pools of anemones and starfish on the reefs here. Feel free to look, but don't disturb these animals by touching them, and avoid walking on the mussels. Climbing on Haystack Rock is banned to protect seabird habitat.

If you're ready to return on the short loop through town, walk 0.3 mile back to a beach access where a huge pipe emits a creek beside blocky motels. Walk up this access a block and turn left on Hemlock Street for 0.8 mile, passing quaint cottages on your way back to downtown.

If you choose instead to continue along the beach, a good goal is Hug Point Wayside—especially if you can arrange a 5-mile car shuttle so you only have to walk one way.

The beach here is actually a historic wagon route. Before the coast highway was built, settlers reached the community of Arch Cape by driving south along

Haystack Rock.   Opposite: Cannon Beach shops.

this beach. The most dangerous narrows was Hug Point, named because drivers had to hug the headland to pass even at the lowest tide. Nearby Humbug Point won its name when travelers mistook it for the tricky headland and rounded it easily, only to see the real Hug Point ahead. About 1920, frustrated locals blasted a narrow roadbed around Hug Point just above the waves. Today the ledge gives hikers dry passage except at high tide, when waves block the route altogether.

If you make it around Hug Point you'll find a hidden cove where Fall Creek cascades into a pool beside 2 short, sandy caves. A few hundred yards beyond is the railed trail up to Hug Point Wayside's parking lot. To drive here, simply take Highway 101 south of Cannon Beach 5 miles.

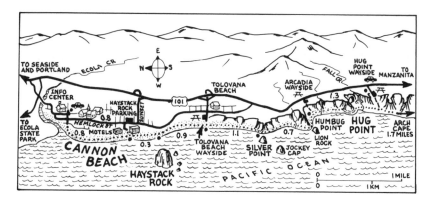

Phlox cushion along the trail.

9   Saddle Mountain

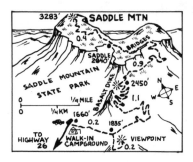

Difficult
5.2 miles round-trip
1620 feet elevation gain

Highest point in northwest Oregon, this saddle-shaped peak commands a panorama from the ocean to the truncated cone of Mt. St. Helens. The climb is especially popular in May and June, when wildflowers fill the mountain's meadows with the richest floral display in the entire Coast Range. Avoid the steep path after mid-winter ice storms.

The Columbia River basalt forming Saddle Mountain erupted 15 million years ago near Idaho, poured down the Columbia's channel, and fanned out to the sea. Here the lava puddled up in a deep bay. When the Coast Range later rose, erosion stripped away the surrounding soft rock, turning the erstwhile bay into a mountain. The summit still has a lumpy, pillow-shaped surface typical of lava cooled quickly by water.

To find the trailhead, take Highway 26 west of Portland 66 miles (or east of Seaside 10 miles), and turn north at a state park sign. Follow a winding, one-lane paved road uphill 7 miles to its end at a picnic area and 10-site tent campground.

The path starts in a forest of alder and salmonberry. Flowers line the trail in spring: 5-petaled white candyflower, red bleeding hearts, green stalks of fringecup, 3-petaled white trilliums, wild lily-of-the-valley, and pairs of white fairy bells. Old 8-foot stumps recall 1920s logging and 1930s fires.

After 0.2 mile a large unmarked side trail to the right leads 0.2 mile to a bare-topped rock outcrop with the park's best view of Saddle Mountain itself.

Continuing on the main trail, you'll switchback steeply up 1.1 mile to a narrow spine of rock running up the mountain like a stone wall. This basalt dike is actually part of the same lava flow that formed the rest of the mountain. Here, however, the tremendous weight of the flow extruded molten lava down into cracks in the ground, where the lava developed the hexagonal fractures typical of slow-cooled basalt. Exposed by erosion, the dike now resembles a long stack of cordwood.

Another half mile's climb brings you to the wildflower meadows on the peak's upper slopes. Footbridges allow you to cross these fragile rock gardens without damaging them. Several rare flower species, including Saddle Mountain bittercress (a pink, 4-petaled mustard) are found almost exclusively on this summit. The alpine habitat here has served as a refuge for Ice Age species that have vanished elsewhere in Western Oregon. Flower picking is prohibited.

Blooms you're likely to spot include red Indian paintbrush, blue iris, purple larkspur, yellow buckwheat, blue daisy-like aster, white meadow chickweed, and cushions of bluish phlox. Perhaps the strangest flower is the chocolate lily, with a big, mottled brown bell drooping from a 1-foot stalk.

At the 2.2-mile mark you'll cross the mountain's saddle, with a dizzying view down 1200 feet to your car. Cables anchored along the final 0.4-mile pitch help you climb the steep slope to the top's railed viewpoint. The coastal panorama extends from Nehalem Bay in the south to Astoria's bridge and the mouth of the Columbia River in the north. On clear days, Cascade snowpeaks from Mt. Jefferson to Mt. Rainier shimmer to the east.

Saddle Mountain.

Creek at Sunset Wayside.

10　　Sunset Wayside

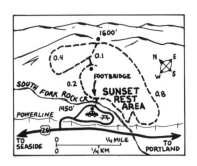

Easy
1.5-mile loop
150 feet elevation gain

Most travelers on busy Highway 26 overlook this quiet trail in the woods behind the Sunset rest area. It's a good place to stretch your legs on the trip to the coast, and the pebbly creek bank is a perfect spot to let car-bound kids loose.

Find the rest area 45 miles west of Portland (or 35 miles east of Seaside), between mileposts 28 and 29. Drive all the way around the wayside's parking loop to a big signboard describing the Sunset Infantry Division to whom the wayside is dedicated.

The trail starts behind the signboard, crosses the broad South Fork Rock Creek on a 100-foot bridge, and promptly forks. Turn left to start the loop. Once a nature trail describing logging history and ecology, the route is now missing many of its original numbered posts.

The alder forest here has salmonberry bushes with edible orange berries in summer. Shamrock-shaped *oxalis* (sourgrass) carpets the ground. In fall, the pinwheel-shaped leaves of vine maple turn fiery red. A few blackened 7-foot-thick stumps attest to the logging and fires that ravaged this area in the first half of the 20th century. In fact, most of this loop trail follows old logging roads, now nicely overgrown with trees.

The trail has numerous unmarked forks, but if you keep left at all junctions you'll hike the complete 1.5-mile loop. Near the end of the loop you'll descend through a powerline clearing before returning along the creek to the footbridge.

11 Four-County Point

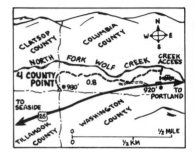

Easy
1.6 miles round-trip
100 feet elevation gain

At only one spot in all of Oregon can you stand in 4 counties at once. An easy walk on a woodsy trail from Highway 26 leads to this geographical vortex, a granite slab where the corners of Clatsop, Columbia, Tillamook, and Washington counties meet.

The hike is so short that it can be used simply to break up the drive from Portland to the coast. Or you can combine this hike with the loop trail 6 miles down the road at Sunset Wayside (Hike #10) to fill out the day.

Drive Highway 26 west of Portland 39 miles (or east of Seaside 41 miles) to a green hiker-symbol sign on the north shoulder at the end of a guardrail between mileposts 34 and 35. There is no trailhead pullout, but the paved shoulder is wide enough for parking.

The trail descends into a grove of 5-foot-thick Douglas fir with vine maple and sword fern. After 100 yards the main trail turns left, while a spur continues straight a few yards to the pebbled shore of North Fork Wolf Creek, the only access to this pretty, alder-lined stream. The main trail follows a wooded bluff above the creek. After a quarter mile the path turns briefly right on a powerline access road, then ducks back into the woods. The trail never quite escapes the traffic noise of Highway 26. The trail ends at the monument, a flat stone marker set here in 1982 amidst a mossy forest of second-growth Douglas fir and salal.

Four-County Point trailhead.

12   Banks-Vernonia Railroad

Easy (to Buxton Trestle)
3 miles round-trip
200 feet elevation gain

Moderate (shuttle to Horseshoe Trestle)
5.3 miles one-way
500 feet elevation gain

A showpiece of the rails-to-trails movement, Banks-Vernonia Linear State Park consists of 21 miles of abandoned railroad converted to a wide. well-graded path through the forested Coast Range foothills.

Parts of the route are chiefly of interest to bicyclists, horseback riders, and distance joggers, but the secluded central portion includes 2 colossal timbered trestles that make good day-hike goals. The path is open year-round and is remarkably quiet, considering it's just 30 minutes from Portland.

The railroad line was built in the 1920s to haul lumber to Portland from the Oregon-American mill in Vernonia. After the mill closed in 1957, a steam excursion train briefly operated here. The rails were torn up in 1973.

A 1.5-mile sampler takes you to a picnic area in a meadow below the huge Buxton trestle. Drive Highway 26 west of Portland 28 miles to a BP gas station near milepost 46 and turn north onto Fisher Road. After half a mile turn right onto gravel Pongratz Road for 0.8 mile. The trailhead's on the left, just before a mailbox numbered 48465.

The broad, graveled trail, closed to motor vehicles by a cable between posts, briefly skirts farm fields before ducking into a forest of second-growth Douglas fir, bigleaf maple, and bracken. Wild iris flags the route with blue in spring.

Mileposts mark quarter-mile intervals. After 1.5 miles you'll reach the 600-foot-long framework of the Buxton trestle over Mendenhall Creek. It's too

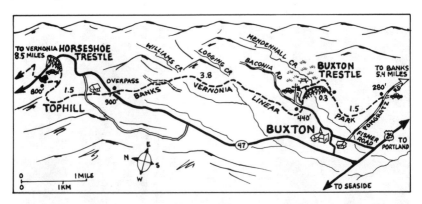

Buxton trestle. Opposite: Thimbleberry bloom.

dizzying and dangerous to cross; instead, take a side trail to the right to a picnic area in a lovely creekside meadow—a good turnaround point for a short hike.

If you'd prefer to hike a longer section, try the 5.3 miles between the Buxton trestle and the Horseshoe trestle. To start, turn off Highway 26 onto Fisher Road for 0.8 mile to Buxton and curve right on Baconia Road for 0.6 mile to the start of gravel, where the trail crosses the road. Fifty feet beyond, a driveway on the right leads to the Buxton trestle parking area.

After inspecting the trestle, walk back to the trail crossing and head west. The quiet, wooded route spans creek canyons on cuts and fills, some of them 100 feet deep. Expect to see deer. After 3.8 miles (near milepost 10, according to the trail's marker system) you'll cross Highway 47 on a steel footbridge. For the next half mile the railbed passes the backyards of a few rural mobile homes. Then the trail crests at Tophill Pass in an enormous 1990 clearcut and gradually descends 0.6 mile to a fork. Ahead a few hundred yards is the amputated Horseshoe trestle, which ends in mid-air 100 feet above Highway 47. To the left, the trail descends to the Tophill trailhead parking lot.

If you're driving to the Tophill trailhead to leave a shuttle car, turn off Highway 26 at the sign for Vernonia and follow Highway 47 north 6.4 miles.

Other Hiking Options

The trail continues 8.5 miles north from the Tophill trailhead to Anderson Park in downtown Vernonia, but the route parallels Highway 47. The southern end of the 21-mile trail also has highway noise. Because of private land south of Pongratz Road you have to drive along Pongratz and Pihl roads 1.3 miles to the Manning trailhead. Then the trail parallels highways 26 and 47 through farmfields 4.1 miles to a bridge over Dairy Creek, just outside Banks.

13 Cape Falcon

Easy (to Short Sand Beach)
1.2 miles round-trip
100 feet elevation gain

Moderate (to Cape Falcon)
5 miles round-trip
300 feet elevation gain

Difficult (shuttle to Arch Cape)
8 miles one-way
1200 feet elevation gain

For more than 12 miles, the Oregon Coast Trail traverses the old-growth rainforests and craggy capes of Oswald West State Park. Here are 3 options for day hikers: a short stroll to a secluded beach, a moderate hike to Cape Falcon's vista, and an 8-mile trek through the forests to the community of Arch Cape.

Start by driving Highway 101 south of Seaside 18 miles (or north of Tillamook 30 miles) to a small wooden "Oswald West State Park" sign marking the day-use parking lot. It's on the east side of the highway, a bit south of milepost 39. Park at the far left end of the lot and take a paved path under the highway bridge. The trail follows Short Sand Creek through a old-growth rainforest of mossy alder, hemlock, red cedar, and spruce. Douglas squirrels scold from the 6-foot-thick trunks. Salal, salmonberry, and 3 varieties of ferns line the path.

After 0.3 mile ignore a left-hand fork to the campground. Continue 200 yards to the Oregon Coast Trail, a junction marked by a large post.

For the short hike, turn left and follow "Beach Access" pointers for 0.2 mile to Short Sand Beach. On the way you'll cross a dramatic 70-foot suspension footbridge over Necarney Creek and finally hop across driftwood logs to the secluded strand in cliff-rimmed Smuggler Cove, a favorite spot for surfers.

If Cape Falcon's your goal, backtrack 0.2 mile from Short Sand Beach to the big junction where you first met the Oregon Coast Trail. This time head north, cross through a picnic area, and keep left at an unmarked fork. This path has a few muddy spots where it winds through the woods. Then it heads out the cape, gaining views of Neahkahnie Mountain (Hike #14). Finally reach a junction in a field of wind-trimmed salal bushes. For the Cape Falcon viewpoint, turn left on a 0.2-mile spur trail that becomes increasingly panoramic and rugged before petering out near the tip of the salal-covered headland.

If you're not ready to turn back yet, continue north on the Oregon Coast Trail. The next 1.2 miles pass 3 cliff-edge viewpoints framed by twisted old-growth spruce. After this the trail climbs steeply inland through viewless woods.

If your goal is Arch Cape, hike onward and upward. The path climbs over a broad, 1000-foot ridge where the forest was leveled by a 1982 windstorm, and then drops to a crossing of Highway 101. On the far side, the trail briefly follows an abandoned road before climbing to a broad pass and switchbacking down to the Arch Cape Creek suspension footbridge and the trailhead.

To leave a shuttle car here, drive 4 miles north of the Os West parking lot to

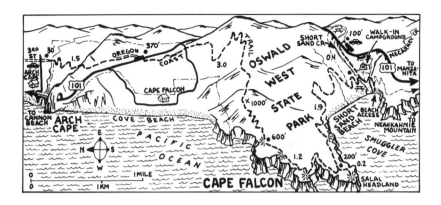

the far end of a tunnel, turn right on Arch Cape Mill Road for 0.4 mile, and park on the shoulder at Third Street. The trail begins as a gravel road to the right.

Other Hiking Options

Oregon Coast Trail trekkers sometimes hike this section from north to south instead. To find the trail from Cannon Beach (Hike #8), hike the beach south past Hug Point 1.7 miles and turn left under the highway bridge at Arch Cape Creek.

Cape Falcon. Opposite: Oxalis (sourgrass).

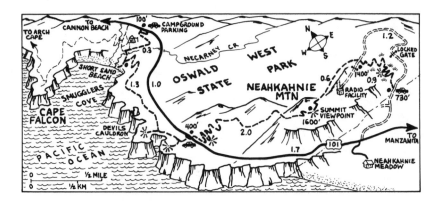

14   Neahkahnie Mountain

Moderate (to summit viewpoint)
3 miles round-trip
900 elevation gain

Difficult (shuttle to campground)
5.1 miles one-way
1000 feet elevation gain

Left: Neahkahnie Mountain from Cape Falcon.

Neahkahnie mountain juts 1600 feet above the beach. Indians thought it a viewpoint fit for gods, and named it with the words *Ne* ("place of") and *Ekahni* ("supreme deity"). White men shroud the peak with legend as well. Treasure seekers sift the beach at the mountain's base, spurred by tales of gold buried by sailors from a shipwrecked Spanish galleon. The discovery here of a strangely inscribed block of beeswax, possibly of Spanish origin, adds to the speculation.

Drive Highway 101 south of Seaside 20 miles (or north of Tillamook 28 miles) to a brown hiker-symbol sign opposite the Neah-Kah-Nie subdivision, between mileposts 41 and 42. Turn east on gravel 0.4 mile to a wide spot with a small "Trailhead Parking" sign on the right. The trail starts at a gray post on the left. Steep switchbacks lead up through meadows 0.9 mile to a ridgetop junction. Continue straight on a path that contours 0.6 mile around the wooded back of the mountain before emerging at the summit meadow viewpoint.

Most hikers return as they came. But if you can arrange a car shuttle, it's worth continuing down the far side of the mountain. This portion, muddy in spots, descends 2 miles through forest to a crossing of Highway 101. If you want to park a shuttle car here, look for a gray post at a viewpoint pullout 0.2 mile south of milepost 40. But as long as you're shuttling a car, you should take it another mile to the Oswald West campground parking lot. Then you can hike the very scenic 1.3-mile stretch of the Oregon Coast Trail to Short Sand Beach. From there, keep right at junctions for 0.3 mile to the campground parking lot.

15 Nehalem Bay

Moderate
5.2-mile loop
No elevation gain

Right: Nehalem Bay from spit.

Shorebirds and seals outnumber people on the beach rimming Nehalem Bay's dune-covered peninsula. Drive Highway 101 south of Seaside 22 miles (or north of Tillamook 26 miles) to milepost 44, just south of Manzanita. Follow signs a mile to Nehalem Bay State Park's entrance and keep straight for another 1.7 miles to a picnic area at road's end. A day-use parking fee is charged.

A sandy path leads through a grassy foredune to the broad beach. Neahkahnie Mountain's cliffs (see Hike #14) loom to the right at the end of the strand. A drunk captain and inexperienced crew sailed the British 3-masted *Glenesslin* into those cliffs on a calm, sunny day in 1913; rusted iron parts remain. Legends say a 16th-century Spanish galleon also foundered here, and that survivors buried the ship's treasure beneath a dead man to frighten looters.

Walk left along the beach 2.3 miles to Neahlem Bay's jetty. A 1990 archeological dig here unearthed a Salish salmon-fishing camp from 1300-1600 AD. Walk inland along the jetty's edge 0.5 mile to a broad bayshore beach where 50 harbor seals often lounge. It is illegal to harass these marine mammals. Even approaching within 100 yards will set them galumphing toward the bay.

On a low bluff to the left, a "Restroom" sign marks an outhouse and picnic table at the end of the spit's inland horse trail, a 4-wheel-drive track overgrown with Scotch broom. This is a possible return route, but the scenery and bird-watching's better if you simply continue along the soft bayshore beach 2.2 miles to the park's boat ramp and follow the paved road 0.2 mile left to your car.

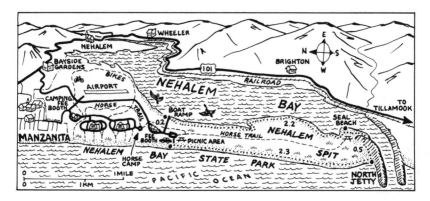

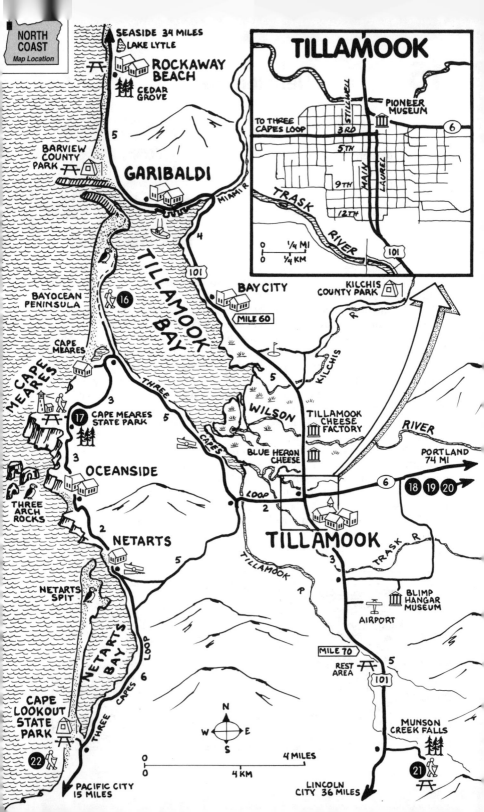

Tillamook Holstein dairy cow.

TILLAMOOK

Five rivers meander across dairy pastureland to Tillamook Bay in this coastal county touted as the "land of cheese, trees, and ocean breeze." To the south, Highway 101 takes an inland shortcut, but the Three Capes Scenic Route provides a coastal loop past Cape Meares, Cape Lookout, and Cape Kiwanda.

Cheese Factories
When local dairymen in the 1880s tired of having their butter spoil before it reached Portland and San Francisco on unreliable ships, they built their own sailing ship and started making cheddar cheese. Today the Tillamook Cheese factory, 2 miles north of Tillamook on Highway 101, is one of Oregon's most popular tourist stops, with a self-guiding tour, a deli, and a gift shop. Daily hours are 8-8 in summer, 8-6 in winter. The Blue Heron French Cheese Company, a mile south, keeps the same hours, but features Camembert and Brie.

Blimp Hangar
Navy blimps from this enormous hangar prowled the coast for Japanese submarines during World War II. Twenty stories tall and nearly a quarter mile long, the 1942 hangar remains the largest clear-span wooden building in the world. After the war, a sawmill operated here for 30 years, entirely indoors. Today the colossal hangar houses an excellent collection of rare World War II aircraft, including barrage balloons and fighter planes. Daily hours are 9 to dark from mid-May to mid-October; otherwise, 10-5.

Cape Meares State Park
A lighthouse, a bluff-top picnic area, and the odd-limbed Octopus Tree are the top attractions in this park on the Three Capes Loop west of Tillamook. The 1890 lighthouse is open to visitors 11-4 daily from May through September, and is open 11-4 on weekends in March, April, and October. See Hike #17.

Cape Lookout State Park
This picturesque park on the Three Capes Loop stretches from a massive, cliff-edged headland to the tip of the 5-mile-long Netarts sand spit. In the middle is a beachside picnic area and a popular 250-site campground (summer camping reservations accepted). See Hike #22.

Pioneer Museum

Displays at this restored 1905 Tillamook County courthouse include quilts, Indian artifacts, a stagecoach, a blacksmith shop, a pioneer house, and an operating steam-powered donkey logging engine. A cut above average, the museum at 2106 Second Street is open daily 8-5; Sunday hours are 12-5.

Oceanside

Clinging to a steep seafront hillside like a fishing village in the Outer Hebrides, this hamlet on the Three Capes Loop has kept its 1920s charm. Life here revolves around the beach, Roseanna's Cafe, and the Anchor Tavern.

Three Arch Rocks

Half a mile to sea from Oceanside, 220,000 birds of 13 species nest on these wave-carved islands. Murres crowd the ledges. Sea lions loll nearby. Protected by Theodore Roosevelt as a national wildlife refuge in 1907, the area's 17 acres of islands are now an official wilderness. But the wildlife is being endangered by people who won't settle for watching through binoculars from Oceanside's beach. People venturing closer than 1000 feet by boat, sailboard, kayak, jet ski, scuba gear, and airplane are causing panicked animals to flee.

Rockaway Beach

The broad, breezy beach in this tourist village keeps kite shops hopping. Most popular beach access is the state park picnic area at First Avenue in mid-town. On 12th at the north edge of town is a boat ramp for freshwater Lake Lytle (powerboats permitted). On the south edge of town on 6th is a 25-acre old-growth cedar grove protected by the Nature Conservancy.

Garibaldi

Tillamook Bay's major port, this fishing town was named by a fan of Italian freedom fighter Giuseppe Garibaldi. Once a small coastal railroad supplied Garibaldi's mill with logs. Now the line hauls tourists. The Fun Run excursion train leaves Garibaldi Sat-Sun at 10am and 1:30pm from late May to mid-October for 3-hour round-trips north to Nehalem Bay.

Three Arch Rocks from Netarts Spit.   Opposite: Tufted puffin.

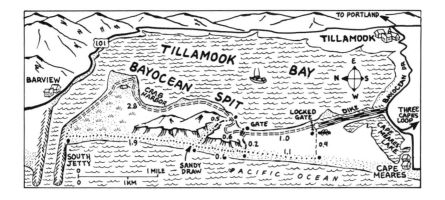

16   Bayocean Spit

Moderate (to sandy draw)
3.9-mile loop
100 feet elevation gain

Difficult (to jetty)
8.1-mile loop
No elevation gain

The scenic, sandy peninsula sheltering Tillamook Bay not only has some of the coast's best birdwatching, it's the site of one of Oregon's strangest ghost towns. Sample the sights on a 3.9-mile loop that's easy enough for hikers with children. Or plan a longer, 8.1-mile loop to the jetty at the spit's tip.

The ghost town story begins in 1907, when a Kansas City realtor named T. B. Potter platted the "Queen of Oregon Resorts" on the sandy spit. The city of Bayocean soon boasted a hotel, grocery, bowling alley, and the largest indoor saltwater swimming pool on the West Coast. Visitors were ferried from Portland by ship. Hundreds of lots were sold. Then one night Mrs. Potter reported that her husband had gone violently insane. He was never seen again. Development ceased.

In 1917, when construction of Tillamook Bay's north jetty changed ocean currents, street after street of the town began eroding into the sea. A 1932 jetty extension sped the process. By 1952 Bayocean Spit was an island, wiped clean of its city. Ironically, a dike built in 1956 to protect the bay caused the spit to regrow, creating Cape Meares Lake.

From Highway 101 in downtown Tillamook, follow "Three Capes Scenic Route" signs 7 miles to a big signboard on the right describing the Bayocean Spit. Turn right on a gravel road along a dike for 0.9 mile to a big parking area.

The trail starts as an old gated road through the Scotch broom along the bayshore. If you bring a bicycle you can ride this flat road out the spit to the jetty, but hikers see more birds and can take the loop along the beach.

So walk the road for a mile. Along the way, watch the bay for ducks and long-necked loons. Great blue herons stand like sticks in the mudflats. Curlews stride along the shore, probing the sand with long thin bills.

After a mile you'll reach a road gate at the base of a forested hill. Turn left here on a sandy path that ducks through salal and shore pine 0.2 mile to the beach. (If you try to hike the loop in reverse, this trail at the edge of the forested hill will be hard to find.) Head right along the beach 0.6 mile to a big sandy gap in the forested bluff on the right.

If you're ready to head back on the shorter loop, turn inland through the grassy dunes in this draw. After 0.3 mile the sandy opening narrows to a trail that descends into the forest. The path dives through dense salal before emerging at the bayshore road. Your car is 1.6 miles to the right.

If you'd prefer the long loop, continue along the ocean beach 1.9 miles to the jetty. Loons, tufted puffins, and brown pelicans often fish in the bay mouth. Turn right for a few hundred yards to find the start of the bayshore road. While you're following it 4.4 miles back to your car, scan across the bay to spot Garibaldi's docks to the left and the distant roof of the huge Tillamook blimp hangar to the right.

Bayocean Spit from Cape Meares.   Opposite: The Octopus Tree.

17 Cape Meares

Easy (to light and Octopus Tree)
0.6 mile round-trip
100 feet elevation gain

Moderate (from beach to Big Spruce)
3 miles round-trip
500 feet elevation gain

An 1890 lighthouse and an ancient spruce forest top this dramatic bluff. The headland's name honors British Captain John Meares, who built a fur-trading fort in Nootka, Alaska and sailed south in 1788 questing for the great river of the Northwest. He overlooked the Columbia and turned back here.

For a short stroll to the lighthouse, drive west from Tillamook 10 miles (or north from Pacific City 26 miles) following "Three Capes Scenic Route" signs, and take the Cape Meares State Park entrance road 0.6 mile to a turnaround. A wide paved path straight ahead leads 0.2 mile to the short white lighthouse. Its spectacularly prismed, 1-ton lens was hand-ground in Paris in 1887, shipped around Cape Horn, and finally pulled up here by mules. You can climb the tower (and visit the gift shop inside) between 11 and 4 daily from May through September. In March, April, and October it's only open weekends.

To the south, the view extends past Three Arch Rocks to Cape Lookout. To the north, the view includes Pyramid Rock and (closer to shore) Pillar Rock, crowded with hundreds of black-and-white nesting murres in May and June.

Return to your car, cross the parking lot, and walk past the restroom to find the short, wide path to the Octopus Tree, a 12-foot-thick spruce with big, odd limbs. For a longer stroll, walk halfway around the tree to find a smaller path that continues half a mile to the highway, passing several viewpoints.

So far you'll have walked less than an hour. For a more substantial hike, drive

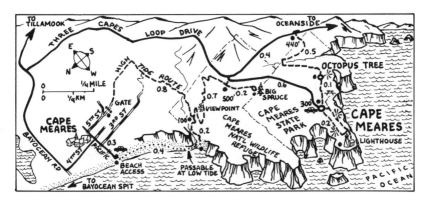

Cape Meares lighthouse.   *Opposite: Tillamook Burn snags on Elk Mountain.*

back to the Three Capes Loop highway, turn left toward Tillamook for 2 miles, turn left on Bayocean Road 0.7 mile, curve left onto 4th Street 0.4 mile, and turn left on Pacific Street to a beach access in the old-timey village of Cape Meares. Two hiking routes climb from here to the cape itself: a scenic low-tide route along the beach and a longer high-tide path through brushy backwoods.

If the tide's at all low, walk left along the beach 0.4 mile to its end at a promontory. At low tide, you can round this headland to a gravel beach in a secluded cove. Scramble up this beach's bank to find the trail that climbs 0.9 mile to the start of the lighthouse road, passing viewpoints of the Bayocean Spit (Hike #16) along the way. Keep right at the trail junction beside the road to continue 0.2 mile to trail's end at Big Spruce, a 16-foot-thick, 193-foot-tall giant over 400 years old. Return as you came.

If the tide's high you'll have to start this hike differently. From the beach access in the town of Cape Meares, walk up Pacific Street to Fifth Street, turn right on this gravel road for 200 yards, and continue straight on a gated, grassy spur signed "Keep Out; Water System." This public path, a bit too muddy for tennis shoes and a bit too brushy for shorts, meanders 0.8 mile through scrub to join the low-tide route above the gravel beach.

18   Kings Mountain

Difficult (to Kings Mountain)
5.4 miles round-trip
2780 feet elevation gain

Difficult (to Elk Mountain)
4.2 miles round-trip
2000 feet elevation gain

Very difficult (both peaks)
11.6-mile loop
4100 feet elevation gain

Steep, rugged trails climb to sweeping Coast Range viewpoints atop Kings Mountain and neighboring Elk Mountain. In May and June, wildflowers brighten the upper ridges. Below, ancient snags and regrowing forests recall the Tillamook Burn fires of the 1930s and '40s. For an athletic challenge, connect the 2 summits via a ridgecrest hiking route, partly on old roads.

To find the Kings Mountain trailhead, drive Highway 6 west of Portland 49 miles (or east of Tillamook 25 miles) to a brown hiker-symbol sign at a pullout just east of milepost 25. The unsigned but obvious trail leads up into a mossy alder forest with sword ferns and tiny, 5-petaled candyflower. After a mile the trail steepens sharply and the forest shifts to drier Douglas fir woods. At the 2.4-mile mark the path climbs into a glorious ridgecrest meadow of red Indian paintbrush, blue larkspur, wild strawberry, purple penstemon, cushions of bluish phlox, and the huge white plumes of beargrass. Summit views extend from Mt. Hood to the ocean beyond Tillamook Bay. Hikers can sign a register kept in a blue plastic tube. The trail continues toward Elk Mountain, but if you're planning to tackle this difficult traverse, it's best to start at the other end.

To find the Elk Mountain trailhead, drive Highway 6 to milepost 28 and turn north at a sign for Elk Creek Forest Park. After 0.3 mile, pass the primitive campground on the left and continue straight across a bridge. Beyond the bridge

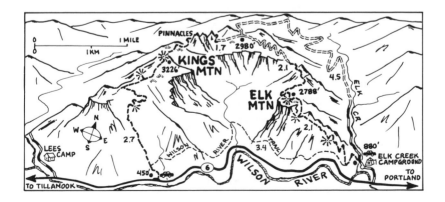

Fog on Elk Mountain.   Opposite: University Falls.

100 feet you'll find the trail on the left, marked by a blue dot on a tree.

This path scrambles up a steep, rocky crest with all the subtlety of a bobsled run. Loose scree makes the route especially treacherous. As consolation, there are lots of orange Indian paintbrush and viewpoints. After dipping across 4 saddles, reach the summit meadow of beargrass and Cascade lilies.

If you're continuing on the still more difficult traverse, take the path that dives off the far side of Elk Mountain's summit. For the next mile you'll often have to use your hands to follow the scrambly ridgecrest route, at times atop a narrow rock hogback. Then continue on an old road 1.5 miles to a junction in a pass and turn left for 1.7 miles to Kings Mountain's summit and the start of a long descent. A quarter mile before reaching Highway 6, turn left on the Wilson River Trail (open late 1999) for 3.4 miles to complete the loop back to your car.

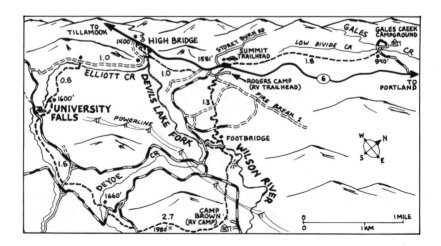

19 University Falls

Difficult
8.4-mile loop
1200 feet elevation gain

(Refer to map on previous page)

At the crest of the Coast Range, where the devastating Tillamook Burn fires of 1933, 1939, and 1945 began, the regrowing state forest is decidedly not a wilderness. Motorcycles and all-terrain vehicles whine through the woods. Logging roads scar the slopes. So it is surprising to find this eminently hikable footpath here, looping around the Wilson River's headwaters to University Falls, a 100-foot fan-shaped cascade in a quiet alder grotto.

Drive Highway 6 to the Coast Range summit at milepost 33, west of Portland 41 miles (or east of Tillamook 33 miles). Park in a large pullout on the north side at a sign for Storey Burn Road. The trail starts directly across the highway from this sign. Walk up the trail 100 yards, cross the entrance to another huge parking area (an all-terrain vehicle staging area known as Rogers Camp), walk a hundred yards up a dirt road marked "Fire Break 1," and turn right on the trail proper.

Motor vehicles are banned on this path, and although horses and mountain bikes are allowed, you're unlikely to meet any. Throughout the 8.8-mile loop, the trail is identified by blue dots spray-painted on trees. Follow these dots carefully, because the route crosses 11 logging roads and 10 motorcycle trails.

After 1.3 miles you'll reach a T-shaped trail junction at the bank of the Devils Lake Fork, a lovely green creek shaded by alders. Turn left to a log footbridge, cross the creek, and turn left again. After this, you'll hike 2.7 miles through second-growth Douglas fir woods (often interrupted by roads, powerlines, and clearcuts) before crossing another scenic creek. This time it's Deyoe Creek, with a plank footbridge and a nearby bench that's a good spot for lunch.

Another 1.6 miles, and many road crossings, bring you to an X-shaped trail junction. To the left 100 yards is University Falls—impressive in spring's high water, but a mere trickle by late summer. To the right is the continuation of the loop, now called the Gravelle Trail.

Beyond the falls 0.8 mile the path crosses a creek and joins a motorcycle road for a mile. Then fork to the right, cross the Devils Lake Fork Wilson River on a new log bridge, and continue a mile up to your car.

Other Hiking Options

To extend the hike, start at the Gales Creek Campground. A trail along a pre-1933 railroad grade climbs 1.8-mile through deep woods to the Highway 6 summit trailhead at the start of the loop.

20 Hagg Lake

Easy (south shore)
3.2 miles round-trip
50 feet elevation gain

Moderate (north shore)
6.6 miles round-trip
150 feet elevation gain

Difficult (around lake)
13.1-mile loop
200 feet elevation gain

Fishermen and waterskiers have long since found Hagg Lake, the reservoir created in this rural Coast Range valley near Forest Grove in 1975. But relatively few hikers have discovered the charms of the 13.1-mile footpath around the lake, even though it's just a half hour's drive from Portland.

Short walks along either the north or south shore lead through old-growth forests and grassy fields with lake vistas. Visit March to June for the best woodland wildflowers. Skip summer weekends if you're bothered by the whine of powerboats.

From Freeway 217 in Beaverton, turn west for 12 miles on Highway 8 through

Hagg Lake.   Above: Trillium.

Hillsboro to Forest Grove. Then turn left for 5 miles on Highway 47 (toward McMinnville) and turn right at a "Hagg Lake" pointer for 3 miles to the park's fee booth. A parking fee is charged here from late April through September.

For a short hike on the quiet, south shore of the lake, drive past the fee booth 0.3 mile and turn left across the dam (toward Boat Ramp C) for 0.8 mile to a small pullout on the right with a red post inscribed "Trail."

The path hugs the shore amid young alder and Douglas fir. In spring expect big, 3-petaled white trilliums and droopy, 6-petaled fawn lilies. Ignore left-hand side trails; they lead to the road. In 0.6 mile you'll cross an arm of the reservoir on a huge log and a footbridge. After another mile, cross the end of a second reservoir arm on a zigzagging 90-foot bridge and reach an X-shaped junction. The lakeshore trail turns right to several picnic tables amidst scenic lakeside firs—a good lunch spot and turnaround point.

For a longer hike that avoids the summertime parking fee, turn left at the fee booth and park in an open field designated for free parking. From here, walk cross-country up the grassy face of the reservoir's earthen dam to the spillway. Cross the paved road atop the dam, step over a guardrail, follow the bouldery lakeshore 200 yards, and turn right for 50 yards up a steep dirt path to an abandoned parking area. Another 50 yards to the left is the official lakeshore trailhead, a wooden staircase that leads into old-growth woods.

After 1.3 miles, cross the paved parking area at Boat Ramp A and continue, sticking close to the lakeshore. Wear boots to cross a few muddy spots; poison oak makes off-trail detours unwise. After another mile briefly join the highway (opposite Nelson Road). Keep left past a red trail post to continue on the path, which passes 4 picnic tables in the woods before entering a broad, grassy field. In 0.4 mile a bench at the tip of a grassy promontory offers perhaps the best view of the lake anywhere.

For a moderate hike, turn back at the bench. If you're confident you can manage the 13.1 miles around the lake, press onward. Note, however, that the lakeshore path crosses abandoned farm fields (now maintained as elk pasture) for much of the next 6 miles. In a few spots the trail parallels the road closely, and 1.4 miles of the loop follows the road itself.

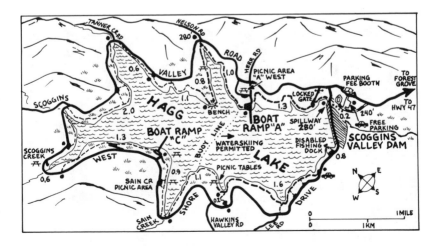

21   Munson Creek Falls

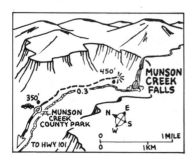

Easy
0.6 miles round-trip
100 feet elevation gain

The Coast Range's tallest waterfall plunges 266 feet into an old-growth forest canyon. It's just off Highway 101, but surprisingly few travelers discover this small county park and the easy trail along rushing Munson Creek to the base of the slender, 5-tiered cataract. The falls are named for Goran Munson, who came from Michigan to settle near here in 1889.

Drive Highway 101 south of Tillamook 8 miles. Just before milepost 73, turn left for a mile at a sign for Munson Creek Falls. After the narrow road turns to gravel, fork right 0.4 mile to a small turnaround with a few picnic tables.

The large trail at the end of the turnaround ambles along the creek amidst 5-foot-thick red cedars, huge alders, and bigleaf maples with moss-draped branches. Watch for yellow monkeyflower, graceful lady ferns, red elderberries, and pink salmonberries.

After 0.3 mile the trail ends at a picnic table with a view of the top third of Munson Creek's long waterfall. It's no use trying to see the rest of the falls by scrambling up through brush on slippery logs, either. Tillamook County plans eventually to build a trail to a more satisfying viewpoint higher in the canyon.

Munson Creek Falls.

Neskowin's beach and Cascade Head from the mouth of Nestucca Bay.

NESKOWIN

The shore between Tillamook and Lincoln City is the quietest stretch of coastline within a 2-hour drive of Portland. Long beaches and headlands here remain delightfully pristine. Highway 101 detours inland, approaching the beach only at the posh cottages of Neskowin, where the downtown consists of a single general store, a restaurant, and 2 golf courses.

Three Capes Loop

A coastal alternative to the inland portion of Highway 101, this scenic route south of Tillamook passes sandy Cape Kiwanda, cliff-edged Cape Lookout, and lighthouse-topped Cape Meares. The route also skirts three estuaries (Nestucca Bay, Sand Lake, and Netarts Bay), and visits three villages (Pacific City, Netarts, and Oceanside).

Sand Lake

Sand Lake resembles a coastal river bay without a river. It's best known for the dune landscape to its north, where all-terrain vehicles roar out from their staging area at the Forest Service's Sand Beach Campground. But the estuary itself is actually a quiet haven for coastal wildlife. To explore a small area of grassy, motor-free dunes on the spit between Sand Lake and the ocean, head for the picnic area beside the Forest Service campground.

Whalen Island County Park

The best access to Sand Lake's birdwatching, canoeing, and kayaking is in this very beautiful, often overlooked little park. It's right on the estuary, across a bridge from the Three Capes Loop Drive, 6 miles north of Pacific City. The park includes a tidy campground, picnic area, and boat ramp.

Cape Kiwanda

This accessible, popular headland near Pacific City shelters the area's busiest beach. With the morning's outgoing tide, fishermen back boat trailers across the sand to launch dories dramatically through the waves. Jet skiers zoom past like spacemen riding vacuum cleaners through the surf. Hang gliders soar from sand dunes atop the cape's neck. Pedalers on rented recumbent tricycles cruise the strand. Hikers explore the cape's wave-sculpted tip (see Hike #23). To find the beach access, drive a mile north of Pacific City on the Three Capes Loop.

Nestucca Bay

Canoeing and kayaking on this relatively undeveloped, many-armed estuary is best when winds are low. Start at any of 3 launch sites: at Straub State Park (see Hike #23), on the road between Pacific City and Highway 101, and where Highway 101 crosses the Little Nestucca River.

Mount Hebo

Once a radar base scanned the skies from this 3176-foot, flat-topped mountain. The base is gone, but the panorama from the summit meadows remains. Either hike there from the campground at Hebo Lake (Hike #25), or drive to the view. The paved road to the top starts beside the Hebo Ranger Station, just off Highway 101 on Highway 22.

Cascade Head

The meadowed capes at Cascade Head can only by reached on foot (see hikes #28 and #29), but non-hikers have other options. The Salmon River estuary at the foot of the cape is a labyrinth of winding waterways, perfect for canoe or kayak exploration. Launch at the Savage Park boat ramp on Three Rocks Road (see the map for Hike #27). For a scenic drive through the Cascade Head Experimental Forest, take Slab Creek Road (an old, 11-mile section of Highway 101) from Otis to Neskowin.

Nestucca Spit in Bob Straub State Park.

22   Cape Lookout

Moderate (to tip of cape)
5 miles round-trip
400 feet elevation gain

Moderate (to south beach)
4 miles round-trip
800 feet elevation gain

Easy (shuttle to picnic area)
2.3 miles one-way
800 feet elevation loss

Like an unfinished dike to Hawaii, this narrow, cliff-edged cape juts 2 miles straight out into the Pacific Ocean. At the trailhead atop the cape, hikers have 3 choices: walk out to the viewpoint at the cape's tip, descend to a secluded beach at the southern base of the cape, or amble north along the bluffs to the state park's popular picnic area and campground. The trails have muddy spots unsuitable for tennis shoes.

The cape itself dates back 15 million years, when lava flows from Eastern Oregon poured down the Columbia River and fanned out. All along the northern Oregon Coast, tough remnants of that massive basalt flood have survived to form headlands and islands.

From downtown Tillamook, head west on 3rd Street and follow signs for Cape Lookout State Park 13 miles. Continue past the campground turnoff 2.7 miles to the signed trailhead turnoff on the right. (If you're driving here from the south, take the Pacific City exit of Highway 101 and follow the Three Capes Loop 16 miles north to the top of a pass and the trailhead sign.)

To hike to the tip of the cape, take the left-hand trail at the end of the parking lot and keep straight at a junction 100 yards beyond. The dense forest of gnarled old spruce and hemlock trees shelters ferns, salal, salmonberry, and candyflower, an edible little 5-petaled white bloom with delicate pink stripes.

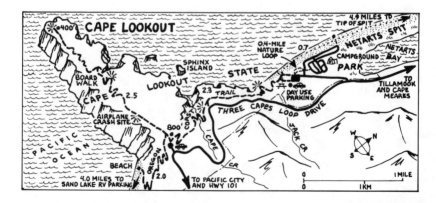

Sphinx Island from the Oregon Coast Trail.   Opposite: Wild lily-of-the-valley.

The first view south, after 0.6 mile, is just above the site where a B-17 bomber crashed into the cape's 800-foot cliffs on a foggy day in 1943. If the weather's clear, you can spot Haystack Rock off Cape Kiwanda, as well as Cascade Head and distant Cape Foulweather.

Another 0.6 mile brings you to a railed overlook with your first view north. Note Three Arch Rocks off Cape Meares and the blue silhouette of Neahkahnie Mountain. Next the trail detours above a cove where the old path slid into the sea in 1992. A boardwalk helps hikers cross mudpits on the new route.

At the tip of the cape, red Indian paintbrush, white yarrow, and scarlet fireweed brighten a clifftop meadow 400 feet above the waves. A red buoy moans offshore. Bring binoculars to watch for gray whales here from December to June. Up to 20,000 migrate from Alaska to Mexico each year. Sometimes as many as 30 per hour round this prominent cape. Remember to save some energy for the return hike uphill to the trailhead.

If you'd rather try a less heavily used path from this trailhead, take the Oregon Coast Trail either south or north. To the south the path switchbacks 2 miles down to a beach that stretches to the Forest Service campground at Sand Lake. The first 2 miles of this beach are quiet, but the last 2 are open to cars.

To the north of Cape Lookout, the Oregon Coast Trail descends gradually through an old-growth spruce forest with views of Sphinx Island, to the picnic grounds at the state park's day-use parking area. For an easy hike, leave a shuttle car here (a parking fee is charged) and hike this 2.3-mile trail all downhill.

Other Hiking Options

For a difficult trek from the campground, walk the beach 4.9 miles to the tip of Netarts Spit, where seals and shorebirds often hang out. The spit has views of Netarts, Oceanside, and Three Arch Rocks. It's not easy to return on a loop because the muddy shores of Netarts Bay are largely unhikable.

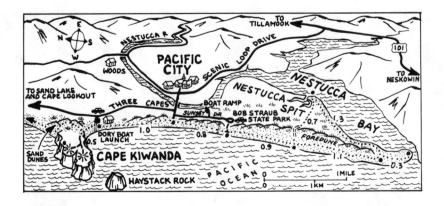

23 Pacific City

Easy (to Cape Kiwanda)
1 mile round-trip
100 feet elevation gain

Moderate (around Nestucca Spit)
5.5-mile loop
100 feet elevation gain

Best known for its dory fishing fleet, Pacific City's beach offers a number of attractions for hikers. Start with a short stroll at the beach's busy north end by Cape Kiwanda. The tidepools, clifftop viewpoints, and sand dunes here are especially popular for hikers with children. For a longer hike, head for Bob Straub State Park at the south end of the beach, where a quieter hiking route circles Nestucca Spit.

Drive Highway 101 north of Lincoln City 18 miles (or south of Tillamook 25 miles) and turn west on the Three Capes Scenic Route for 2.7 miles. In the center of Pacific City, turn left for 2 blocks across a river bridge, and then turn right for a mile to the huge Cape Kiwanda parking lot on the left.

Fishermen here launch dories directly through the waves, taking advantage of the natural breakwater created by Cape Kiwanda and massive Haystack Rock, a mile offshore. Summer mornings you can watch fishermen back their trailered boats into the shallows, slide them off, and then race to jump aboard. The tricky procedure is reversed when the fleet returns in mid-day.

A short walk takes you to the foot of the wave-sculpted yellow sandstone cape. At low tide you can explore the tide pools and shallow caves along its base. For a viewpoint, climb past a signboard on a sand slope to a junction atop the bluff. Both forks of the trail deadend in 200 yards at views of surf-smashed cliffs. Do not leave the trail or venture beyond the viewpoints; every few years self-styled adventurers slip to their deaths here.

If you want to cross the headland, return to the beach and hike up through the dunes farther inland. Here you'll reach a windy, sandy pass where hang gliders launch to sail down the far slope to cars waiting on the beach below.

For the longer hike around the Nestucca Spit, return to your car and drive a mile back toward Pacific City. At the junction by the bridge, jog right onto Sunset Drive and continue 0.8 mile to the road's end at turnaround in Bob Straub State Park. The park prohibits horses and camping.

The path starts by the restrooms and climbs across a grassy foredune to the wide beach. Head left for 2.3 miles to the end of the spit. Cars are allowed on this stretch of beach, so you'll see tire tracks and probably will find a few fishermen parked at the spit's tip. When you follow the beach left to the quiet bayshore side of the peninsula, however, you'll leave motorized disturbances behind. The breath-holes of clams dot the soft white beaches of the still bay. On your left, grassy dunes gradually give way to a young forest of spruce, shore pine, and Scotch broom.

North of the spit's tip 1.6 miles, the bayshore beach finally ends where the tide flats of a branching estuary inlet cut into the peninsula. Here you'll need to bushwhack left through tall grass and clumps of shore pines to complete the loop. Follow the sound of surf until you reach an open area in the middle of the peninsula. This deflation plain can be a bit marshy in winter. Then head for a sandy tire track cutting across the tall foredune ahead. Take this track to the beach and turn right to return to the parking area, marked by a driftwood post on the beach, 0.2 mile before the first beachfront house.

Haystack Rock and Cape Kiwanda.   Opposite: Rented recumbent tricycles.

24 Niagara Falls

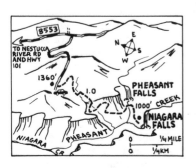

Easy
2 miles round-trip
360 feet elevation gain

Two 100-foot waterfalls spill into Pheasant Creek's secluded box canyon. An easy 1-mile path descends along a wooded creek to viewpoints at the falls' base.

Drive Highway 101 south of Tillamook 15 miles (or north of Lincoln City 28 miles) to the village of Beaver near milepost 80, and turn east on a paved road along the upper Nestucca River. After a 6.7-mile drive through pastoral dairy farmland, keep right at the settlement of Blaine. Now watch the odometer. In another 4.8 miles (between mileposts 11 and 12), turn right on an easy-to-miss paved road through a fenced field. This narrow road passes signs stating "8533" and "Niagara Falls Trail" and then turns to gravel. Go straight on the main road at all forks for 4.3 miles to another easy-to-miss junction at a pass. Turn right past a small "Trail" sign for 0.7 mile to a parking area on the left.

The trail sets off downhill through a forest of Douglas fir, salal underbrush, sword ferns, and the mossy arches of vine maple. Spring brings big 3-petaled trilliums, 5-petaled candyflower, and the delicately belled stalks of wild lily-of-the-valley. Look for yellow monkeyflower on creek banks.

The path crosses a splashing creek 3 times on footbridges, then traverses down a canyon slope to the base of Pheasant Falls' lacy 100-foot fan. Another 100 yards brings you to a picnic table at a viewpoint of Niagara Falls, a gauzy 130-foot ribbon launching off the lip of a vast amphitheater of sheer rock cliffs. The layers exposed here reveal that this rock was formed by a series of basalt lava flows.

Niagara Falls.   Opposite: View west from Mt. Hebo.

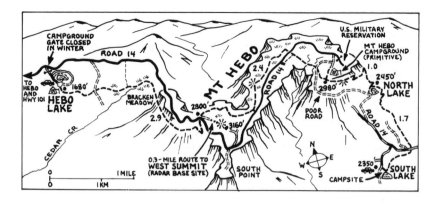

25   Mount Hebo

Difficult (to west summit)
6.4 miles round-trip
1500 feet elevation gain

Difficult (shuttle to South Lake)
8 miles one-way
1400 feet elevation gain

    Views from the 3-mile-long, meadowed plateau atop Mt. Hebo stretch from Tillamook Bay and Cape Lookout to Pacific City's Haystack Rock. This coastal mountain is so high that snow often blocks access in January and February. By May the meadows are colored with wildflowers. Like Saddle Mountain to the north, this plateau is a remnant of a gigantic, 15-million-year-old basalt lava flow that spilled from Eastern Oregon to the sea.

    Surprisingly, Indians crossing from the Willamette Valley to the coast found it easier to scale this mountain and cross its high meadows than to cut their way through the lowland rainforests. Pioneer Hiram Smith and a crew of Tillamook settlers improved the Indians' steep path in 1854. It remained the major horse route across the Coast Range until a lower elevation wagon road was built in 1882. The Forest Service rediscovered the historic path in 1975, upgraded it, and opened the 8-mile Pioneer-Indian Trail from Hebo Lake to South Lake in 1984.

    Much of the route traverses a dense, 8000-acre Douglas fir forest planted in 1912 after a devastating fire. This was one of the Forest Service's first reforestation efforts, and unwisely relied on seed collected in the distant Rocky Mountains. Today the trees are not nearly so large as similar-aged, native Douglas fir stock better adapted to Oregon's coastal climate.

Drive Highway 101 south of Tillamook 19 miles (or north of Lincoln City 24 miles) to Hebo and turn east on Highway 22 for 0.3 mile. Just before the Hebo Ranger Station, turn left at a sign for Hebo Lake. Follow twisty, paved Road 14 uphill 4.7 miles, fork to the right at the Hebo Lake Campground entrance, and keep right for 0.2 mile to the trailhead parking area. From mid-April through October, expect to pay a $3-per-car day use parking fee here. The rest of the year the campground is gated closed, adding 0.2 mile to the hike.

For a quick warm-up, you might want to stroll 0.5 mile on the wheelchair-accessible gravel path and boardwalk around Hebo Lake. The main Pioneer-Indian Trail starts at a signboard on the opposite side of the parking lot from the picnic shelter. This trail climbs for 2.9 miles, crossing a gravel road and a bracken-filled meadow, before reaching paved Road 14 at a saddle.

If you haven't arranged a car shuttle to the far end of the trail, your best bet is to take a 0.3-mile side trip up to Mt. Hebo's west summit for the view, and then to return as you came. To find this route, walk across Road 14 and turn to the right up a steep, abandoned road closed by an earth berm. This track peters out in a steep meadow of thimbleberry and bracken fern, but climb onward to the flat summit, the bulldozed site of a large Cold War-era radar station. Now only the sweeping view and a cluster of microwave relay towers remain.

If you do have a shuttle car, or if you're game for a long hike, simply continue straight across Road 14 on the continuation of the Pioneer-Indian Trail. The path contours around the mountain and follows posts across a broad plateau with meadows and viewpoints. Wild strawberries and Indian paintbrush grow here. It's also home to the threatened silverspot butterfly.

The path crosses Road 14 again, passes a spur to the tiny, primitive Mt. Hebo Campground, and descends steeply to brush-rimmed North Lake. Keep left and continue 1.7 miles through the woods to trail's end at a campsite beside South Lake. If you intend to drive a shuttle car here, be warned that part of the road is rough. From Hebo Lake, continue 3.3 miles up paved Road 14 to a summit, fork right on a narrower continuation of Road 14 for 2 miles, turn right onto a rough dirt road past a "14" sign, and soon turn right again. After 1.6 bumpy miles join a good gravel road. Continue 0.4 mile and then turn right for a final 0.3 mile to the trailhead pullout on the left.

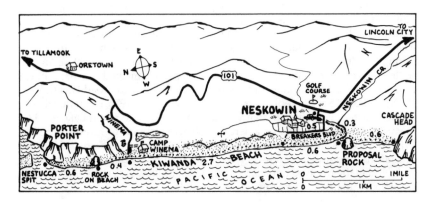

26   Neskowin

Proposal Rock.

Easy (to Proposal Rock)
1.4-mile loop
No elevation gain

Easy (Camp Winema to Porter Pt)
2 miles round-trip
No elevation gain

(Refer to map on previous page)

This beachfront village has been known as a romantic hideaway since the 1800s, when a sea captain is said to have rowed his lady love to Proposal Rock to pop the question. The forested little island is still a good place for an old-fashioned query. These days the rock is accessible on foot from Neskowin's beach at all but the highest tides.

Drive Highway 101 south of Tillamook 33 miles (or north of Lincoln City 10 miles), turn west at a small "Neskowin" pointer, and go straight 100 yards to the Neskowin Wayside. From the far left end of the parking lot, walk across a street and follow a paved path straight along Neskowin Creek 0.3 mile to Proposal Rock.

Expect to wade to visit the rock, since it diverts Neskowin Creek. In fact, the sandy creek lapping the rock's base is good place to let kids splash around a bit—warmer and safer than in the surf. The creek's name derives from the Salish word *Ne* ("place of") and *skowin,* reported to mean "plenty fish."

If you want to climb Proposal Rock, a steep scramble trail at its right-hand edge leads up through spruce, alder, salal, and salmonberry to the top.

At very low winter tides, the stumps of a sunken cedar forest emerge on the beach, evidence of massive earthquakes that drop Oregon's coastline about 6 feet at intervals of 500 to 1000 years, according to geologists.

To tour Neskowin on a short loop, turn right along the beach for 0.6 mile. Head inland at a railed beach access just beyond a row of 11 identical condominiums. Turn right on paved Breakers Boulevard, pass 7 blocks of nice old cottages, and turn left on Salem Avenue to your car.

For a longer hike, you could simply walk north along the beach to its end at the Nestucca River. But that's a tiring trudge in loose sand. To skip to the highlight of that trek, drive 4 miles north of Neskowin on Highway 101, turn left on paved Winema Road for 0.6 mile, and park at a beach access. From here it's a fun 1-mile stroll north to the driftwood jumbled at the river mouth beneath the cliffs of Porter Point. This is a quiet, wild spot, where you're almost certain to see seals, cormorants, and loons.

27 Cascade Head Inland Trail 🌲🌲

Difficult
6 miles one-way
1200 feet elevation gain

While the most heavily used trails on Cascade Head (Hikes #28 and 29) lead to clifftop meadows overlooking the rugged shoreline, this longer inland trail through the rainforest provides a less crowded alternative, but lacks views.

From the junction with Highway 18 (just north of Lincoln City) drive 1 mile north on Highway 101, turn left at Three Rocks Road, and immediately park by a trail sign on the right. The path switchbacks uphill through a second-growth spruce forest with pink salmonberry, red thimbleberry, and clusters of red elderberry in summer. In spring look for white woodland blooms: trilliums, oxalis, and wild lily-of-the-valley. Much of the trail follows ancient roadbeds, regrown with alder. Expect a few muddy spots and some distant highway noise.

The entire trail is in the Cascade Head Experimental Forest, where logging-oriented research has cut many of the area's old-growth trees. A stately grove of 6-foot-thick Sitka spruce remains in a hidden glen where springs feed the headwaters of Calkins Creek, 2.9 miles along the trail. A boardwalk crosses a skunk cabbage dale here.

After 3.6 miles, turn right on gravel Road 1861 for 100 yards. The trail's final 2.4-mile section descends through woods to a red barricade and brown hiker-symbol sign at a Highway 101 pullout 1 mile south of Neskowin.

If you'd prefer to leave a shuttle car at the Road 1861 trail crossing, turn west off Highway 101 on Cascade Head Road (1861) for 1.2 miles and look for a post.

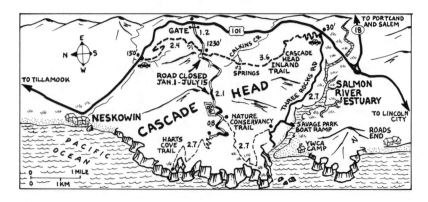

Harts Cove.   Opposite: Salmonberry along Cascade Head's inland trail.

28   Harts Cove   

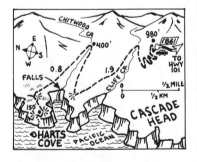

Moderate
5.4 miles round-trip
900 feet elevation gain
Open July 16 through Dec 31

Cascade Head won its name when sailors spotted the waterfalls cascading from its oceanfront cliffs. The trail down to Harts Cove leads to a viewpoint of one of these dramatic falls. But the path also features an old-growth spruce forest, a flower-filled blufftop meadow, and a rocky shore where sea lions bellow. To protect endangered butterflies and wildflowers on the headland, the road to the trailhead is gated closed January 1 to July 15.

From the junction with Highway 18 (just north of Lincoln City), drive north 4 miles on Highway 101. Just before a crest, turn left on gravel Cascade Head Road (Road 1861) and follow "Harts Cove" pointers 4.1 miles to a parking lot at road's end.

The well-graded trail switchbacks down through a young hemlock forest 0.7 mile to a footbridge over pretty Cliff Creek. Next the path contours amid 6-foot-thick Sitka spruce and hemlock giants. Spring blooms here include big, 3-petaled trilliums, double fairy bells, and stalks of wild lily-of-the-valley. Fall brings orange chanterelle mushrooms.

A bench at the 1.4-mile mark offers a glimpse ahead to Harts Cove's headland. Don't take a brushy side path down to the left in the hopes of a better view; it doesn't have one. Instead continue on the main trail. In half a mile you'll cross a bridge over Chitwood Creek, and in another 0.6 mile you'll enter the headland's fabulously scenic meadow, once part of the Taggard homestead.

Take the leftmost of several paths down the grassy bluff to find a cliff-edge viewpoint overlooking Harts Cove and Chitwood Creek's waterfall. The sea lions you hear so clearly are out of sight around a promontory.

To reach the shore (on a rugged path not suitable for children), climb back up from this viewpoint 50 yards to a junction and head seaward. A scramble trail descends to the lava rock edge of the headland, where deep water gently rises and falls, exposing a bathtub ring of barnacles, starfish, and sea palms.

Chitwood Creek waterfall.

29   Cascade Head Preserve

Easy (from upper trailhead)
2 miles round-trip
160 feet elevation gain
Open July 16 through Dec 31

Moderate (from lower trailhead)
3.4 miles round-trip
1100 feet elevation gain
Open all year

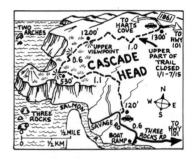

Cascade Head's panoramic, blufftop wildflower meadows were threatened by commercial development in the 1960s, but fans of the wild headland rallied to purchase the fragile area and donate it to the non-profit Nature Conservancy for preservation. Ironically, the impact of up to 10,000 nature-loving visitors a year now threatens the meadows' ecology. If you hike here, please *stay on the trail.* Even spreading out a picnic may inadvertently trample the meadow's rare checkermallows (5-petaled pink wildflowers) or the violets that serve as food for the threatened Oregon silverspot butterfly's caterpillars.

The Nature Conservancy's 2.7-mile trail zigzags up through the steep meadows from a lower trailhead off Three Rocks Road (open all year) to an upper trailhead on Road 1861 (gated closed Juanuary 1 to July 15). Flower picking, hunting, camping, fires, bicycles, and dogs are banned.

To find the lower, year-round trailhead, drive Highway 101 north 1 mile from the interchange where highways 101 and 18 join (just north of Lincoln City). Then turn left on Three Rocks Road for 2.2 miles and turn right on one-lane, paved Savage Road for 0.5 mile to a wooden sign on the right. Parking along the narrow shoulder here is limited to 10 cars. Others must park 0.6 mile back down the road at a county boat ramp.

The trail climbs through a forest of large, gnarled spruce for 1.1 mile to a meadow with a breathtaking view across the Salmon River estuary. In the distance are Cape Foulweather and Lincoln City's Devils Lake. Then the path steepens and climbs 0.6 mile to an upper viewpoint, a good turnaround spot.

An easier route to the meadows starts at the upper trailhead, closed half of each year. To find it from the interchange where Highways 101 and 18 join, drive north 4 miles on Highway 101. Just before a crest, turn left on gravel Cascade Head Road (Road 1861). After 3.3 miles, park at a guardrail on the left.

The nearly level trail ambles through a forest of second-growth Douglas fir, spruce, and alder for a mile before emerging at the meadows. In summer expect white yarrow, plumes of goldenrod, tall pink foxglove, and Indian paintbrush.

A hundred yards into the meadow the trail crests at the upper viewpoint. Most hikers will find it hard to turn back here. Remember, the farther you continue down the steep meadow trail, the farther you'll have to climb back up. A good compromise is a cliff-edge overlook halfway down, the only viewpoint of the rugged coves and islands to the north.

30 Baskett Slough Refuge

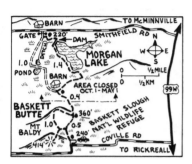

Easy (to Baskett Butte)
1.5-mile loop
200 feet elevation gain
Open all year

Moderate (to Morgan Lake)
4.2-mile loop
260 feet elevation gain
Open May 1 to September 30

Each fall 22,000 dusky Canada geese fly from Alaska's Copper River delta to winter in the Willamette Valley. This refuge west of Salem welcomes them with diked ponds and unharvested fields of corn, rye grass, and wheat. Not surprisingly, the area has become a hit with other bird species, too. A short loop hike here visits a viewpoint and an oak forest. A longer loop to the birds at Morgan Lake is open May through September. Pets and flower picking are banned.

From Salem, take Highway 22 west to Rickreall, turn north on Highway 99W for 1.8 miles, and turn left on gravel Coville Road 1.4 miles to the trailhead parking lot on the right. If you're coming from Portland or Corvallis, look for the Coville Road turnoff on Highway 99W between mileposts 56 and 57.

Walk up the wide, mowed trail 200 yards and fork left. Old apple trees, wild rose bushes, and pale blue flax flowers line the path. Expect the chirp of crickets, the hollow coo of mourning doves, and the squawk of ring-neck pheasants.

After another 200 yards you'll reach a fork at a pass. To the left is the grassy summit of Mt. Baldy and a view across the Willamette Valley's patchwork of farms to the rumpled green Coast Range. Take the right-hand fork to find the mowed loop trail around Baskett Butte and into an oak forest. Beware of the abundant, triple-leaved poison oak plants masquerading as tree seedlings here.

At the 1-mile mark reach a T-shaped junction. To the right is the quick route back to your car. Turn left for the longer loop, open from May through September. This path descends to an ancient barn, now colonized by zooming swallows. Follow trail signs to the right, along Morgan Lake, and back along a service road to end the loop at the swallow barn. Along the way look for redwing blackbirds perched on cattails, polliwogs in the ditches, and beaver-like nutria in the ponds.

Morgan Lake.

Little Luckiamute River.   Below: Columbine.

31   Little Luckiamute River

Easy (to first clearcut)
2 miles round-trip
100 feet elevation gain

Difficult (to waterfalls)
8.2 miles round-trip
900 feet elevation gain

This pretty river splashes beneath mossy bigleaf maples and stately Douglas fir, deep in the Coast Range west of Salem. The first mile of the trail along the river passes gravelly beaches and wading pools—perfect for a hot summer day or an easy winter walk with the kids. For a longer hike, continue upstream 3.1 miles, partly through old clearcuts, to waterfalls in a forest canyon.

To find the trailhead, drive to Rickreall; it's 10 miles west of Salem, where Highway 22 crosses Highway 99W. From this crossroads, follow signs 4 miles to Dallas, and then follow signs to Falls City another 9 miles. At the far end of this secluded village, just before the main street turns left across a bridge, go straight on Black Rock Road. Keep left in 0.4 mile at a fork, go straight another 3.3 mile on gravel, and park just before a yellow gate at a river bridge. Don't drive onward even if the gate is open, as it can be locked without warning. Walk across the bridge and up the road 200 yards to the trailhead on the left.

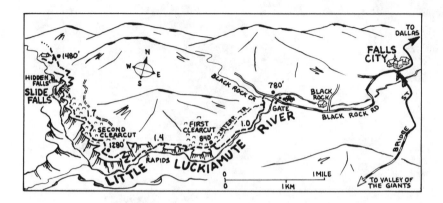

The path begins with a footbridge over Black Rock Creek. After 100 yards, keep left at a fork. Lady ferns, salmonberry, and shamrock-like oxalis crowd the lush forest's floor. Beware of stinging nettles (resembling tall, ragged mint plants). Summer blooms include bleeding hearts and red columbine.

After 0.7 mile a sign indicates that the trail crosses from Bureau of Land Management land to Willamette Industries timberland. If you're hiking with kids, this is a good place to turn back. Beyond, the path climbs through a rough 1989 clearcut to a T-shaped junction. To the right is an optional return route, an interpretive trail describing timber company forest management.

Turn left for the longer hike to the falls. This trail is a little rough, but easy to follow. It skirts the clearcut, follows the river through uncut woods for a lovely mile, then switchbacks up to a second, larger clearcut. Logged in 1990, then burned and planted with Douglas fir, this mile-long slope has regrown with silk tassel—tough, pungent bushes in the same genus as oaks. The Chemeketans, a Salem hiking club, arduously cleared and rebuilt the trail here after the logging.

Shortly after reentering uncut woods, pass a viewpoint above a 40-foot slide falls. Next the trail climbs to a steep canyon slope above the roar of a hidden waterfall. At a trail junction turn left to a campsite by a lovely bedrock riverbank with cool pools and refreshing little cascades. A scramble trail continues upstream from the junction, but the falls make a good turnaround point.

Valley of the Giants.

32   Valle y of the Giants

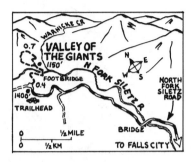

Easy
1.5-mile loop
400 feet elevation gain

This ancient grove, towering above the rushing headwaters of the Siletz River, is home to some of the largest trees in Oregon. While the hike here is not difficult, the drive is. Plan a full hour to negotiate the 28 miles of confusing, unmarked gravel logging roads between Falls City and the trailhead.

Start by driving to Rickreall, where Highway 22 from Salem crosses Highway 99W between Corvallis and McMinnville. From this intersection, follow signs 4 miles to Dallas, and then follow signs to Falls City another 9 miles. At the far end of this village, curve left across a bridge onto Bridge Street. In 0.7 mile the street turns to gravel, and in another mile it becomes a one-lane timber company road, where log trucks rumble on weekdays.

A total of 14.9 miles from Falls City, the road turns sharply left to avoid a locked gate with a "Keep Out" sign. This is the site of Valsetz, a logging company town built as the terminus of the Valley & Siletz Railroad. In the 1980s the company that owned the town removed the buildings, drained the neighboring millpond lake, and gated the road to keep out nostalgic former residents.

Just 200 yards after turning left at the gate, turn right at a T-shaped junction. (Remember this turn; it's easy to miss on your return drive.) Keep right around the old Valsetz lakebed, now full of snags, foxglove, and alder.

A total of 8.2 miles from the gate you'll cross a one-lane wooden bridge over the South Fork Siletz River. Beyond the bridge 0.2 mile take an uphill fork to the right. In another 0.3 mile, keep left at a fork. Now keep left at all junctions for 4.9 rough, potholed miles to a bridge over the North Fork Siletz River. Continue on the gravel road another 1.1 mile to a fork, and finally turn right for 0.5 mile to a sign for the Valley of the Giants Trail.

The trail itself descends among 450-year-old, 10-foot-thick Douglas firs, some rising 150 feet to their first branch. In June marbeled murrelets roost on the thickest of the high branches here. These small black-and-white birds spend the rest of their lives at sea. They only fly inland to lay their eggs, without benefit of a nest, on mossy, flat-topped branches 150 feet up in giant trees. A shortage of suitable old-growth trees has left the birds on the verge of extinction.

The path descends to the North Fork Siletz River, crosses on a steel footbridge, heads left past a picnic table, and then forks for a final, 0.7-mile loop through the area's grandest stand of big trees. White woodland flowers beneath the giants include star-flowered smilacina, queens cup, trillium, and oxalis.

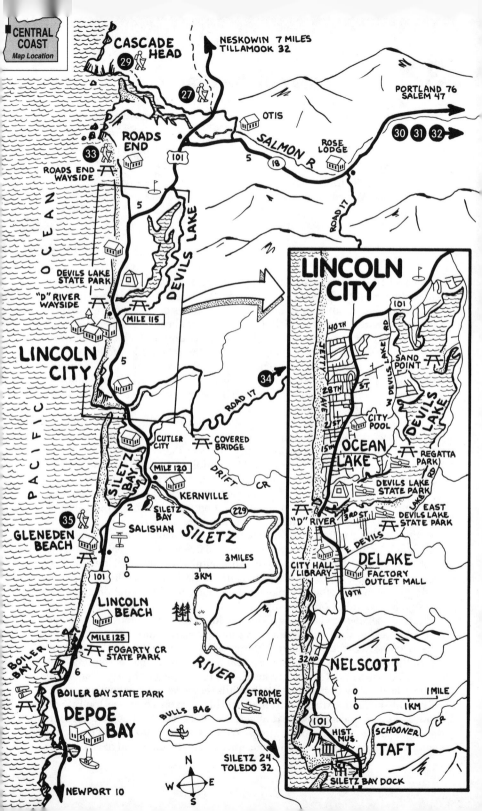

Siletz Bay and the Taft district of Lincoln City.

LINCOLN CITY

The longest town on the Oregon Coast, Lincoln City formed when 5 coastal communities voted to consolidate in 1964. Local entrepreneurs began billing their heavily-developed coastline as the "20 Miracle Miles." Then-governor Mark Hatfield dubbed the zone the "20 Miserable Miles," and in the resulting uproar many of the most garish motel signs and billboards were removed.

The area's natural scenery does border on the miraculous. Behind the beach, Devils Lake and Siletz Bay retain much of their pastoral setting. To the south, the seashore crinkles into a series of scenic coves at Fogarty Creek and Boiler Bay. Just beyond lies Depoe Bay, a quaint fishing village with the world's smallest harbor.

Oceanlake District

Shops line Highway 101 In the northernmost of Lincoln City's 5 boroughs. Best bets include the coffee at Cafe Roma's bookstore on North 16th Street, the maple bars at the Colonial Bakery on 17th, the indoor public swimming pool off 22nd, and the Siletz tribe's cavernous, flashy Chinook Winds casino on 40th.

Devils Lake

Indian legends of a hungry lake monster gave this freshwater lake its name. Despite the monster threat, waterskiing and swimming are popular in the relatively warm lake. Interest in water sports took a temporary dive when weeds choked the lake, apparently flourishing on seepage from lakeshore cottages. The introduction of weed-eating carp cleared the plants so successfully that the city has celebrated a Grass Carp Festival annually since 1986.

Just north of the D River bridge is the 100-campsite Devils Lake State Park (summer reservations accepted), with paddleboat and sailboard rentals nearby. On the opposite shore is East Devils Lake State Park, a day-use area with picnic tables and a boat ramp heavily used by waterskiers. To explore the quieter north end of the lake by canoe or sailboard, launch at Sand Point Park's beach (off East Devils Lake Road) or at one of the city parks along West Devils Lake Road.

D River Wayside

Shortest river in the world, the D River flows a mere 200 yards from Devils Lake to the sea. The state wayside at the Highway 101 river bridge provides access to a busy—and reliably windy—beach. One of the world's largest kite festivals is held here each year on a September or October weekend, bolstering Lincoln City's claim to be "Kite Capital of the World."

Delake district

Once a city in its own right, the Delake district now is home to Lincoln City's library and city hall at South 9th and a large mall of factory outlet stores at 14th.

Nelscott district

This beach community is named for Nelson and Scott, the developers who founded it in 1926. The district's old-fashioned, literate ambience inspired local mystery author M. K. Wren to set several of her popular murder stories in a cat-dominated used bookstore. Bookish haunts and antique shops still abound.

Taft District

The area's best seal watching and family beach fun is at the Siletz Bay dock in Lincoln City's Taft district. To find it, turn west 2 blocks at the South 51st Street traffic light near milepost 118. Taft's old city hall on Highway 101 now houses the free North Lincoln County Museum, open Wed-Sun noon-4.

Siletz Bay

Sawmills once poisoned this estuary, but time and care have brought about a remarkable recovery, with great blue herons and snowy egrets stalking among the driftwood on the bay's mudflats. A new wildlife refuge encompasses the grassy tidal plain southeast of Highway 101's Siletz River bridge. The hottest birdwatching, however, is from Cutler City's bayfront park (turn west off Highway 101 by the Lumbermen's store at the south end of Lincoln City).

Siletz River

Tidewater backs 18 miles up the forested canyon of this untamed river. For a scenic 62-mile loop drive, take paved Highway 229 upriver to the village of Siletz (headquarters of the Siletz Indian Reservation), continue to Toledo, turn right to Newport, and return along Highway 101.

For an easy 8-mile canoe exploration of a wild, roadless riverbend known colorfully as the Bulls Bag, leave a shuttle car at Strome Park, an unmarked gravel boat launch 14 miles up Highway 229 from Highway 101. Then drive another 4 miles upstream and launch at Morgan County Park's ramp.

Fogarty Creek State Park

Picture-perfect and protected from the wind, this park 6 miles south of Lincoln City features a cliff-rimmed beach where a lazy creek meanders past a climbable sea stack. A trail under a Highway 101 bridge leads to picnic tables and a parking area in a spruce forest. A day-use fee is charged.

Boiler Bay State Park

The explosion of a gas torch blew up the *J. Marhoffer* as she sailed past this rugged, lava-rimmed bay in 1910. The captain steered the flaming ship to the rocks, where, inspired by the courage of the captain's wife, all hands escaped to shore. All that remains of the ship is a barnacled boiler and driveshaft, accessible on the bay's rocky reef at low tide.

Low tide also exposes some of Oregon's richest tidepool life here. A short, rough trail down to the reef starts beside the Boiler Bay Bakery (incidentally, a source of outstanding breads, soups, and pastries). The official Boiler Bay State Park parking area, with lawns, picnic tables, and blufftop viewpoints, is half a mile farther south on Highway 101. This is a good spot to bring binoculars and watch whales; several spouters have taken up year-round residence nearby.

Depoe Bay

In picturesque Depoe Bay, whale watching boats thread their way from the world's smallest natural harbor through a rock channel to the sea. At high tide a spouting horn in a smaller chasm nearby sprays saltwater across Highway 101; don't park where the road is wet. Among the arcade-like row of gift shops lining the highway you'll find Oregon's smallest state park (itself a shop selling Oregon-made wares), several used bookstores, and the Siletz Tribal Smokehouse, featuring smoked fish. Down at the bay's docks, a small Coast Guard station with 44-foot ships is open to visitors Mon-Sat 4-8pm and Sun 1-8pm.

The town's name honors a Rogue River Indian who was forcibly moved to the Siletz Reservation and then lived near here. He spent so much time hanging around the Army depot in Toledo, however, that soldiers dubbed him Depot Charley. A later attempt at decorum upgraded the moniker to Charles DePoe.

Cormorants dry their wings at the Roads End headland (Hike #33).

Roads End.

33   Roads End

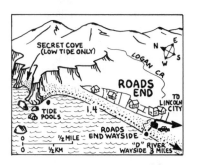

Easy
2.8 miles round-trip
No elevation gain

Even when Lincoln City's beaches are crowded or windy, this sheltered strand just north of town is surprisingly quiet. With tidepools, islands, and a headland with a hidden cove, it's a fine place for a romantic stroll.

Take Highway 101 to the Lighthouse Square shopping center at the north end of Lincoln City and turn onto Logan Road. (If you're coming from Portland or Salem, drive 2.7 miles south from the intersection of Highways 101 and 18.) Follow Logan Road a mile to Roads End State Park, a parking lot on the left.

A short path descends to the beach at the pebbly mouth of a lazy little creek. Hike to the right. For the first mile, the beachfront bank is topped by a jumble of quaint old cottages. Then the beach narrows to its end at a massive headland.

The tough black basalt lava of the promontory's tip has protected a long, striped orange cliff of softer sedimentary rock that curves back along the beach. Other fragments of lava form ragged islands, where comic, long-necked cormorants dry their black wings atop guano-stained roosts. At low tide, look in pools here for starfish, mussels, and anemones—but don't disturb these animals.

Also at low tide, it's possible to clamber around the headland's tip to a secret cove's beach. Tarry here and you'll be trapped until the next low tide.

34   Drift Creek Falls

Easy
3 miles round-trip
340 feet elevation gain

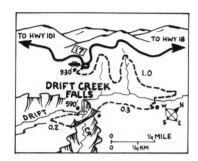

Newest trail in the Lincoln City area, this well-graded path descends through the woods to a dramatic, 150-foot suspension footbridge beside a 100-foot waterfall. The packed gravel path is passable even for strollers and wheelchairs. Trail Park passes are required at the trailhead. They cost $3 per car day or $25 per season, and are available at Forest Service offices.

From Lincoln City, take Highway 101 to milepost 119 at the south edge of town, turn east onto Drift Creek Road for 1.5 miles, turn right at a T-shaped junction, and 0.3 mile later, fork uphill to the left onto one-lane Drift Creek Camp Road (alias Road 17). In another 0.8 mile turn uphill to the left again. Then continue 9.1 twisty, paved miles to the large trailhead parking area on the right.

If you're coming from Portland or Salem, take Highway 18 toward the Coast, but turn left onto Bear Creek Road in the hamlet of Rose Lodge, 5 miles short of Highway 101. Then follow Bear Creek Road (which becomes Road 17) 8 miles.

The trail descends through a second-growth Douglas fir forest with sword ferns, red huckleberries, vine maple, and salal bushes. In early spring, big white trilliums and tiny white oxalis bloom here. After a mile the trail crosses a 20-foot-wide creek amid alders. The path briefly ducks through a brushy 1988 clearcut before entering an old-growth grove of big hemlock, red cedar, and fir.

At the 1.3-mile mark the trail spans Drift Creek's sudden, curving canyon on a dizzying suspension footbridge, site of a fatal construction accident in 1993. A waterfall beside the bridge spills a ribbon of spray into a misty pool.

Drift Creek Falls.

35 Salishan Spit

Difficult
8.1 miles round-trip
No elevation gain

Sandy peninsulas—known as spits—separate each of Oregon's coastal river bays from the sea. But only here, beside Siletz Bay, has the unstable dunescape been developed into a posh, private resort. Winter storms in 1972 and 1973 cut into the spit, destroying one partially built house and threatening others before bulldozers and truckloads of boulders stopped the erosion.

The spit's beach, of course, remains open to the public, and is almost always empty—except for shorebirds and the nearly 200 harbor seals that lounge at the peninsula's tip. Perhaps the most fun part of the hike, though, is ogling the elaborate and often weird homes built by the well-to-do on a foundation of shifting sand.

If you are staying at Salishan Lodge, or if you are a guest of a Salishan homeowner, you can start your hike at the Marketplace at Salishan, a cluster of upscale shops 3 miles south of Lincoln City on Highway 101 (near milepost 122). Park behind the gas station and follow a private nature trail along the dike separating the golf course from Siletz Bay. In half a mile the path crosses Salishan Drive to the beach.

If you don't have connections at Salishan you'll have to start a bit farther away, at the public beach access in Gleneden Beach. To find it, drive 0.8 mile south of Salishan, turn west onto Wessler Street at a sign for Gleneden Beach State Park, and drive 0.2 mile to a huge parking lot and small picnic area.

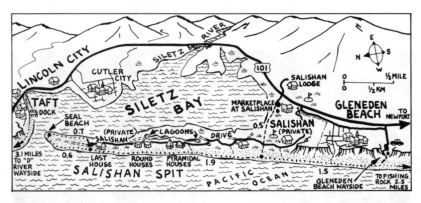

Harbor seals at the tip of Salishan Spit.   *Opposite: Salishan homes.*

A short paved trail descends through a wind-dwarfed spruce forest to a soft sand beach flanked by crumbling orange sandstone bluffs. Wet-suited surfers often catch waves here in the mornings. Seal heads peer from the surf.

As you hike to the right along the beach, the horizon ahead is dominated by the dark green cape of Cascade Head (Hike #29), and the Inn at Spanish Head, a 10-story concrete-and-glass bookshelf leaning against the cliffs of Lincoln City.

After a mile, the bluff ends and Salishan begins. The daring, angled rooflines of the uniformly gray houses here seem clipped from 1960s *Sunset* articles. Pass a pair of pyramidal palaces, then a duo of round domiciles, and, at the 3.4-mile mark, the last house. Another 0.6 mile brings you to the end of the spit, opposite the Taft dock. Disturbing the seals here is illegal, so don't venture too near.

Continue around the bayshore half a mile until the beach turns to mud. Then turn right across driftwood to the end of paved Salishan Drive. If you're a guest at the resort, you can return on a loop along this private road, rather than merely on the public beach. If you take the road, you'll pass lagoons and picturesquely placed houses for 1.9 miles. When you reach the golf course, either turn left on the nature trail to the Marketplace at Salishan, or turn right on a path to the beach.

Newport's Yaquina Bay Bridge.

NEWPORT

This romantic port is one of the oldest resort towns on the Coast. Top attractions include a world-class aquarium, 2 historic lighthouses, and a bustling bayfront. There's plenty of room for guests; Newport has more oceanview hotel rooms than any other city between San Francisco and Seattle.

Bay Front

In the quaint old streets along Yaquina Bay, whale watching tour offices, fish canneries, and clam chowder restaurants rub shoulders with commercial tourist attractions such as the Wax Works, Ripley's Believe It Or Not, and the Undersea Gardens. At the west end of the Bay Front, near Newport's bridge, an active Coast Guard station offers free daily tours from 1-4. At the east end are the Embarcadero docks, where you can charter a boat or rent crab nets.

Oregon Coast Aquarium

Not to be missed, this modern aquarium features large outdoor exhibits of playful sea otters, curious seals, and chattering sea birds. Indoors are hands-on exhibits, a video theater, a gift shop, a cafeteria, and a huge Plexiglass tank of pulsing jellyfish. New in 1996 is a giant tank with Keiko, the killer whale made famous in the movie *Free Willy*. Follow signs from the south end of Newport's bridge. Open daily 9-6 from Memorial Day through Labor Day; otherwise 10-5.

Hatfield Marine Science Center

If the Oregon Coast Aquarium seems too crowded—or too expensive—drive a block farther to this more sedate research center, reopened in January 1997 after 2 years of remodeling. Here are carefully labeled exhibits of Oregon marine species, including an octopus lurking in a tank by the door. Hours are 10-6 daily; 10-4 in winter.

Newport's Lincoln County Museum.

Yaquina Head

Inside Oregon's tallest lighthouse, built in 1873, narrow spiral stairs lead visitors up to a dizzying view. The lighthouse's scenic cape, Yaquina Head, was preserved in 1980 when Congress bought the headland from a gravel company that had planned to quarry it to sea level. Today the cape features an interpretive center, stairs to a cobble beach, and an all-accessible tidepool loop trail through a portion of the old quarry. A viewpoint beside the lighthouse overlooks islands teeming with cormorants, murres, tufted puffins, and seals. Whale watching is excellent here too. Drive 3 miles north of Newport on Highway 101 and turn left. Expect a $5-per-car day use fee. See Hike #37.

Otter Crest Scenic Route

This twisty portion of old Highway 101 traces the cliffy face of Cape Foul-weather below the modern highway. English explorer Captain Cook named the cape on a stormy day in 1778. The old road passes an artistic 1930s bridge, a viewpoint atop Otter Crest, and the entrance to Devils Punchbowl State Park—a panoramic picnic area on a cave-riddled sea bluff (see Hike #36).

Beverly Beach State Park

A short trail from this popular park leads under a Highway 101 bridge to long, often windy Beverly Beach. The 279-site campground is open all year, with reservations accepted in summer. The park includes a picnic area and 0.9-mile loop trail along Spencer Creek. See Hike #36.

Historic Museums

An 1895 Victorian mansion and a neighboring log cabin hold the Lincoln County Historical Society's exhibits of pioneer artifacts. Located 1 block east of Highway 101 in Newport's Old Town, the free museum is open Tue-Sat 11-4.

Toledo

Toledo lost its county courthouse to rival Newport in the mid 1900s. Today this well-preserved, off-the-beaten-track milltown features antique shops.

South Beach

Construction of the Oregon Coast Aquarium in 1992 woke up this sleepy Newport suburb south of the Yaquina Bay bridge. A cluster of shops beside the South Beach Marina includes the popular Rogue Ale microbrewery. A mile down the road, amid the beachfront's grassy dunes, South Beach State Park offers 254 campsites and a network of trails (see Hike #38).

Nye Beach

Art galleries, B&Bs, and romantic beachfront hotels cluster near 3rd and Coast streets in Newport's historic Nye Beach district. Best bets include the Sylvia Beach Hotel, a 1910 classic renovated with a literary theme, and the Cosmos Cafe, a funky coffee shop with an off-beat gallery. The Newport Visual Arts Center at 239 NW Beach Drive hosts juried art exhibits; it's free, and open noon-4 daily in summer (otherwise 11-3). The nearby Newport Performing Arts Center (777 W Olive) stages concerts, plays, and festivals.

Yaquina Bay

Flamboyant entrepreneur Colonel T. Egenton Hogg whirled into Newport in the 1870s promoting a transcontinental railroad that he claimed would turn the town into a new San Francisco. When canny locals responded by demanding high prices for his railroad right-of-way, Hogg angrily built his terminal 4 miles short of the city and instead ferried rail tourists the final miles across Yaquina Bay to the beach. Today a scenic, 14-mile bayside road between Newport and Toledo passes the abandoned railbed's trestle pilings. Oyster farms dot the route. For the bay's best birdwatching, however, park at the far left corner of the Hatfield Marine Science Center and stroll the short Estuary Trail to viewpoints.

Sea otter at the Oregon Coast Aquarium.

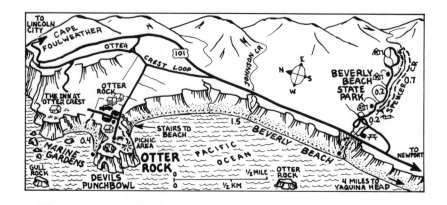

36   Devils Punchbowl

Easy (to the Devils Punchbowl)
1.1 miles round-trip
100 feet elevation gain

Moderate (to Beverly Beach)
4.3 miles round-trip
150 feet elevation gain

When 3 wave-carved caves met underneath the yellow sandstone bluffs of Otter Rock, their roofs collapsed, leaving a gigantic "punchbowl" at the tip of the panoramic headland. For an easy walk that's fun even with kids, explore the punchbowl from above and below, passing tidepools along the way. For a longer hike, walk the beach south to a woodsy loop beside the campground at Beverly Beach.

To start, drive 8 miles north of Newport (or 15 miles south of Lincoln City) on Highway 101 to the Devils Punchbowl State Park turnoff between mileposts 132 and 133. Then follow signs 0.7 mile to the park's day-use parking area.

Park the car and walk up the road a block—past a chowder restaurant and some shops—to a fenced overlook. What looks like orange paint on the punchbowl's sides is natural lichen. The bowl's soft sandstone would erode much quicker, but it's stacked atop an ancient lava flow of tough black basalt. The same lava flow left the many flat islands and reefs visible from here. Walk left around the picnic area to pick up more views on the way back to your car.

To visit the inside of the punchbowl and the Marine Gardens tidepools, walk 2 blocks along C Street (the other street by the parking lot). Just past the street's "Dead End" sign, take the trail to the left down through spruce woods to a hidden, quarter-mile-long beach. Low tide here exposes vast rock shelves where starfish and anemones crowd the cracks. Don't touch these animals, and don't walk on the mussels. Also beware of the extremely slippery green seaweed.

At the left end of the beach you can sneak into the Devils Punchbowl through either of 2 caves, though one is blocked at high tide.

For the longer hike along Beverly Beach, return to your car and cross the road to a 97-step staircase descending the other side of Otter Rock's headland. The beach here is a hot spot for surfers, and nicely sheltered from the north winds that bedevil many a summer beach picnic. Walk south along Beverly Beach 1.5 miles to pebbly Spencer Creek and turn inland on a trail underneath the Highway 101 bridge. Don't cross the creek to the picnic area unless you've left a shuttle car there. Instead go straight to a campground fee booth (where you can pick up a nature trail brochure) and continue straight on a campground loop road to site C5T. Here a wide nature trail crosses Spencer Creek on a footbridge. The heavily used path loops 0.7 mile through second-growth alder and spruce along the creek's bank before ending at campsite E9T. Turn left and walk back to the beach along the campground road.

Marine Gardens.   Opposite: Inside the Devils Punchbowl.

37 Newport Lighthouses

Easy (Yaquina Head exploration)
2.6 miles round-trip
300 feet elevation gain

Easy (Old Town tour)
3-mile loop
250 feet elevation gain

Newport's two historic lighthouses are both popular tourist destinations, but they also serve as starting points for easy hiking explorations of Newport's scenic coast. Begin at the Yaquina Head lighthouse, on a dramatic cape with a modern interpretive center. Then drive into town to visit the older Yaquina Bay lighthouse, where a 3-mile loop takes you through Old Town to the bayfront.

To find Yaquina Head, drive 3 miles north of Newport on Highway 101 and turn left. Stop at the headland's entrance booth to pay the $5-per-car fee, and then continue half a mile to the large Interpretive Center parking lot on the right. After touring the displays here, walk or drive another 0.3 mile to a small parking area and turnaround at road's end, near the headland's tip.

From there, a short, paved path leads to the 1873 Yaquina Head lighthouse, Oregon's tallest. Climb the 93-foot tower's spiral stair to the lantern room, with its two-ton lens of curved glass prisms. A deck at the tower's base overlooks islands where cormorants, murres, and seagulls nest. Watch for whale spouts.

Next return to the parking turnaround and take a staircase down to an

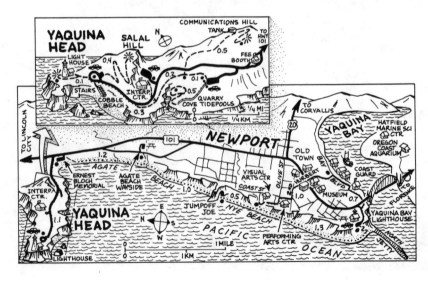

Yaquina Head from Jumpoff Joe's tunnel. *Opposite: Yaquina Bay Lighthouse.*

unusual beach of black basalt cobbles, where you'll find tidepools at low tide. Harbor seals lounge on nearby islands. Then return to the parking turnaround. Near the restrooms you'll find a trail that switchbacks 0.4 mile up through wildflowers to Salal Hill and a bird's-eye viewpoint of the entire cape.

Before leaving Yaquina Head, drive down to the Quarry Cove trailhead for a 1-mile hike on concrete paths through a former gravel quarry, converted in 1994 to wheelchair-accessible tidepools.

To visit Newport's older Yaquina Bay lighthouse, drive back to Highway 101 and turn south through town. Immediately before the Yaquina Bay Bridge, veer right at a state park sign to a picnic area below the turreted 1871 lighthouse. Newport's oldest building, it's open for free tours daily 11-5.

Locals claim the Yaquina Bay Lighthouse is haunted, a tale aided by the fact the building was abandoned after only 3 years of use. Planners had intended for a supporting lighthouse to be placed 10 miles north at Cape Foulweather, but a local Army colonel ordered it built nearer instead, on the more accessible Yaquina Head. The mixup left the older Yaquina Bay lighthouse superfluous.

For a walking tour of Newport, go down stone steps from the picnic area to the beach and head north along the sand 1.3 miles. When you reach the historic Nye Beach district (heralded by Nye Creek and a pair of quaintly-painted historic hotels), walk up to a plaza atop a concrete street turnaround. Climb stairs to the right past the Newport Visual Arts Center gallery (open daily in the early afternoon) and go straight on Cliff Street to the funky Cosmos Cafe and the Newport Performing Arts Center. Here jog left a block on Olive, turn right on Coast Street a block, go left on Second Street for 3 blocks, and then angle to the right on Hurbert Street to Highway 101 in Old Town. Continue on Hurbert Street, which turns into Canyon Way and passes the Canyon Way Bookstore, a labyrinthine wonderland hiding an award-winning restaurant.

At the end of Canyon Way, turn right along the bayfront past wharves, fish canneries, and the original Mo's restaurant. Skirt the grounds of a historic Coast Guard station and duck under the Yaquina Bay Bridge to return to your car.

38 South Beach

Easy (Estuary Trail)
0.7 mile one way
No elevation gain

Easy (Mike Miller Trail)
1-mile loop
100 feet elevation gain

Easy (to South Jetty)
2.1-mile loop
No elevation gain

These 3 short trails just south of Newport visit an estuary, an old-growth forest, and a jetty. The paths are easy enough that you can hike all of them in an afternoon. But pick just one if you're hiking with kids or if you're planning to round out the day with a visit to one of the aquariums here.

The easiest of the 3 paths traces the edge of Yaquina Bay's estuary. Drive to the south end of Newport's Yaquina Bay Bridge and follow signs to the Hatfield Marine Science Center, a research center with lots of public exhibits and well-labeled tanks of Oregon marine species. Park by the "Nature Trail" sign at the far left end of the parking lot.

The paved path is accessible even to strollers and wheelchairs. Trail brochures are out of print, but interpretive signs describe the estuary ecosystem. You're sure to spot great blue herons and shorebirds. At low tide, clam diggers often work the mud flats ringing the bay here.

The Estuary Trail curves through head-high yellow lupine and Scotch broom for 0.4 mile to a long boardwalk across an arm of the estuary. The odd tubrous plant greening the mud flats here is pickleweed, a globally rare, edible species that thrives on saltwater and is sometimes collected as a salty salad green. Just beyond the boardwalk, the path ends at a road. Either follow the road 2 blocks to the Oregon Coast Aquarium or simply return as you came.

To try a 1-mile loop through an old-growth coastal forest, drive 1.2 miles south of the Yaquina Bay Bridge on Highway 101, turn left at a sign for the Mike Miller Park Educational Area, and follow a gravel road 0.2 mile to a parking area and map board. This trail loops through a stand of 6-foot-thick hemlock and spruce. Twice the path crosses a long, marshy pond on scenic footbridges. Look here for osprey nests made of sticks on the tops of tall snags.

If you'd rather hike on the beach, drive Highway 101 south of the Yaquina Bay Bridge 1.4 miles, turn right at a sign for South Beach State Park, and drive straight 0.5 mile to the day-use parking area. Park by the restrooms and cross the grassy foredune to a broad, white-sand beach. Hike to the right 0.9 mile to the Yaquina River's South Jetty. Huge brown pelicans plummet into the water here, spearing fish with their bills. Gulls and other seabirds lurk nearby, hoping for leftovers. Climb up on the jetty for a view across the busy ship channel to the Yaquina Bay Lighthouse. A row of pilings upriver marks the route of a railroad that brought jetty rock here.

Pilings lining Yaquina Bay's South Jetty.   *Opposite: Brown pelican.*

To return on a loop, follow the jetty-top road inland 0.3 mile. Look for a sign on the right marking a trail into the grassy dunes. Take the left fork of this sandy path 0.2 mile to a paved trail. Walk 50 yards left on the paved trail to a signpost.

Here you have a choice. The shortest route back to your car is to turn right on a 0.7-mile bark dust path across the sandy deflation plain. For a longer loop, keep left at all junctions. This route follows the Cooper Ridge Trail on a low wooded rise around the campground 1.3 miles to the entrance fee booth. From there, a half-mile walk along the road completes the loop to your car.

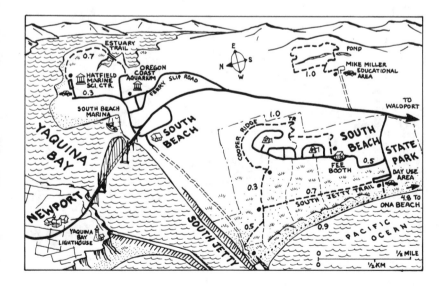

CENTRAL
COAST
Map Location

NEWPORT

TOLEDO

Oregon Coast Aquarium

SOUTH
BEACH

SOUTH BEACH
STATE PARK 38

MILE 145

2 ELK CITY RD

YAQUINA

RIVER

HOLIDAY
BEACH

7

101

1000 LINE RD

FOREST

LOST
CREEK

50

10

ONA BEACH
STATE PARK

39

2

N BEAVER CR RD

4

N ELKHORN RD

50

MILE 150

ONA

6

51

SEAL
ROCK
S.P.

SEAL ROCK

51

SEAL
ROCK

5

A
T
I
O
N
A
L

DRIFT

CREEK

40

DRIFT

5087

3

MILE 155

ALSEA
BAY

CREEK

WILDERNESS

3460

ALSEA BAY
BRIDGE INTERP.
CTR.

DRIFT

41

3449

3446

PATTERSON

WALDPORT
RANGER
STATION

WALDPORT

ALSEA

3446

3

101

4

RISLEY CR RD

ALSEA 33
CORVALLIS 5

5

WACONDA
BEACH

7

34

RIVER

42 43 44 45

BEACHSIDE STATE PARK

N

MILE 160

W   E

TILLICUM BEACH

S

0   3 MILES

YACHATS 4

0   3 KM

Waldport's new Alsea Bay Bridge.

WALDPORT

Waldport's name derives from the German word *Wald* ("forest"). Appropriately, the forest begins just behind the area's long, quiet beaches and extends inland to the old-growth groves of Drift Creek Wilderness and Marys Peak.

Alsea Bay Bridge Interpretive Center

Waldport's original Alsea Bay Bridge, built in 1936 by luminary state engineer Conde McCullough, won a place on the National Historic Register in 1981 for its graceful arches. But the bridge was replaced ten years later when engineers found that salt air had weakened its concrete. At the south end of the new span's single, nostalgic arch is a surprisingly interesting interpretive center with photographs and models telling the story of Waldport and its bridges. The free museum is open daily 9-4 except in winter, when it's closed Sundays and Mondays. Saturdays at 2, rangers lead guided walks along the bayfront and help visitors cast miniature concrete bridge models in the sand.

Seal Rock State Park

From the small picnic area in this blufftop park, a short paved trail descends to a sandy cove sheltered by rocky islands. Low tide exposes vast rock flats with tidepools. Bring binoculars to spot seals lounging on offshore reefs.

Ona Beach State Park

One of the most pleasant picnic areas on the coast, this park has lawns, a looping river, and trails across a bridge to a sandy river mouth. See Hike #39.

Alsea Bay

No jetties tame the mouth of the Alsea, so the river can still be capricious. A 1983 storm swept nearly a thousand feet off the end of the Alsea spit, undermining oceanfront homes. Today it's fun to watch seals basking on the mudflat islands that emerge from the estuary at low tide. Birdwatching is best at high tide, when rising water scoots shorebirds to the bank, where they're easier to spot. Crabbing is also popular. Rent crab pots and boats at The Dock of the Bay, on the waterfront in Waldport's Old Town.

Seal Rock. Opposite: Old-growth forest in the northern Drift Creek Wilderness.

39   Ona Beach and Seal Rock

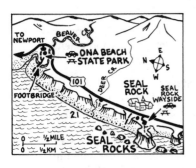

Moderate
4.2 miles round-trip
100 feet elevation gain

The Ona Beach picnic area and the island-ringed headland at Seal Rock rank among the most scenic spots on the central Oregon Coast. Although you could visit them by car, why not hike from one to the other along a quiet beach?

Start at Ona Beach State Park, near milepost 149 on Highway 101, south of Newport 7 miles. From the parking area, take the large paved trail straight ahead, past picnic lawns and restrooms. Cross a footbridge over lazy, looping, 100-foot-wide Beaver Creek. Then turn left along the bluff-edged beach toward Seal Rock. The beach narrows at high tide, so watch for waves.

Strangely, the lava forming Seal Rock matches flows found near Idaho in Hells Canyon. Odder yet, a dozen headlands on the northern Oregon Coast are composed of identical rock. Geologists say this proves Seal Rock is the toe of one of the largest lava floods in Earth's history. Fifteen million years ago, when the North American continent buckled as it rammed westward over the Pacific Ocean floor, immense flows of Columbia River basalt welled up through cracks near Hells Canyon. The lava puddled up in Eastern Oregon before surging through the Columbia Gorge and fanning south along the coast to here.

When you reach Seal Rock, do not try to climb directly up the headland's slippery face. Instead, at a small creek just before the next-to-last blufftop house (0.3 mile short of the cape) take an unmarked path up a draw to a highway guardrail near Grebe Street, 300 yards from the entrance to Seal Rock State Park's picnic area. Short, paved trails from the picnic area lead to a viewpoint on the headland's neck and down to a beach and tidepools on the south side.

40 Drift Creek North

Difficult
8-mile loop
1400 feet elevation gain

So few ancient forests have survived in the Coast Range that Drift Creek's wilderness canyon really stands out. Three trails descend through the old growth to this wild coastal stream, overhung with mossy maples. The northern Horse Creek Trail described here is slightly longer than the other routes (see Hike #41), but it passes the biggest trees and concludes with a lovely creekside loop that doesn't require fording the bridgeless stream. All of the paths head downhill, so save some energy for the climb back to your car.

To start, drive 7 miles north of Waldport on Highway 101 to Ona Beach State Park, turn right on North Beaver Creek Road for 1 mile to a fork. Veer left for 2.7 miles to a T-shaped junction, and turn right onto one-lane, paved North Elkhorn Road. At another T-junction in 5.8 miles, turn left onto Road 50 for 1.4 miles. Then fork right onto gravel Road 5087 for 3.4 miles to the trailhead.

Don't start hiking at the road barricade, but rather on the path by the registration box. Nearly level for the first mile, this trail sets off through a rare, almost pure stand of old-growth western hemlock trees up to 5 feet in diameter. Later you'll pass 7-foot-thick Douglas fir and Sitka spruce. In spring look for white wildflowers: 6-petaled queens cup, shamrock-leaved oxalis, and wild lily-of-the-valley. In fall, orange chanterelle mushrooms dot the path's edge.

After a distant glimpse of the ocean at the 2-mile mark, the trail heads

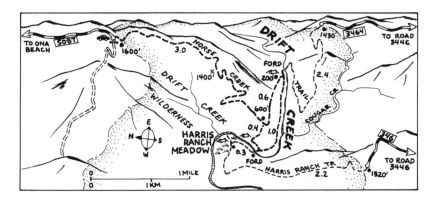

Drift Creek.   Opposite: Bedrock pools near the lower Drift Creek ford.

seriously downhill, switchbacking 1.6 miles to a T-shaped junction in a creekside salmonberry thicket. There's a bouldery ford 100 yards to the left, but don't take it. Instead turn right and follow the Harris Ranch Trail downstream. After 1 mile this pleasant path also leads to a ford, this time at a bedrock creekbank. Don't wade here either. Climb to the right on an unofficial trail that leads 150 yards to a large campsite on a forested bench above the creek. From here head straight uphill on a rough path 0.4 mile to the Horse Creek Trail. Turn left to return.

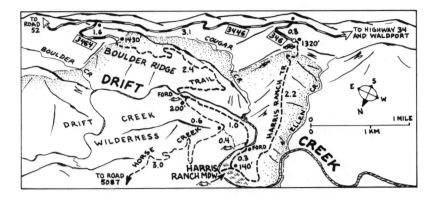

41   Drift Creek South

Moderate (to Harris Ranch)
4.4 miles round-trip
1200 feet elevation gain

Difficult (shuttle to Boulder Ridge)
5.9 miles round-trip
1300 feet elevation gain

(Refer to map on previous page)

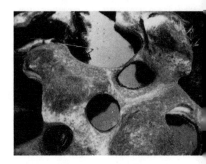

Overhung with mossy bigleaf maples, Drift Creek meanders through the densely forested canyons of the Coast Range's largest wilderness area. For the easiest route to the creek, hike the Harris Ranch Trail down to an ancient homestead meadow in a creek bend. If you want to continue, you can ford the creek and climb the Horse Creek Trail to a different trailhead—just a 5-mile car shuttle away from the first. The hikes end uphill, so save some energy for the home stretch.

To start, drive Highway 34 east of Waldport 6.9 miles (or west of Corvallis 57 miles) to an Alsea River bridge. Turn north on narrow Risley Creek Road (alias Road 3446) for 4.1 miles, always taking the larger fork at junctions, and then veer left onto gravel Road 346 for 0.8 mile to the Harris Ranch Trailhead.

The path sets out through an old-growth rainforest of alder, 5-foot-thick Douglas firs, and droopy-limbed red cedars. Underbrush here includes salmonberry, vine maple, and lady fern. After 2.2 miles downhill, the trail enters a field of bracken and blackberries—a pre-World War II homestead pasture gone wild.

Don't overlook a faint, unmarked junction at the start of the meadow. For the shorter hike, keep straight at this junction to find a large, lovely campsite beneath big streamside cedars. The bare bedrock banks of Drift Creek are great for picnicking or sunbathing. Red crawdads crawl through the shallows.

For the longer hike, turn right at the meadow junction and keep right for 0.3 mile to a ford. Crossing the creek here requires a chilly, knee-deep wade. Rarely, after mid-winter rains, the creek isn't passable at all.

On the far shore, the trail continues upstream through a mossy forest of spruce and maples for 1 mile to another ford. The creek here is smaller and full of boulders, so hikers can usually cross dry-footed in summer and fall. The Horse Creek Trail on the far shore climbs steadily 2.4 miles up Boulder Ridge to the end of gravel Road 3464. To find this trailhead from Highway 34, drive Risley Creek Road (alias Road 3446) a total of 7.2 miles, taking the larger fork at all junctions, and turn left on Road 3464 to its end.

Other Hiking Options

It's possible to hike from these trails to the northern Drift Creek Wilderness trailhead described in Hike #41, but shuttling a car to that trailhead requires a 33-mile drive on slow, twisty backroads.

42   Marys Peak   

Easy (road to summit)
1.2 miles round-trip
340 feet elevation gain
Open April through November

Easy (Meadow Edge Trail)
2.2-mile loop
500 feet elevation gain

Moderate (East Ridge Trail)
5-mile loop
1250 feet elevation gain

Highest spot in the Coast Range, Marys Peak's wildflower-dotted summit meadows command views from the ocean to the Cascades. Four different trails ascend this mountain, ranging from easy paths to long, hard climbs. When winter whitens the summit, the road to the observation point is plowed for sledders and skiers. Sno-park permits are required when there is snow, and the rest of the year you'll need a Trail Park pass (available at outdoor stores).

Kalapuya Indians sent young men to the summit in quest of guiding spirit visions. The mountain's Indian name, Chateemanwi ("place where spirits dwell"), survives in the name for nearby Chintimini Creek. Numerous Marys have been credited for the peak's mysterious English name.

Indian legend offers an explanation for the summit's unusual alpine wild-flowers and noble fir forest—rare in the Coast Range. Apparently the trickster god Coyote stole Panther's wife, and Panther retaliated by kidnapping Coyote's son. In his anger, Coyote dammed the Willamette and flooded all but this peak's summit, which he spared as a refuge for plants and animals. Botanists see a thread of truth in the tale. Oregon's climate has warmed over the past 6000 years, forcing once-common Ice Age species to retreat to this mountaintop "island."

The easiest and only crowded hike at Marys Peak is the 0.6-mile stroll up a gated gravel service road from the observation point parking lot to the summit, beside 2 radio relay buildings. On a clear day, views extend from the ocean to

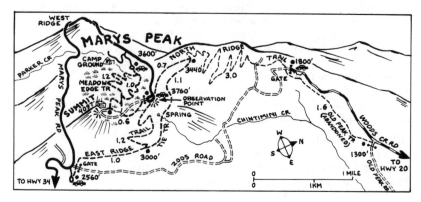

Marys Peak summit meadows.   Opposite: Old-growth forest on the East Ridge Trail.

Mt. Rainier and Mt. Thielsen. July colors the summit meadows with red Indian paintbrush, purple penstemon, white yarrow, and blue butterflies.

To find the observation point trailhead, take Highway 20 west of Corvallis through Philomath, fork left onto Highway 34 for 8.8 miles and turn right on paved Marys Peak Road 9.5 miles to its end. (From Highway 101 at Waldport, take Highway 34 inland 48 miles and turn left.)

But why jostle with crowds? The Meadow Edge Trail is only a mile longer and offers a far quieter, more interesting loop to the summit. To start, drive Marys Peak Road only 8.8 miles up from Highway 34, turn right at the Marys Peak campground entrance, and 100 yards later fork left to a picnic area and trailhead. Keep left when the path splits after 150 yards. The trail climbs along the margin between a rare grove of huge, old-growth noble fir and a meadow. After 0.7 mile turn left at a junction, and 80 yards later turn right, to climb to the summit viewpoint. To finish the loop, head back down and keep left at all junctions.

The moderate East Ridge Trail climbs across a slope of dense, old-growth Douglas fir to the peak's high meadow views. Start this hike by driving the Marys Peak Road only 5.5 miles up from Highway 34. At an "East Ridge Conner's Camp" pointer, turn right to a trailhead parking lot. The well-graded path soon enters a stand of 5-foot-thick fir with June wildflowers: 3-leaved vanilla leaf, white starflower, and yellow Oregon grape. After a mile, fork left and climb 1.2 miles to the observation point parking lot. (A detour here will take you up the gravel road to the actual summit.) To return on a loop, walk to the far end of the parking lot past a picnic table and take the North Ridge Trail down a forested crest 0.7 mile. At an unmarked junction, turn sharply right onto the Tie Trail, which passes a small spring and traverses back to the East Ridge Trail.

Other Hiking Options

The most challenging route up Marys Peak, the North Ridge Trail, switchbacks up through dense forest to the observation point parking lot, gaining 2000 feet in 3.7 miles. To find the trailhead, drive west from Corvallis through Philomath, fork right on Highway 20 for 1.8 miles (to milepost 48), and turn left on Woods Creek Road 7.6 miles to a locked gate.

43   McDonald Forest

Moderate
4.8-mile loop
900 feet elevation gain

Left: Willamette Valley viewpoint.

This 11-square-mile Oregon State University research forest includes 6 self-guiding nature walks. Because the short loops often overlap, it's tempting to combine them. The tour described here visits many of the area's highlights—an old-growth forest, a lake, and a dramatic viewpoint of the Willamette Valley.

Drive Highway 99W north of Corvallis 5 miles (or south of Monmouth 16 miles), turn west onto Arboretum Road for 0.8 mile, and turn west again at a Peavy Arboretum entrance sign. Then keep left at all forks for 0.3 mile to a gravel parking area before a locked orange gate.

Walk back downhill 100 yards to a brochure box for the Forest Discovery Trail, a loop introducing some of the arboretum's plants. Walk up the trail and take a right-hand fork amid second-growth Douglas fir, bigleaf maple, and sword fern. Keep uphill at other junctions: first jog to the right 100 yards on a gravel road, then fork right, then cross an unmarked trail, and finally reach an X-shaped junction. You'll want to turn left here along the Section 36 Loop, but first detour 100 yards to the right to pick up a trail brochure at the Forestry Club Cabin.

Brochure in hand, set out on the Section 36 Loop. This path gradually climbs 1.2 miles through clearcuts and experimental ponderosa pine plantations to a gravel road and a brochure box for the Powder House Trail. Turn left along the road 0.4 miles to its end at a hilltop with a sweeping view across the Willamette Valley to Mt. Hood and Mt. Jefferson. Spot the Three Sisters above Albany.

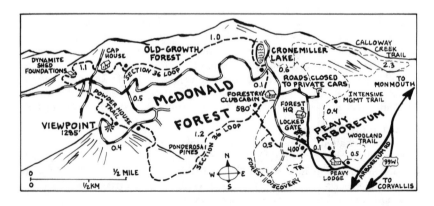

The Powder House Trail descends from this viewpoint, crosses 3 gravel logging roads, passes the foundations of a dynamite storage building, crosses another road beside a dynamite cap storage shed, and descends through a lovely, mossy grove of 6-foot-thick Douglas fir giants. After a downhill mile, turn right at an X-junction and skirt the shore of Cronemiller Lake, a tree-rimmed reservoir where foresters hold annual log-rolling competitions. At the lake's far end, turn briefly right on a gravel road to find a sign for the trail to the Forestry Club Cabin. From there, walk down either the road or the trail 0.5 mile to your car. Four other McDonald Forest hikes are described on pages 231-232.

44 Finley Wildlife Refuge

Easy (Woodpecker Loop)
1.2-mile loop
100 feet elevation gain

Easy (Mill Hill Loop)
2.9-mile loop
100 feet elevation gain

Easy (Beaver Pond Loop)
3-mile loop
No elevation gain
Open May 1 to October 31

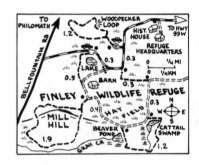

When the draining of Willamette Valley wetlands led to a decline of dusky Canada goose populations in the 1960s, the U. S. Fish and Wildlife Service used money from the sale of duck hunter stamps to convert this 8-square-mile farm into a bird-friendly patchwork of ponds, woodlands, and farmfields.

Since then 3 easy loop trails have been laid out so hikers can enjoy this rural birdland. Here too is the 1855 farmhouse of John Fiechter, a German whose success in the California gold rush financed a Greek Revival clapboard classic. Furnished with antiques, the restored home is open 1-5 on summer Sundays.

Drive Highway 99W south of Corvallis 10 miles (or north of Monroe 5 miles) to a Finley Refuge sign at milepost 93. Turn west on a gravel road for 0.7 mile, and then turn left on Finley Refuge Road for 1.5 zigzagging miles to the Fiechter House. To start the easiest of the 3 hikes, continue 0.9 mile and turn right at a sign for the Woodpecker Loop.

Named for the 5 woodpecker species that might be seen in this varied habitat, the broad gravel path begins in a grassy field with blackberries and wild roses, forks left through oak woodlands, climbs amid second-growth Douglas firs, and spans a boggy swale on a boardwalk. Near loop's end is an observation deck built around a huge oak. Views extend across the Willamette Valley to the Halsey mill, the Coburg Hills, and the snowy tips of Mt. Jefferson and the Three Sisters.

For the other 2 loop trails, drive 0.6 mile farther along Finley Refuge Road and park on the left in a gravel lot overlooking a fenced, bird-filled lake. Follow Mill Hill Loop signs to the right. In 0.3 mile, turn right along a gravel road for

300 yards to a junction at a curve. If Mill Hill's your goal, turn right at a "Trail" pointer, follow a mowed path straight to Gray Creek, and keep right around the low, wooded hill to complete the loop.

If you'd prefer the longer Beaver Pond loop (closed November 1 to April 30 to protect geese), stick to the gravel road at the Mill Hill turnoff. Follow the road 0.4 mile across a farmfield, and turn right at another "Trail" sign. This path passes a diked pond with ducks and nutria (alas, no beaver), makes several left turns, passes a diked cattail pond, and returns to the road. Turn right on the road 0.3 mile to a curve, turn left along a hedgerow another 0.3 mile, and turn right across a field to find the road back to your car.

45   Alsea Falls

Easy (to Alsea Falls)
1.9-mile loop
250 feet elevation gain

Moderate (to Green Peak Falls)
3.5-mile loop
400 feet elevation gain

Half the fun of visiting this Coast Range waterfall is discovering the scenic road that leads here between the rustic, time-forgotten hamlets of Alsea and Alpine. At the falls themselves you'll find a small campground, a well maintained picnic area, and a loop trail completed by Boy Scouts in 1994.

Many visitors here drive the South Fork Road as an unhurried alternate route to or from the Coast. If you're coming from the Willamette Valley, drive Highway 99W just north of Monroe (or 16 miles south of Corvallis), turn west at a sign for Alpine, follow Alsea Falls signs 12.7 paved miles, turn right into the camping area entrance, and keep left 100 yards to the trailhead. If you're coming from Highway 101 at Waldport, head inland on Highway 34 for 39 miles to the town of Alsea, turn right 0.9 mile at a sign for Lobster Valley, turn left on South Fork Road for 8.5 miles (including 2 miles of gravel), drive past the Alsea Falls picnic area, and turn left into the campground at an "Alsea Falls Recreation Area" sign.

Don't cross the footbridge across the river (the loop's return route). Instead start at a trail sign on the left beside a park maintenance garage. This riverside path ambles among second-growth hemlock and Douglas fir. Below them are giant old stumps, sword fern, moss-draped vine maple, shamrock-like oxalis, and salal bushes. Look for crawdads in the river.

Keep right on a wide trail through the picnic area. Near the last picnic tables, detour a few steps to the right to an overlook at the top of the 20-foot falls. Then continue straight on a small trail that switchbacks down 100 yards to a deep pool at the base of the falls. There is no bridge, so hikers with small children might want to turn back here.

Alsea Falls.   Opposite: Alder cones.

Clamber across the river on the bouldery logjam at the lower end of the pool. Then continue downstream on a rougher, narrower trail through an old-growth forest. Beware of 3-leaved poison oak here. The tread improves at a junction.

If you're ready to return via a loop, turn right on a path that climbs along the river's north shore 1 mile to the footbridge by your car.

If you'd like to extend the hike by taking a side trip to Green Peak Falls, turn left at the junction. In 200 yards the trail becomes a road. Continue straight, join a larger gravel road, ignore dirt bike paths up to the right, and in 400 yards meet the entrance road to McBee Park, a rundown picnic area owned by a timber company. Turn right on the entrance road for 100 feet, but promptly turn right through a picnic site and follow a muddy dirt-bike trail along Peak Creek. This trail becomes a very nice footpath that climbs up and down through an old-growth grove to a viewpoint of Green Peak Falls' 60-foot waterslide. A steep scramble path descends to a pool at the falls' base.

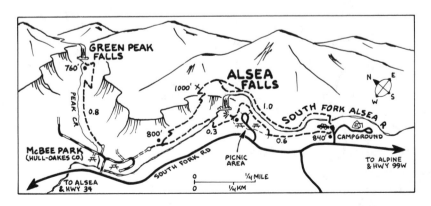

CENTRAL COAST
Map Location

WALDPORT 5 MILES

TILLICUM BEACH

SAN MARINE

101

4

YACHATS TRAIL

46

SMELT SANDS WAYSIDE

YACHATS

YACHATS

MILE 165

YACHATS OCEAN RD

3

SIUSLAW

YACHATS RIVER RD

YACHATS RIVER

VIEWPOINT

CAPE PERPETUA AUTO TOUR ROUTE

54

PERPETUA

VISITOR CENTER

CAPE PERPETUA

47

DEVILS CHURN

GWYNN CR

55

5590

KELLER CREEK

CUMMINS CR

48

CUMMINS CREEK

NEPTUNE STATE PARK

STRAWBERRY HILL

BOB CR

CUMMINS RIDGE

55

BOB CR PULLOUT

MILE 170

49

WILDERNESS

5694

NATIONAL

TENMILE CREEK

AUDUBON PRESERVE

56

STONEFIELD BEACH

9

TENMILE CREEK

OCEAN BEACH

ROCK CR

ROCK CREEK

ROCK CREEK

ROCK CREEK WILDERNESS

BIG CREEK

MILE 175

PONSLER WAYSIDE

57

BIG

WASHBURNE STATE PARK

CREEK

50

FOREST

DEVILS ELBOW STATE PARK

HECETA HEAD

CAPE CR

N
W   E
S

2

1

SEA LION CAVES

MILE 180

FLORENCE 11 MILES

0   3 MILES
0   3 KM

Cape Perpetua from Yachats Ocean Drive.

YACHATS

When Indians from 5 far-flung tribes were corralled onto this rocky shore below Cape Perpetua in 1856, they named the spot Yachats (pronounced YAH-hots), meaning "at the foot of the mountain." The reservation was disbanded in 1875, and the remaining Indians were sent north to Siletz. Today an upscale, quiet little resort town clings to the dramatically rugged coastline here.

Yachats

Hollywood has filmed Yachats' wave-pounded coast often enough that even big-name stars have discovered this little town's funky coffeeshops, romantic bed & breakfast inns, and surprisingly suave restaurants. A restored 1927 church and museum in a cute log cabin is open daily 10-4 on Third Street, a block west of Highway 101. At the north edge of town, Smelt Sands Wayside overlooks a rocky shore with spouting horns, smelt fishermen, and an 0.7-mile wheelchair-accessible trail (Hike #46). At the south edge of town, the scenic, 1-mile Yachats Ocean Drive loops from Highway 101, passing a glorious picnic area and beach access at the mouth of the Yachats River.

Cape Perpetua

Cape Perpetua confronts the sea with a 700-foot cliff. Highway 101 clings to a ledge with viewpoints of the rugged lava shore between Yachats and the Heceta Head lighthouse. The black rock here erupted as part of a broad, undersea shield volcano over 40 million years ago. The rise of the Coast Range has lifted much of the 2000-foot submarine mountain above the waves.

Just south of the cape, stop at the Siuslaw National Forest's free Cape Perpetua Visitor Center for excellent interpretive displays, a short movie, and advice from helpful staff. First-rate hiking trails start here (hikes #47 and 48), but if you're short on time, drive Highway 101 north 0.3 mile to a parking area for the Devils Churn, a lava chasm that funnels waves to photogenic crashes. On the opposite side of the highway, a paved road leads to a small campground. Keep left on this road's various forks to drive to the top of Cape Perpetua, where a short stroll leads to a 1930s stone shelter with an unmatched view. On the same road, follow brown-and-white auto tour signs to discover a scenic, paved, 18-mile back route to Yachats.

Neptune State Park

South of Cape Perpetua 2 miles, this picnic area amid windswept spruce accesses a small but beautiful beach at the mouth of Cummins Creek. Head south along the shore 0.4 mile, scrambling over 3 small lava headlands, to discover a large cave. Or drive Highway 101 a mile south to the park's far end, and park at the Strawberry Hill turnout for the area's best tidepooling, views of seals on nearby rocks, and access to another beach.

Washburne State Park

This overlooked, 66-site campground is open all year, and often has room when bigger state campgrounds are full. Trails lead to a quiet beach and a creekside meadow popular with elk (Hike #50).

Devils Elbow State Park

In a picturesque cove below the Heceta Head lighthouse, this picnic area features a small beach at the mouth of Cape Creek, mussel-covered rocks at low tide, and islands crowded with sea birds. A day-use fee is charged. Trails lead up to the lighthouse and under Cape Creek Bridge's 220-foot arch (Hike #50).

Sea Lion Caves

One of the few really worthwhile commercial attractions on the coast, this 100-foot-tall, sea-washed grotto still has dozens of wild, resident sea lions, despite the 200,000 tourists who ride an elevator down to see them each year.

Lighthouse keeper's house at Devils Elbow State Park.   Opposite: Acorn barnacle.

46 Yachats

Easy
1.4 miles round-trip
50 feet elevation gain

This easy path traces Yachats' rocky shoreline past spouting horns and crumbling bluffs to a long, broad beach. The trail exists today only because a landowner blocked access to the traditional smelt fishing rocks here in the late 1970s. Outraged local senior citizens checked county books and discovered a forgotten 19th-century right-of-way for an unbuilt county road. After a decade-long legal battle, fought all the way to the Oregon Supreme Court, the route was turned over to the State Parks for an official trail in 1990.

Drive Highway 101 to the north end of Yachats and turn west at a State Parks sign onto Lemwick Lane. The gravel lane leads to the turnaround at Smelt Sands Wayside. Walk north on a broad, graveled path. After 100 yards, watch for 2 spouting horns on the left. These geyser-like sprays shoot from cracks in the lava that have been widened by waves. The trail passes in front of a motel and ambles through fields of wind-mown salal, yarrow, and matted spruce trees.

After 0.7 mile the path crosses a house's gravel driveway and descends steps to a broad beach. If it's not too windy, this is a good place to let kids clamber on the barnacled rock headland or splash in the creek snaking across the beach. If you want a longer hike, hard-packed sand extends 6.3 miles to the Governor Patterson picnic area at the edge of Waldport. More realistic goals are the grassy dunes beside Vingie Creek in 0.8 mile or the concrete stairs up a low orange bluff to the Tillicum Beach picnic area in 2.7 miles.

47 Cape Perpetua

Easy (to tidepools and Devils Churn)
1.8-mile loop
100 feet elevation gain

Easy (to Giant Spruce)
2 miles round-trip
100 feet elevation gain

Moderate (to viewpoint at shelter)
3 miles round-trip
700 feet elevation gain

Most tourists at Cape Perpetua merely watch the visitor center's movie and drive on. They're missing a lot. Trails fan out from the visitor center toward old-growth forests, tidepools, and historic viewpoints you'll never see from a car window. The 3 easy hikes described here are short enough that a sturdy hiker can cover them all in an afternoon. Expect a $3-per-car parking fee.

English explorer Captain Cook named the cape in 1778 while sailing into the teeth of a storm. Irritably, he noted in his journal that the same cape had loomed before him for 5 days straight. It was March 11, the holy day of St. Perpetua, and the faith-tested martyr's name apparently struck a chord.

Start by driving Highway 101 south of Yachats 3 miles (or north of Florence 23 miles) to the Cape Perpetua Visitor Center turnoff between mileposts 168 and 169. All 3 of the hikes begin at the visitor center's front door. For the shortest walk, follow the "Tidepools" pointer on a big map board to the left.

This completely paved trail descends to a tunnel under Highway 101 and then forks. To the left is a 0.4-mile loop that visits lava tidepools, a spouting horn that sprays at high tide from a undersea cave in Cooks Chasm, and a white shell mound (or "midden") left by a village of mussel-gathering natives as long ago as 6000 years. Collecting marine animals is banned here now.

If you take the other trail fork by the tunnel, you'll cross a footbridge and then walk along the highway shoulder 250 yards to a "Cape Cove Trail" sign on the

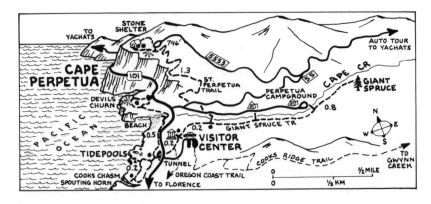

View from Cape Perpetua's stone shelter.   *Opposite: Sea anemones in a tidepool.*

left. An unpaved spur of this path descends to a small, hidden beach. Keep straight another 0.2 mile to reach staircases down to tidepools and the Devils Churn. This seething, 50-wide slot began as a crack in the lava, but millennia of wave erosion expanded it to a long cave and then collapsed the roof. From here, the trail climbs to a Highway 101 parking lot. Walk 100 feet along the lot's edge and descend an unmarked trail to the right to return on a loop.

For the next easiest hike from the visitor center, follow a "Giant Spruce" pointer on a path to the right and keep right at all junctions for a mile. You'll follow a broad gravel trail along alder-lined Cape Creek, just opposite a campground. The 15-foot-thick Sitka spruce at trail's end sprouted some 400 years ago atop a rotting log, and as a result its arching roots now frame a tunnel.

For the most difficult, and most rewarding, of the 3 short hikes described here, follow the "Viewpoint" pointer 0.2 mile from the visitor center, turn left across Cape Creek, cross 2 paved roads, and switchback 11 times up a ridge to viewpoints in Cape Perpetua's wildflower meadows. Blue camas, red Indian paintbrush, and a few lupine bloom here in May and June. Keep left at the top to find the stone shelter built in 1933 by the Civilian Conservation Corps. Views extend 37 miles to sea, north to Cape Foulweather, and south 104 miles to Cape Blanco. The summit loop continues through spruce woods carpeted with wild lily-of-the-valley to a parking area. Walk right 100 feet to find the return trail.

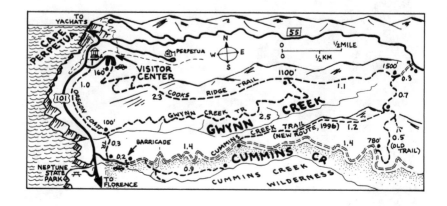

48   Gwynn Creek

Difficult (from visitor center)
5.8-mile loop
11**00 feet** elevation gain

Difficult (from Cummins Creek)
8.1-mile loop
1500 **feet** elevation gain

Some of the most spectacular old-growth Sitka spruce forests on the Coast drape the wild canyons south of Cape Perpetua. A 5.8-mile loop from the visitor center follows the crest of Cooks Ridge and traverses back through Gwynn Creek's secluded valley. The Forest Service charges $3 to park at the visitor center, but there's no fee at the Cummins Creek Trailhead, where a longer loop around the beautiful Gwynn Creek valley begins.

For the short loop, drive Highway 101 south of Yachats 3 miles (or north of Florence 23 miles) to the Cape Perpetua Visitor Center turnoff between mileposts 168 and 169. Park in the overflow parking lot. The Cooks Ridge Trail begins by a map signboard in this upper parking area.

The path climbs along an ancient logging road 0.4 mile and then forks. Either fork is fine, because they rejoin in 0.3 mile at the top of the ridge. From here the trail follows the relatively level crest amid magnificent 6-foot-thick spruce and sword ferns for 1.6 miles to a junction in a saddle. Turn right on the Gwynn Creek Trail, which traverses gradually down a canyon slope.

Under the big trees on this route you'll find lots of orange-brown mushrooms from August to November: delectably edible chanterelles (with orange ribs underneath their caps) and deadly poisonous panther amanitas (with papery white gills underneath).

After 2.5 miles, the Gwynn Creek Trail descends to the creek and a T-shaped trail junction. Turn right to return to the visitor center. This 1-mile section of the Oregon Coast Trail follows the abandoned bed of a 1913 Florence-Yachats wagon road. Though the route is not far above Highway 101, the ocean views are great and the pounding surf drowns out traffic noise.

For the longer loop to Gwynn Creek, drive Highway 101 a mile south of the visitor center. Near Neptune State Park, turn inland at a sign for Cummins Creek Trailhead, and drive 0.3 gravel mile to a parking area at a barricade. The Cummins Creek Trail that begins here is actually an abandoned road that traverses up the canyon without ever approaching the creek.

After walking up the old road 1.4 miles, look for a new trail on the left. Set for completion in 1996, this shortcut will follow a ridgecrest up through old-growth Douglas fir and spruce. If it's not ready, continue walking on the road 1.4 miles and turn left on the old, steep trail. Either way you'll eventually reach a junction with the Cooks Ridge Trail. Turn left here for 1.1 mile, then turn left down the Gwynn Creek Trail 2.5 miles, and turn left again on the Oregon Coast Trail for 0.3 mile to its end at the road, 0.2 mile from your car.

Other Hiking Options

Although the official Cummins Creek Trail doesn't go to Cummins Creek, an unofficial path does. From the parking area barricade, walk up the Cummins Creek Trail 300 yards and fork to the right on a smaller path. After 250 yards this trail hops a small creek and then forks. To the right, a short path deadends at Cummins Creek's bank in alder woods. The left fork continues 0.6 mile up the canyon bottom, scrambling over roots and logs, to its end at a small gravelly beach beside Cummins Creek.

Old-growth spruce on the Cooks Ridge Trail.   Opposite: Chanterelle mushrooms.

49   Cummins Ridge

Difficult
6 miles one-way
1200 feet elevation loss

Left: The lower Cummins Ridge trailhead.

The only official trail in the Cummins Creek Wilderness, this path descends along a densely forested ridgecrest 6 miles. This trip's best if you can arrange a car shuttle, because then you can hike the entire route downhill. A shuttle also avoids the need to hike both ways on the trail's less-interesting lower half —a grassy, abandoned road.

To leave a shuttle car at the lower trailhead, drive Highway 101 to milepost 169 (4 miles south of Yachats or 22 miles north of Florence), turn inland at a "Cummins Ridge Trailhead" sign, and drive gravel Road 1051 for 2.2 miles to a barricade. The overgrown roadbed ahead is the trail.

The upper trailhead is a better place to start your hike, but it's less well marked. To find it, drive Highway 101 to the arched concrete bridge over Tenmile Creek (2.5 miles south of the other trailhead turnoff), and turn inland on gravel Tenmile Creek Road for 2 miles. At a fork where the road becomes paved, turn left on one-lane Road 5694 for 8.2 twisty miles. A quarter mile after the road becomes gravel, turn left on Road 5694-515 for 0.3 mile to its end.

From this upper trailhead, the path gradually descends along a slope of mossy-limbed Douglas fir. Look for yellow monkeyflower and white, 5-petaled candyflower in early summer. After 3 miles, at a junction marked by a rock cairn, turn left on an abandoned, nearly viewless ridgecrest road for the final 3 miles. Blue iris, stalks of purple foxglove, and bracken fern line the route in summer.

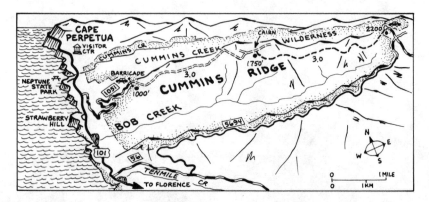

Heceta Head.   Below: Wind-sculpted sand on the beach below the Hobbit Trail.

50 Heceta Head

Easy (from Devils Elbow)
1 mile round-trip
200 feet elevation gain

Moderate (from Highway 101)
2.6 miles round-trip
600 feet elevation gain

Difficult (from Washburne Park)
5.9-mile loop
800 feet elevation gain

Oregon's most photographed lighthouse opened for public tours on its 100th anniversary in 1994; now a new section of the Oregon Coast Trail allows hikers to take their choice of an easy, a moderate, or a longer route to visit the scenic beacon.

Heceta Head (pronounced huh-SEE-tuh) honors Bruno de Heceta, the Portuguese captain of a Spanish ship, who first sighted the cape in 1775. The lighthouse here was the last of Oregon's dozen coastal lighthouses to be built. Bricks for the tower were shipped from San Francisco to Florence, carted down the beach, and hauled over the hills on wagons. The 2-ton Fresnel lens, with 640 delicate, hand-ground prisms, was off-loaded onto the cape by surf boat.

To find the shortest trail to the lighthouse, take Highway 101 north of Florence 12 miles or south of Yachats 15 miles. Just north of a tunnel, turn downhill into Devils Elbow State Park (also known as Heceta Head Lighthouse Viewpoint). A day-use fee is charged in summer, but the picnic area is truly picturesque, with a beach framed by the graceful 220-foot arch of a 1933 highway bridge. Low tide exposes a beach route to rocky islands, but access is banned to protect sea birds.

The lighthouse trail starts at the far end of the parking lot and climbs 0.3 mile through salal meadows and spruce groves to an old road. To the right is Heceta House, a white clapboard, 1893 Queen-Anne-style duplex that once housed the 2 assistant light keepers and their families. Still allegedly haunted by a young woman named Rue, Heceta House is now a bed and breakfast inn with a stunning view. For prices and reservations, call (541) 547-3696.

From Heceta House, walk left along the old road 0.2 mile to reach the lighthouse. When it's open (noon-5pm Monday-Thursday and 11-6pm Friday-Sunday), volunteers lead visitors up the tower's 58 steps to see the massive lens rotating on its ball bearing track. Even if you don't climb the tower, bring binoculars to watch the antics of the 7000 long-necked, black Brandt's cormorants that roost April through August on the rocks below the railed yard. This headland has the species' largest mainland nesting colony. Tufted puffins, now rare here, were once so numerous that they gave Parrot Rock its name.

The two longer hiking routes to Heceta Head Lighthouse avoid the crowds and parking fee of the Devils Elbow picnic area. For the moderate hike, drive 0.9 mile north on Highway 101 from the Devils Elbow turnoff to a paved pullout on the right signed "Overnight Camping Prohibited." Walk 100 feet north and cross the highway to find a Hobbit Trail post. When the path forks after 50 feet, keep left. This trail climbs through an ancient, wind-swept Sitka spruce forest with salal, rhododendrons, and views up the coast as far as Cape Perpetua. Wear boots, because the tread is slick and slippery in spots. After 1.3 miles the path switchbacks down to the lighthouse, the hike's turnaround destination.

For a longer loop hike that visits a beach and a beaver lake, drive 2 miles north on Highway 101 to milepost 176, turn west into the Washburne State Park day use area, and park at the far end of the picnic loop. Take the trail past the restrooms and follow the wide beach 1.2 miles to the left. At a brushy break in the bluffs, just 300 yards before the beach ends, head inland on the Hobbit Trail, named because it tunnels up through the dense spruce forest as if burrowed by one of author J. R. R. Tolkien's fantasy creatures. At a trail junction just before Highway 101, take the Oregon Coast Trail to the right 1.3 miles to the Heceta Head lighthouse and back. To complete the hike with a loop, cross Highway 101 and walk right 100 feet to find a small "Valley Trail" sign. Keep left on this path 1.7 miles to return to your car via an inland route that passes a beaver-dammed lake, China Creek, and the state park campground entrance.

Florence's 1936 Siuslaw River Bridge.

FLORENCE

Dunes lie between the sea and this Siuslaw River port, where quaint shops pack the riverfront's Old Town. Shifting sand hills have backed up dozens of freshwater lakes in the forests nearby. Two of these sinuous lakes bracket popular Honeyman State Park. The dunes south of town are mostly dominated by all-terrain buggies, but all's quiet in the scenic Sutton Creek area to the north.

Old Town

Founded in 1893, this delightful riverfront district between Highway 101 and the docks at the Port of Siuslaw is home to 36 boutiques and a dozen eateries. Parking can be tight on weekends. Start your exploration afoot at the gazebo and fishing dock in the cute pocket park at Laurel and Bay streets. Shops line the waterfront in both directions. First explore under the arched, 1936 Siuslaw River Bridge to the west. Then walk back to the wharf at Mo's chowder restaurant. The 50-passenger Westward Ho! sternwheeler departs here at 2pm for hour-long river cruises.

Shops extend up the side streets, too. Of note are the craft shops in the restored 1905 Florence Grade School at 278 Maple Street and the one-of-a-kind Fly Fishing Museum at 2nd and Nopal streets.

Jessie M. Honeyman State Park

Kids slide down sand dunes straight into swimmable Cleawox Lake at this extremely popular park. Twenty-foot-tall pink rhododendrons bloom in April in the forest. This is Oregon's busiest state park campground, with 381 campsites. The campground's open year round, but you're unlikely to find a spot on summer afternoons without a reservation. The park's 4 day-use picnic areas include 2 free areas east of Highway 101 on forested Woahink Lake, where a boat ramp caters largely to waterskiers. Parking fees are charged at the 2 Cleawox Lake picnic areas west of Highway 101, but this is where you'll find the dunes. There's also a historic 1930s store by a swimming beach where paddleboats are rented in summer. For a map, see Hike #59.

Harbor Vista County Park
The Siuslaw River's twin jetties jut across mudflats and broad beaches to the sea. For the best panorama, stop by the blufftop picnic area and 25-site summer campground in this often overlooked park. Drive Highway 101 to the north edge of Florence, turn west on 35th Street a mile, turn right on Rhododendron Drive a mile, and turn left on North Jetty Road.

North Jetty
After soaking up the view at Harbor Vista, continue a mile to a parking lot at North Jetty Road's end, a good place to let kids play on the beach or clamber on the jetty's boulders.

Weekends from mid-March through October, Seahorse Stagecoach offers hour-long beach rides from here north to Heceta Beach's Driftwood Shores resort. Before Highway 101 was completed in 1936, stages regularly plied the hard, wet sand of low tide. This updated coach has fat rubber tires, a bright red roof, big windows, and a wood stove. Departures still depend on low tides. The 3 white Percheron draft horses work weekdays pulling logs in the forest.

South Jetty
South Jetty Road, a mile south of Florence, divides the dunes into two worlds. North of the road, the river-edged Siuslaw Spit is reserved for hikers and wildlife—notably the thousands of tundra swans that winter in the dune-fringed marshes of the spit's interior. To the south, dune buggies roar through the sand hills from staging areas along the road.

Sutton Creek Recreation Area
Quieter than Honeyman Park, this area 6 miles north of Florence also features lakes, dunes, and forest. A boat ramp along Highway 101 accesses large, forest-rimmed Sutton Lake (waterskiing permitted). Drive west 2 miles from Highway 101 at the recreation area sign to find Holman Vista, a fun picnic area with an observation platform overlooking the dunes beside Sutton Creek. Explorers can reach the beach by wading the creek and crossing the grassy dunes.

Open year-round, 80-site Sutton Campground straddles the creek upstream from Holman Vista. The 39-site Alder Dune Campground and picnic area is only open summers, but features a lake where kids can slide down a dune into the water. An extensive trail network loops through the area (Hike #52).

Darlingtonia Wayside
The insect-eating pitcher plant *Darlingtonia californica* usually grows in bogs in the Klamath Mountains, luring flies and bees into its baseball-bat-shaped green throat with a honey-like smell. A short boardwalk from a picnic area in this forested wayside leads across a bog to one of the strange insectivore's northernmost colonies. Drive 5 miles north of Florence on Highway 101.

Siuslaw Pioneer Museum
Indian and pioneer artifacts are displayed in this converted church building a mile south of Florence on Highway 101. Hours are 10-4 daily except Mondays and all of December.

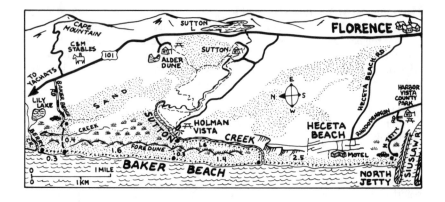

51   Baker Beach

Moderate (shuttle to North Jetty)
5.9 miles one way
No elevation gain

Difficult (to Sutton Creek)
7.3-mile loop
No elevation gain

Left: Baker Beach dunes.

Though quite close to Florence, Baker Beach is a wild stretch of grassy dunes and bird-friendly estuary mostly known only to horseback riders. Hikers can explore the beach on a 7.3-mile loop. If you can arrange a car shuttle, it's fun to wade Sutton Creek and continue south along Heceta Beach, a busier shore lined with cottages and motels, all the way to the Siuslaw River's North Jetty.

Drive Highway 101 north of Florence 7 miles. A ways beyond C & M Stables, turn west on gravel Baker Beach Road for 0.6 mile to its end. Don't take the horse trail on an old road to the left. Instead walk straight ahead on a path through grass-covered sand hummocks with struggling, wind-matted trees. In early summer, blue lupine, wild strawberries, and prickly yellow gorse bloom here.

The sandy path is a bit braided, but follow hoofprints and trail posts 0.4 mile to the beach, hopping a brackish little creek along the way. Note where the trail joins the beach, because the path can be hard to find on your way back.

Turn left along the beach's hard-packed wet sand zone. There are enough sand dollar fragments here that, with patience, you'll find a whole one. The dry sand of the beach's driftwood zone is closed from mid-March to mid-September because the snowy plover, an endangered sandpiper-like bird, nests there then.

After 3 miles you'll reach Sutton Creek, ankle deep where it fans out across the beach. If you've arranged a shuttle to the North Jetty parking lot (see map), wade the creek and continue 2.5 miles.

If you'd rather return from Sutton Creek on a loop, follow the meandering creek inland through grassy, creekside dunes. The estuary is full of graying driftwood logs and stick-like great blue herons. In 1.6 miles, opposite the Holman Vista observation platform (accessible by a knee-deep ford), cut left across the dunes to return to Baker Beach and the route back to your car.

52   Sutton Creek

Easy (to Boldac's Meadow)
1.3-mile loop
30 feet elevation gain

Moderate (to Sutton Campground)
4.3-mile loop
100 feet elevation gain

Right: Holman Vista.

Sand dunes and rhododendron-filled forests line the banks of this meandering creek between Sutton Lake and the ocean. It's a haven for birds and beavers, and a network of loop trails makes it a good place for hikers, too.

Drive Highway 101 north of Florence 5 miles, turn west at a Sutton Creek Recreation Area sign, and go straight on the paved road 2.2 miles to its end at the Holman Vista turnaround. Bring a Forest Service Trail Park pass ($3 per car).

The picnic area here is worth a visit in its own right. A paved, 100-yard trail beside the restrooms leads to a decked observation platform overlooking the creek—where you're likely to see great blue herons. On the horizon, above the grassy dunes of Baker Beach, notice the Sea Lion Caves' entrance building atop a rugged headland. If you don't mind getting your feet wet, it's fun to wade the

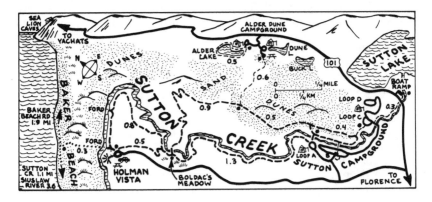

Sutton Creek at Boldac's Meadow.

knee-deep, relatively warm creek and explore across the dunes to the ocean.

For the loop hikes along the creek, however, take a trail cut through the salal bushes behind the picnic area's kitchen shelter. Left-hand forks of this path deadend at creek fords. On a hot day, it's tempting to wade the creek and slide down the dunes on the far shore straight into the water. To hike onward, however, keep straight for 0.8 mile to a bench with a view upstream to a footbridge. For the short loop, turn right at the bench on a half-mile trail that returns through the woods to your car.

For the longer loop, continue into Boldac's Meadow, the site of a vacation resort from the 1930s to the 1970s. Don't cross the footbridge here. Instead continue straight, following a sign for Sutton Campground. After another 1.3 miles along the creek, you'll reach the campground's Loop A. Turn left 100 feet along the road, cross the creek on a footbridge, and then turn right to continue the creekside path. In 0.4 mile, a left-hand fork leads away from the creek on the return route through the soft sand of the dunes. The route generally keeps to the left of a sandy open area, keeping straight for nearly a mile before reentering the woods and switchbacking down to the footbridge at Boldac's Meadow. Turn right to return to your car.

53   Cape Mountain

Easy (to summit)
1.9-mile loop
500 feet elevation gain

Moderate (to Indian shelter)
4 miles round-trip
700 feet elevation gain

Right: Replica of an Indian shelter.

Though designed for horse riders, the well-graded, well-marked trail network on densely forested Cape Mountain has a lot to offer hikers, too.

This coastal mountain was called *Tsahawtita* ("grassy ridge") by Siuslaw Indians because they burned off the forest here to simplify deer hunting. When the Forest Service built a fire lookout on the summit in 1932, the forest grew up and blocked most views. Today the only trailside structure is a *hitsi*, an Indian hunting shelter, reconstructed from a description by an early homesteader.

Drive Highway 101 north of Florence 7 miles. Just beyond C & M Stables, turn inland on Herman Peak Road for 2.8 miles to the Dry Lake Trailhead on the left.

Walk up behind the corral to find the Princess Tasha Trail, which climbs through a mossy coastal forest of 5-foot-thick Sitka spruce and Douglas firs for 0.4 mile to a 4-way trail junction at a pass. Here you could turn right and follow a wooded ridgecrest trail 1.6 miles to the Indian shelter. If instead you turn left and keep left at all junctions for 0.5 mile, you'll climb to Cape Mountain's summit, partly along roads. From there you can backtrack 0.2 mile to the end of a gravel road and turn left on a different trail to return to your car on a loop.

If these options seem too short, go straight at the 4-way junction, following the switchbacking Lookout Loop Trail down through a cedar forest 1.4 miles. From there, trails shown on the map (and on trailside map boards) make possible 4-mile, 5.7-mile, and 7.6-mile loop hikes.

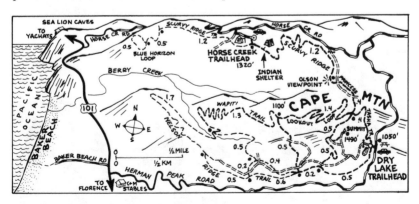

54   Enchanted Valley

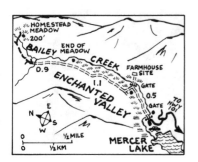

Easy (to end of meadow)
3.6 miles round-trip
50 feet elevation gain

Moderate (to homestead meadow)
5 miles round-trip
200 feet elevation gain

Elk roam the abandoned dairy farm in this coastal valley behind Mercer Lake. Drive Highway 101 north of Florence 5 miles to a "Darlingtonia Botanical Gardens" sign, turn onto paved Mercer Lake Road for 3.7 narrow, twisty miles, and fork left onto Twin Fawn Drive for 0.3 mile to a parking area at road's end.

Cross the gated bridge over Bailey Creek and hike the old farm road up through the valley. The lower part of the meadow is a tall grass wetland with horsetails and skunk cabbage, but farther up you'll pass pink foxgloves, yellow pea-like lotus blooms, blackberries, and red elderberry bushes. At the half-mile mark, by a gate to the old farmhouse site, follow the main road as it cuts left across the meadow and then continues up the valley.

Hikers with children may want to turn back in another 1.1 mile when the valley's meadow ends. But first cross the end of the meadow to a lovely, alder-shaded lunch spot where Bailey Creek splashes out from the forest.

For a longer hike, continue up the old road amid mossy maples and 6-foot-thick Sitka spruce. After half a mile the road fords a small side creek. Here the route dwindles to an elk trail, but if you keep on the main path another 0.4 mile, avoiding 1 fork to the right and then 2 to the left, you'll reach a Bailey Creek crossing. In summer hikers can hop across on slippery rocks. Winter's high water requires a wade. On the far side is an old homestead meadow with half a dozen ancient apple trees. The trail ends here, but a proposed 2-mile connector would climb to the Dry Lake Trailhead on Cape Mountain (see Hike #53).

Enchanted Valley from the farmhouse site.

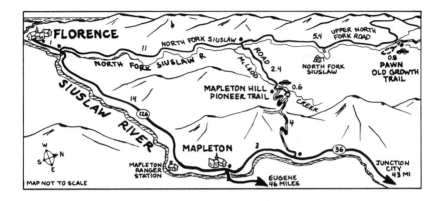

55   Pawn and Pioneer Trails

Easy (Pawn Old Growth Trail)
0.8-mile loop
50 feet elevation gain

Easy (Mapleton Hill Pioneer Trail)
0.6-mile loop
200 feet elevation gain

Right: Pawn Old Growth Trail.

Just a few miles' drive apart, these 2 very short nature trails visit an old-growth forest and a pioneer wagon road. The drive here is half the fun, looping through forgotten homestead valleys of the Coast Range. Take Highway 126 east of Florence 1 mile, turn left onto North Fork Road for 11 miles to a junction, continue straight on Upper North Fork Road for 5.4 miles, and turn right across a bridge onto Elk Tie Road for 100 yards to the Pawn Old Growth Trailhead.

Booklets available at the start of the 0.8-mile loop point out a massive 250-foot-tall Douglas fir, a 500-year-old nursery log sprouting seedlings, and a cave-like red cedar trunk hollowed by fire. It's hard to believe a village stood near here in the early 1900s. After the Coast Indian Reservation was dissolved in 1875, white homesteaders rushed in to stake claims. Four pioneer families set up the town of Pawn, cobbling the name together from the first letters of the families' names: Poole, Akerley, Worthington, and Noland.

When you've finished hiking through the big trees, drive back 5.4 miles and turn left across a bridge onto the North Fork Siuslaw Road 2.4 miles to a "Pioneer Trail" sign on the left, 400 yards after the road turns to gravel.

This trail follows what once was the main route linking the Southern Willamette Valley and the Coast. In 1908, early homesteaders upgraded the steep horse trail to a wagon road with a covered bridge across McLeod Creek and 13 tight switchbacks. The bridge collapsed in a 1929 snow storm, taking a 1926 Chevy into the creek with it. The switchbacking roadbed, now nicely overgrown with mossy alders, bigleaf maples, and droopy-limbed cedars, forms a portion of the 0.6-mile loop trail. Sword ferns and salmonberry line the route, and spring brings trilliums.

Back at the trailhead, complete the loop drive by continuing east on gravel North Fork Siuslaw Road. This is a replacement route built in 1927, with only 7 tight switchbacks instead of 13. When you reach the pass after 1.7 miles, keep left at a junction for another 2.1 miles of gravel. Then turn right on Highway 36. for 3.2 miles to Mapleton, and turn right on Highway 126 to return to Florence.

56 Siuslaw Ridge Trails

Moderate (from Whittaker Creek)
2.6 miles round-trip
800 feet elevation gain

Moderate (from Clay Creek)
2 miles round-trip
600 feet elevation gain

Left: Oregon grape.

These two newly-built Coast Range trails climb through patches of old-growth forest to ridgetop viewpoints. Though the paths are 16 miles apart, they both start at little-known campgrounds on the same paved backroad.

To start the Whittaker Creek hike, drive Highway 126 west of Eugene 33 miles (or east of Florence 26 miles) to a junction between mileposts 26 and 27. Following "Whittaker Cr. Rec. Area" signs, turn south along the Siuslaw River 1.5 miles, turn right for 0.2 mile, and turn right into the recreation area entrance.

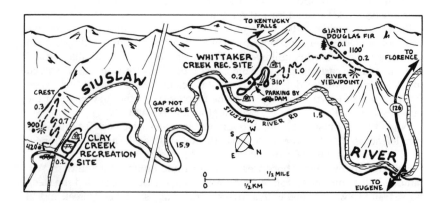

Veer to the right 100 yards and park by a small dam and footbridge. When the campground is closed in winter, park by the gate.

Cross the footbridge over Whittaker Creek and walk left 100 yards on a campground road to an "Old Growth Ridge Trail"sign on the right between campsites 23 and 24. This trail climbs—steeply at times—through a second-growth forest of small Douglas fir trees and large, old-growth stumps. Only toward the top does the trail pass some impressive big trees. Along the way expect white spring wildflowers such as fairy bells, trilliums, and shamrock-leaved oxalis. Yellow wildflowers here are wood violets and Oregon grape.

After climbing a mile you'll reach a ridgecrest junction. The trail to the left ends in 100 yards at a 7-foot-thick, 500-year-old Douglas fir. The trail to the right passes a Siuslaw River viewpoint before ending in 0.2 mile at a bench.

If you'd like to try the other ridge trail, drive back to the Siuslaw River Road, turn right for 15.9 miles, and turn right again at a "Clay Creek Trail" sign. Drive straight past the campground entrance and park on the left just beyond a Siuslaw River bridge. The somewhat rough, narrow trail starts on the opposite side of the road, crosses Clay Creek on flat rocks, and climbs gradually through nice old-growth Douglas fir 0.7 mile to a saddle. Here the trail turns left along the ridgecrest amid red-barked madrone trees 0.3 mile to its end at a viewpoint with a glimpse of the Siuslaw River.

Kentucky Falls (Hike #57).

57 Kentucky Falls

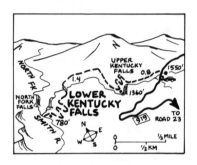

Moderate
4.4 miles round-trip
800 feet elevation loss

Photo on previous page.

Three of the Coast Range's most spectacular waterfalls tumble through the jungly rainforest of this remote Coast Range canyon. Because the trail heads downhill, be sure to save energy for the climb back to the car. Also set aside time for the drive here on twisty backroads.

Start by taking Highway 126 west of Eugene 33 miles—or east of Florence 26 miles. Between mileposts 26 and 27, turn south at a "Whittaker Cr. Rec. Area" sign. In 1.5 miles turn right across a bridge at another Whittaker Creek sign. Follow this paved, one-lane road 1.5 miles and fork left onto Dunn Ridge Road for 6.7 twisty, uphill miles to a T-shaped junction at the end of pavement. Then turn left on Knowles Creek Road for 2.7 miles, turn right on gravel Road 23 for 1.6 miles, and finally turn right on paved Road 919 for 2.6 miles to the trailhead parking area on the right.

(If you're driving here from Reedsport, take Highway 101 north across the Umpqua River, immediately turn right on county Road 48 for 14.5 miles, turn left on North Fork Road for 10 miles, turn right on Road 23 for 9.8 miles, and turn left on Road 919 for 2.6 miles.)

Walk up the road 50 yards from the parking area to find the trail on the left. Beneath the trail's old-growth Douglas firs, look for big white trilliums blooming in April and carpets of shamrock-leaved oxalis with little white blooms in May. In wet areas, look for huge, spiny devils club leaves, delicate red bleeding hearts, and orange salmonberries.

After half a mile the path switchbacks down to the base of tiered, 100-foot-tall Upper Kentucky Falls. In another 1.4 miles the trail ends at an observation deck in a misty grotto where curtains of water spill from the mossy cliffs on either hand. To the right is 100-foot Lower Kentucky Falls. A smaller trail scrambles down 100 yards from the deck to the North Fork Smith River and a better view of North Fork Falls' colossal 120-foot-tall fan.

Other Hiking Options

A 5-mile trail extension is planned down the North Fork Smith River to Road 23, but only the lower portion of this path is complete. To find it, drive 2.6 miles from the Kentucky Falls Trailhead back to Road 23 and turn right for 5.7 miles. Two hundred yards before the road crosses a river bridge, find the trail at the back of a clearing on the right.

Sweet Creek Falls.   Below: Monkeyflower.

58   Sweet Creek Falls

Easy (to Sweet Creek Falls)
2.2 miles round-trip
350 feet elevation gain

Moderate (all trails)
5.2 miles round-trip
650 feet elevation gain

This sleepy Coast Range valley, with its beautiful cascading creek, was settled in 1879 by the Zarah T. Sweets, a family of Oregon Trail pioneers. Portions of an early wagon road have been incorporated in a dramatic new trail past a dozen falls. Four trailheads along the route make it easy to hike the path in segments.

Start by driving Highway 126 to the Siuslaw River Bridge in Mapleton (15 miles east of Florence or 46 miles west of Eugene). Cross the bridge from town and immediately turn west on Sweet Creek Road for 10.2 paved miles. Then take a paved turnoff to the right to the Homestead Trailhead turnaround.

From here a graveled path heads upstream past a split, 10-foot waterfall. Later, the trail hugs a cliff through a canyon full of punchbowl-shaped falls. Four-foot-thick Douglas fir trees tower above the creekside alder and bigleaf maple. Black, robin-sized water ouzels fly just above the creek's surface before plopping underwater to prowl the creek bottom for insect larvae.

After 0.7 mile a path from a second trailhead joins on the left. Continue upstream 0.4 mile to a cliff-edged plunge pool at the base of 20-foot Sweet Creek

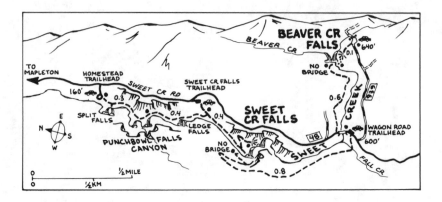

Falls. A spur trail switchbacks up 150 yards to a viewpoint of an upper falls in a thundering slot. From the lower viewpoint, it's possible to cross the bridgeless creek on slippery boulders to reach the unmarked continuation of the trail, but the crossing's tricky enough that most hikers will prefer to turn back.

To hike the valley's upper reaches, drive the paved road 1.3 miles beyond the Homestead Trailhead. Just after a bridge, park at the Wagon Road Trailhead on the left. Across the road, a path heads downstream 0.8 mile to a different viewpoint of Sweet Creek Falls. Just before trail's end, a spur switchbacks down to the bridgeless creek crossing mentioned above.

The 0.6-mile trail segment to Beaver Creek Falls is particularly nice. From the Wagon Road Trailhead, walk across the road's bridge to find a Sweet Creek Trail sign on the right. This portion of the path heads upstream to the base of a fan-shaped waterfall where Beaver Creek and Sweet Creek merge. Although the trail ends here without a bridge, it's not hard to hop the creek. On the far side, a 40-foot scramble up a slippery slope brings you to a railed viewpoint at the end of a very short trail from gravel Road 939. To drive here from the Wagon Road Trailhead, simply continue along the paved road 0.2 mile and take the first fork left for 0.5 mile to a parking area.

Honeyman Park's Cleawox Lake.   Opposite: Ocean view from high dune.

59 Honeyman Park

Easy (dunes exploration)
1.6-mile loop
250 feet elevation gain

Easy (trail between lakes)
2.4 miles round-trip
No elevation gain

Most visitors to this extremely popular park bask in the sand dunes, paddle in the lakes, or bicycle through the campground loops. But perhaps the best way to investigate Honeyman Park's scenery is on foot, either hiking on a loop through the dunes, or walking between the 2 forest-rimmed lakes.

Drive Highway 101 south of Florence 3 miles (or north of Reedsport 18 miles), turn west into the park entrance, and follow "Sand Dunes Picnic Area" signs 0.3 mile to a parking lot where a day-use fee is charged.

A sandy trail at the end of the lot promptly leads to the open dunes beside Cleawox Lake. In summer, kids slide down the sand straight into the swimmably warm water here. Hike through the soft sand to the far end of the lake. Ahead you'll see a "tree island," a forested hill bypassed by the advancing dunes. Because zooming, noisy dune buggies are allowed in the 1.5-mile-wide strip between that tree island and the ocean beach, hikers seldom venture there.

Instead turn left at the end of Lake Cleawox and climb to the crest of a grassy

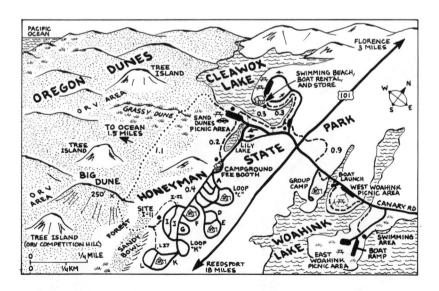

dune. From here you can see south to a second tree island. To its left is the tallest dune in the area, a bare, 250-foot-tall sand hill. Head cross-country 0.5 mile to the wind-rippled summit of this monster dune, where views extend across the undulating sandscape to the sea. Then romp down the steep east face—directly away from the ocean—and duck through a strip of forest on one of several crude, but heavily used sandy paths. In 100 yards you'll emerge in a large sandy bowl rimmed by forest. Cross this basin and climb to the campground trail, marked only by a gap in the rim. The left fork of this sandy forest trail leads you to campsite I-11. From there, turn left on the road and keep left for 0.4 mile to the campground entrance fee booth. Just beyond, a paved trail to the left skirts Lily Lake 0.2 mile back to your car.

If you'd rather hike between the park's lakes—or if you want to avoid paying a day-use parking fee—park at the free East Woahink Picnic Area. To find it, turn east from Highway 101 (away from the campground entrance) onto Canary Road. After 0.5 mile, turn right down the East Woahink entrance road to the large parking area. Walk part way back up the entrance road to find a trail on the left marked "Cleawox Lake Day Use Areas." If you follow these signs and keep left at all junctions for 0.5 mile you'll cross a road bridge, skirt the lakeshore around the West Woahink Picnic Area, cross another road bridge, and duck briefly through the woods to the group camp entrance on Canary Road.

Across Canary Road and 100 feet to the left, the trail resumes. The path tunnels through the coastal forest's salal and rhododendrons, crosses Highway 101, and leads to the paved lakeshore trail at Cleawox Lake. To the right 0.3 mile the lakeshore trail ends at a swimming beach with summer paddleboat rentals and a historic 1930s stone bathhouse converted to a souvenir shop. To the left 0.3 mile is the Sand Dunes Picnic Area—where the dune loop exploration begins.

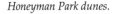

Honeyman Park dunes.

The Hero, *docked by the Umpqua Discovery Center.*

REEDSPORT

The Umpqua River curves to the sea through the largest expanse of coastal dunes in North America. The slowly advancing dunes have backed up more than a dozen large, many-armed freshwater lakes into the forest. The area's main town is Reedsport, but the largest harbor is nearer the ocean at Winchester Bay.

Oregon Dunes National Recreation Area

This is the place to run barefoot along a dune's rippled crest, slide down a sand chute, or watch the wind send a haze of grains sailing off a dune's lip. The recreation area has 36 virtually unbroken miles of beach. Wild rhododendrons up to 20 feet tall fill the forests with pink blooms in April. Birds of 247 species find habitat in the dunes area, especially in the estuaries and the marshy "deflation plains" behind the beach's grassy foredune. While all of the National Recreation Area is open to hikers and horseback riders, few venture into the half where ORVs (off-road vehicles) are allowed to zoom through the sand.

A good first stop is the Oregon Dunes Visitor Center (open daily in summer, weekdays in summer) in Reedsport at the junction of highways 101 and 38. But for a first-hand introduction to the dunes, stop at the Oregon Dunes Overlook 10 miles north of Reedsport on Highway 101. Volunteer hosts here from 10-3 daily in summer give tips on geology, ecology, and recreation.

Umpqua Discovery Center

This modern interpretive center on Reedsport's old riverfront features the Umpqua River's ecology and history. Hours are 9-5 daily. There's an extra charge for a boarding pass to the *Hero*, moored next door, but it's worth it. The historic wooden sailing ship, designed for scientific exploration of Antarctica, preserves the gear and laboratories used by 12 crewmen and 7 scientists in their voyages. Ship tours start every 30 minutes from 10-4 daily.

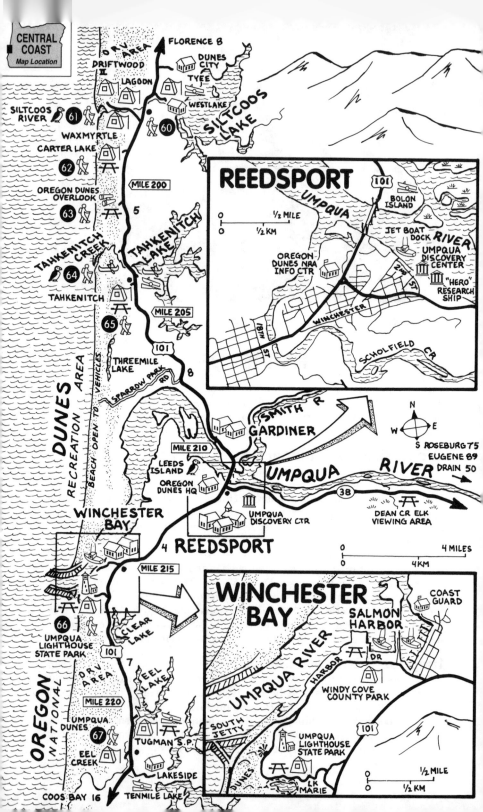

Siltcoos River

Only 3 miles long, this lazy river meanders through the sandy forest between huge Siltcoos Lake and the ocean. Along the way it passes near 4 popular Forest Service campgrounds. East of Highway 101, 14-site Tyee Campground has the river's only boat ramp. Canoe exploration upstream to Siltcoos Lake is easy, but paddling downstream to the sea requires portaging at a low concrete dam. There are 3 large campgrounds west of Highway 101, but Driftwood II is a staging area for noisy off-road vehicles. See Hike #61.

Tahkenitch Lake

Tahkenitch is an Indian word for "many-armed," and indeed this 3-square-mile lake is so sinuous it has nearly 100 miles of shoreline. A boat ramp along Highway 101 is popular with fishermen and waterskiers. A dam blocks lake boaters from exploring Tahkenitch Creek, but if you carry a canoe or kayak 160 yards down the Tahkenitch Creek Trail (Hike #64), you can paddle the lazy creek 2 miles downstream alongside the dunes to the bird-rich estuary.

Dean Creek Elk Viewing Area

A herd of over 100 Roosevelt elk is almost always within sight of this viewing pullout in a pasture beside Highway 38, east of Reedsport 3 miles.

Winchester Bay

Just inside the Umpqua River jetties, Winchester Bay's Salmon Harbor has become Oregon's largest sport fishing marina. The town itself is a salty blend of fish markets, charter boat offices, and tackle shops. Windy Cove County Park, across the street from the marina, has picnic tables and a 98-site campground.

Umpqua Lighthouse State Park

A 2-ton, 800-prism Fresnel lens still rotates atop the 65-foot tower of this 1894 lighthouse, blinking its trademark sequence of 2 white flashes and one red. Groups of 6 may tour the tower Wed-Sat 9-11:30 and 1-3:30, and Sun 1-4:30 from May 1 to September 30 (call 503-271-4631 for info). A stone's throw down the road, the state park has picnic tables, swimming, and a 64-site campground beside little, forest-rimmed Lake Marie (Hike #66).

South Jetty

Two jetties angle together at the south edge of the Umpqua River mouth, enclosing a triangle of saltwater. An oyster and mussel company has set up business here, and it's a good spot for canoeing or birding too. To find it, take Harbor Drive west from Winchester Bay to the Ziolkouski parking area. Beyond this parking lot, Harbor Drive continues 2 miles along the very broad, very flat beach, passing 2 more parking areas. Vehicles aren't allowed on the beach, but the lots are staging areas for off-road vehicle (ORV) exploration inland to the 400-foot-tall Umpqua Scenic Dunes. To visit the dunes on foot, see Hike #67.

Tugman State Park

Resident mallards and geese waddle through the picnic lawns of this state park beside Eel Lake, popular with fishermen and power boaters. The 115-site, forested campground is open mid-April to late October, and is seldom crowded. Drive 10 miles south of Reedsport on Highway 101 and turn inland.

Siltcoos Lake and Booth Island.

60   Siltcoos Lake

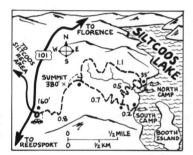

Moderate
4.3-mile loop
600 feet elevation gain

This loop through the woods leads to secluded campsites on the shore of vast Siltcoos Lake. The trailhead parking area is on the inland side of Highway 101, immediately opposite the Siltcoos Recreation Area turnoff 8 miles south of Florence (or 13 miles north of Reedsport) at milepost 198. Forest Service Trail Park passes can be bought here for $3 if you don't have one already.

Take the trail up to the left amid Sitka spruce and Douglas fir. Large sword ferns, slender deer ferns, and orange salmonberries line the path. Many of the huge stumps in the forest still bear springboard notches where loggers stood to cut the trees in the 1930s. Orange chanterelle mushrooms thrive in the second-growth woods from August to November, but do not confuse them with the poisonous, white-gilled panther amanitas also common here.

After 0.8 mile the path heads downhill and forks. Keep right at all junctions for 0.9 mile to South Camp, a single lakeside tentsite surrounded by alder and salmonberry brush. Distant sailboats tilt across the lake. Fishermen troll through the inlets. Across the lake is wooded Booth Island, with a cabin and dock.

Head back up the trail and keep right for 0.5 mile to find North Camp, a nicer collection of 5 lakeshore campsites amid firs. The trails in this camp are a bit confusing. Keep right at every fork until you've visited all 5 campsites. Then turn around and keep right again to find the loop trail back to your car.

If you'd like to canoe to these campsites, drive 1.5 miles north on Highway 101 and turn east at a Siltcoos Lake sign for half a mile to a boat ramp. Paddle 1 mile south to the shore opposite the start of Booth Island.

61 Siltcoos River

Easy
2.6-mile loop
50 feet elevation gain

Right: Snowy plover closure sign.

The estuary where the Siltcoos River loops from the forest to a quiet beach is one of the richest birdwatching sites in Oregon. Even if you have never before seen a kingfisher, an osprey, or an egret, the chances are good you'll spot one here. Along the way, the river trail passes some of the most beautiful scenery in the Oregon Dunes. A special $3 parking fee is charged at the trailhead.

Drive Highway 101 south of Florence 8 miles (or north of Reedsport 13 miles) to the Siltcoos Recreation Area turnoff at milepost 198, and take the paved road 0.9 mile to the Stagecoach Trailhead parking area on the left.

Hike left on the Waxmyrtle Beach Trail between the Siltcoos River and the road 0.2 mile and turn right across a campground entrance bridge over the river. On the far side, turn right again on a riverside trail. Look here for kingfishers perched on branches above the water. These robin-sized birds with oversized heads and pointed bills suddenly dive into the water to spear fish.

Ignoring left-hand spur trails from Waxmyrtle Campground, you'll climb along a bluff edge with a sweeping view across the estuary. If a black-and-white hawk-like bird cruises past, it's probably an osprey. The stork-like birds standing stilt-legged in the river shallows are snowy egrets (if white) or great blue herons (if gray).

The trail leaves the shore pine woods, joins an abandoned sandy road, and follows it to the beach. Turn right 0.2 mile to the river mouth. The dry-sand-and-

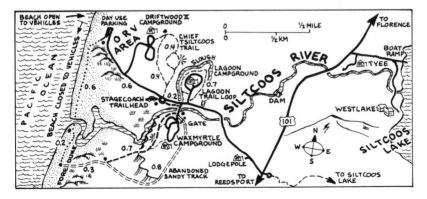

The Siltcoos estuary from the Waxmyrtle Trail.

driftwood zone near the river is off limits from March 15 to September 15 because snowy plovers lay their eggs there then. These rare birds resemble sandpipers but have a white shoulder yoke and search for food in dry sand rather than near the waves. A 1994 survey found the number of snowy plovers on the Oregon Coast had dropped to just 60.

You can return as you came, of course, but to make a loop, take off your shoes and wade calf-deep across the river where it fans out across the beach. Then hike 0.6 mile north along the beach, head inland following footprints across the start of the grassy foredune, cross the day-use parking lot, and follow the paved road 0.6 mile to your car.

Other Hiking Options

The Lagoon Trail loops 0.7 mile around Lagoon Campground, tracing the bank of an oxbow slough that once was part of the Siltcoos River. Birds and boardwalks make the walk pleasant. The trail starts opposite the Waxmyrtle Campground entrance bridge. Yet another short loop, the 0.8-mile Chief Tsiltcoos Trail, begins opposite the Stagecoach Trailhead and explores an ancient, forest-overgrown sand dune beside Driftwood II Campground's ORV area.

62 Carter Lake Dunes

Easy (from Carter Lake)
1.8 miles round-trip
100 feet elevation gain
Open June through September

Moderate (from Taylor Lake)
2.7-mile loop
100 feet elevation gain
Open all year

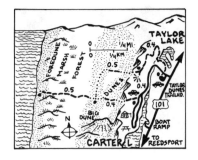

Here you can hike across the range of coastal dune ecosystems—forest, high dunes, foredune, and beach—in less than a mile. Because the popular Carter Lake Campground trailhead is gated closed in winter, there's an optional trailhead at nearby Taylor Lake. Trail Park passes can be bought at both sites.

Drive Highway 101 south of Florence 9 miles (or north of Reedsport 12 miles) and turn west at the Carter Lake Campground entrance road. The Taylor Dunes Trailhead is on the left, but if it's summer and you're eager to get to sand, keep right for 0.4 mile to a parking area just before the first campsite.

From here, the Carter Dunes Trail climbs 200 yards through forest to the open dunes. If you've brought kids, you might detour 400 yards left to explore a giant 120-foot dune. To reach the beach, however, keep heading seaward, following posts with blue-striped tops. The route crosses areas of sand, shore pine forest, and Scotch broom. Just before the beach you'll cross a deflation plain that's marshy in winter, abuzz with mosquitoes in June, and abloom with big, blue king's gentians in August. Before exploring the beach, memorize where the unmarked trail crosses the foredune. The Siltcoos River is 1 mile to the right and Tahkenitch Creek is 4 miles left.

If you start instead at the Taylor Dunes Trailhead, you'll skirt a small lake and climb 0.4 mile to a dunes viewing platform at the end of the graveled path. From here follow posts through the sand 0.5 mile to the Carter Dunes Trail. Turn right for the beach. To make a loop on your way back from the ocean, go straight to the Carter Dunes Campground and walk left 0.4 mile along the road to your car.

Carter Lake Dunes.

63 Oregon Dunes

Easy (to ocean)
2.2 miles round-trip
150 feet elevation gain

Moderate (to Tahkenitch Creek)
4.8-mile loop
250 feet elevation gain

Visitors who simply photograph the view from the Oregon Dunes Overlook are missing the best scenery in this seafront Sahara. It's just over a mile from the overlook's picnic area to a remote, windswept beach. Even better is a 4.8-mile loop hike to beautiful Tahkenitch Creek, through dunes and tree islands.

Looking across the dunes, it's easy to wonder why this part of the coast has so much sand in the first place. Rivers are pulverizing rocks all the time, and grains of the toughest minerals—especially transparent quartz—are carried to sea as sand. Oregon's offshore sand beds are 70 to 180 feet thick. Storms and waves dredge some of this sand up to the beach each spring. Along most of the Coast, headlands and bluffs block the prevailing west winds from blowing the sand farther inland. But here, in the lowlands between Florence and Coos Bay, wave after wave of wind-driven dunes have marched ashore. Each onslaught buries forests before gradually petering out and sprouting forests of its own.

Man accidentally changed the dunes' traditional cycle by introducing European beachgrass in 1910. Originally intended to stabilize sand near jetties and railroads, the stubborn grass spread along the beach, creating a 30-foot-tall foredune. Because this grassy dike stops sand from blowing off the beach, the inland dunes have been cut off from their supply of sand. The last dunes still marching eastward are expected to disappear within a century. Already they have left behind a broad deflation plain, a marshy area stripped by winds to

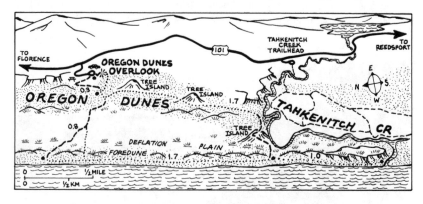

Tahkenitch Creek from the Oregon Dunes loop.   Opposite: Sand dollar and scallop shell.

wet sand. As brush and trees take root on the plain, a young, half-mile-wide forest is growing up between the beach and the dunes.

To find the Oregon Dunes Overlook, drive Highway 101 south of Florence 10 miles (or 11 miles north of Reedsport). Expect a $1 parking fee. From the parking area's turnaround, take a paved path to the right. This trail switchbacks 0.3 miles down through the forest into the dunes themselves.

Once in the open sand, head toward the roar of the ocean, first following posts in the dunes and then a trail across the deflation plain. In early summer look at the edge of the young forest for the blooms of yellow Scotch broom, white coast strawberry, and blue seashore lupine.

Crest the foredune and head left along a remote, windswept stretch of beach. Seals peer from the waves. Pipers and gulls run ahead along the waves' edge. Shells of razor clams, scallops and sand dollars litter the beach.

After 1.7 miles, turn inland at a brown hiker-symbol sign atop the foredune. This path touches a bend of lazy Tahkenitch Creek, curves left across a willow marsh full of driftwood logs, and climbs around the shoulder of a tree island—a forested hill surrounded by dunes. After another stunning viewpoint of Tahkenitch Creek, this time where the dunes are shouldering the creek aside, the trail vanishes into the open sand. Head straight across the sand to find trail posts marking the route along the left side of 2 tree islands. After a mile of hiking in loose sand, climb back to the Oregon Dunes Overlook and your car.

64   Tahkenitch Creek

Easy (short loop)
1.6-mile loop
50 feet elevation gain

Easy (middle loop)
2.6-mile loop
70 feet elevation gain

Moderate (long loop)
4.2-mile loop
80 feet elevation gain

An easy trail network follows this lovely, lazy creek's meanders through the dunes to a wild, driftwood-strewn estuary. Start by driving Highway 101 south of Florence 12 miles—or north of Reedsport 9 miles—to the Tahkenitch Creek Trailhead between mileposts 202 and 203. Trail Park passes can be bought here.

Park at the end of the turnaround and hike down through a coastal forest of Douglas fir, evergreen huckleberries, and rhododendrons. Cross an 80-foot bridge over the languid creek, ignore several right-hand spurs leading down to the creek, and cross a sandy opening to a junction marked by a post.

To hike the loop, veer to the right into shore pine woods. After 300 yards don't miss a right-hand spur that leads to the hike's best creek viewpoint—a sandy bend walled by sheer, 80-foot dunes. Look on the shore for yellow monkeyflowers in summer, and deer hoofprints year round. Then continue on the loop nearly half a mile to a post marking another junction.

For the shortest loop hike, turn left here. If you're still going strong, however, turn right. This right-hand path follows a long sandy opening with a few abandoned telephone poles—all that remains of the Coast Guard road built along the shore in World War II to spread the alarm in case of a Japanese invasion.

After 0.6 miles you'll reach a T-junction and another possible shortcut route back to the car. Turn right to continue the long loop, cross a boardwalk over a

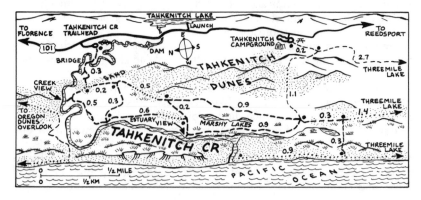

bog with frogs and blue gentians, and 200 yards later climb a short spur to the right to a sweeping overlook of Tahkenitch Creek's braided, grassy, driftwood-littered estuary.

Another 0.9 mile brings you to a 4-way trail junction. To finish the 4.2-mile loop, turn sharply left. If you'd like to detour to the ocean first, turn right and skirt a marsh for 0.3 mile to find an 0.3-mile path through the foredune to the beach. Avoid areas marked as snowy plover nesting sites. Their habitat in the driftwood zone near the creek's mouth is off limits March 15 to September 15.

Tahkenitch Creek from the estuary viewpoint.   Opposite: Coast strawberry.

65 Tahkenitch Dunes

Moderate (to dunes and ocean)
3.2 miles round-trip
400 feet elevation gain

Difficult (to Threemile Lake)
6.5-mile loop
650 feet elevation gain

In addition to huge sand dunes and a secluded ocean beach, this hike offers an optional return route through the forest, passing a remote, 3-mile-long lake.

Drive Highway 101 south of Florence 13 miles (or north of Reedsport 8 miles), turn west into Tahkenitch Campground, keep left to the far end of a loop, and park by a trail sign at a small picnic lawn. Trail Park passes can be bought here.

The path that starts here climbs 0.2 mile amidst 20-foot-tall rhododendrons that bloom in April and May. At a junction, turn right for another 0.4 mile to the open dunes. If you're hiking with kids, it might be best to make these dunes your destination, rather than vowing to reach the ocean. A huge dune invites exploration. And if you keep to the right along the forest edge when you first enter the open dunes, you'll climb a sandy valley to the top of a 250-foot sand slide through the woods—a kid-friendly shortcut back to the campground.

For a more substantial hike, however, follow posts across the open dunes toward the ocean. This route leads to a trail through a shore pine forest. Keep straight at a junction with the Tahkenitch Creek trails, skirt a marshy lake for 0.3 mile, and turn right for 0.3 mile through grassy dunes to the beach.

For the loop, head left on the broad beach 1.3 miles. When you spot a trail sign atop the foredune, take a path inland 0.4 mile to a signpost in the open dunes. The loop trail turns left here, but first continue straight 200 yards to a viewpoint on a sandy bluff above Threemile Lake. The lake is in fact 3 miles

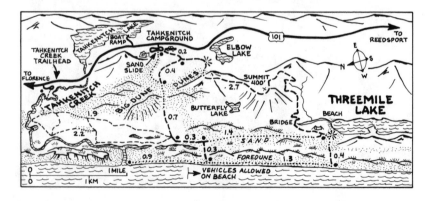

Threemile Lake.   *Opposite: Salal blooms.*

long, but it's wedged between such steep slopes that the best access to the lakeshore's beach is a 200-foot sand slide straight down from this viewpoint.

To continue the loop, ignore a Tahkenitch Creek sign pointing left across the dunes. Instead climb past a campsite in the woods overlooking Threemile Lake. The final 2.9 miles of the loop traverse second-growth woods, climbing along a ridge where chanterelle mushrooms sprout in fall. After passing a viewpoint of Elbow Lake, the path heads back down to Tahkenitch Campground.

66   Lake Marie

Easy
1.4-mile loop
50 feet elevation loss

The stroll around this lovely little lake in Umpqua Lighthouse State Park hardly takes an hour. But it's easy to fill out the day by exploring the Umpqua Dunes, swimming in the lake, camping, or examining the nearby lighthouse.

Start by driving Highway 101 to milepost 217 (south of Reedsport 5 miles or

Lake Marie.   Opposite: The Umpqua Dunes.

north of Coos Bay 22 miles). Follow signs for Umpqua Lighthouse State Park west a mile, bypass the campground entrance, and park at a lakeshore picnic area on the left. Walk down to the small swimming beach and turn right on a shoreline path cut through 8-foot walls of coastal shrubbery, including April-blooming rhododendrons and 2 kinds of bushes with tough-skinned, edible blue berries—salal, with 3-inch leaves, and tiny-leaved evergreen huckleberry.

After 0.2 mile the path forks. Take a detour on the right-hand spur. This fork soon emerges from the forest at the Umpqua Scenic Dunes, a 7-mile-long stretch of sand hills. Unfortunately, dune buggies are allowed to zoom through the areas near the park, so be on guard if you decide to trek half a mile west through the sand to reach the ocean beach at Harbor Drive's Ziolkouski parking area.

Back at Lake Marie, if you take the trail's other fork (and keep left and at all other junctions), you'll circle the lake back to your car in another 0.8 mile, passing an old-growth grove of 4-foot-thick Sitka spruce along the way.

There is no trail to the Umpqua River Lighthouse, but if you drive 0.2 mile up the road from the picnic area you can park at a viewpoint by the 65-foot tower—built in 1894 after a shaky start. When California Gold Rush miners trekking overland from Oregon discovered gold on the Klamath and Rogue rivers in 1850, a ship of entrepreneurs led by Heman Winchester sailed from San

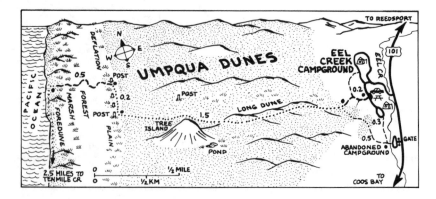

Francisco to find the mouths of those rich rivers. They wound up here, liked it, and stayed. Six years later, the Oregon Territory's first lighthouse was built on the sandy spit across the Umpqua River. After an 1861 storm toppled the tower into the river, the current lighthouse was built in a safer spot atop this bluff.

67 Umpqua Dunes

Difficult
4.8 miles round-trip
100 feet elevation gain

(Refer to map on previous page)

The biggest dunes in Oregon stretch west of Eel Creek Campground in a vast seafront Sahara. No off-road vehicles disturb the immense quiet here. Although the hike from Eel Creek to the beach begins and ends on marked paths, most of the route crosses a stark, trackless dunescape of wind-rippled sand.

Start by driving Highway 101 south of Reedsport 11 miles (or 16 miles north of Coos Bay). Near milepost 222, turn west into Eel Creek Campground. Keep left for 0.3 mile and park on the left. Trail Park passes can be bought at a box.

The Umpqua Dunes Trail that starts here climbs through a forest with thick coastal underbrush—rhododendrons, evergreen huckleberries, and salal. Ignore stairs up to the left and a later campground trail to the right. In 0.2 mile you'll reach open sand. Because no markers guide the way to the ocean, the best bet is to climb the long, tall, dune in front of you. This is an oblique dune, named because it forms at an oblique angle to both the summer's northwest winds and the winter's southwest storms. Constantly moving, oblique dunes can be hundreds of feet tall and over a mile long. The sandy troughs on either side of this one have beachgrass, dwarf blue lupine, and an occasional marshy pool.

Follow the long dune's crest nearly a mile toward a tree island—a forested hill bypassed by the shifting sand. Skirt the tree island's right-hand edge and continue straight half a mile to the line of trees marking the edge of the deflation plain. Winds off the ocean stripped this plain down to wet sand, allowing grass, shrubs, and trees to sprout. In summer, look for yellow monkeyflowers here.

Turn right along the plain's grassy edge, following blue-striped trail posts set at 100-yard intervals. At the fourth post turn left on a path that ducks through a shore pine forest, crosses a marsh on a plank bridge, and crests the grassy foredune to the broad, nearly empty beach.

If you still have lots of energy, you can head left along the beach 2.5 miles to the scenic, rarely visited mouth of Tenmile Creek. Otherwise return as you came, finding your way back across the open sand by heading first to the tree island's left edge and then toward 2 gray water tanks on a forested hill far inland.

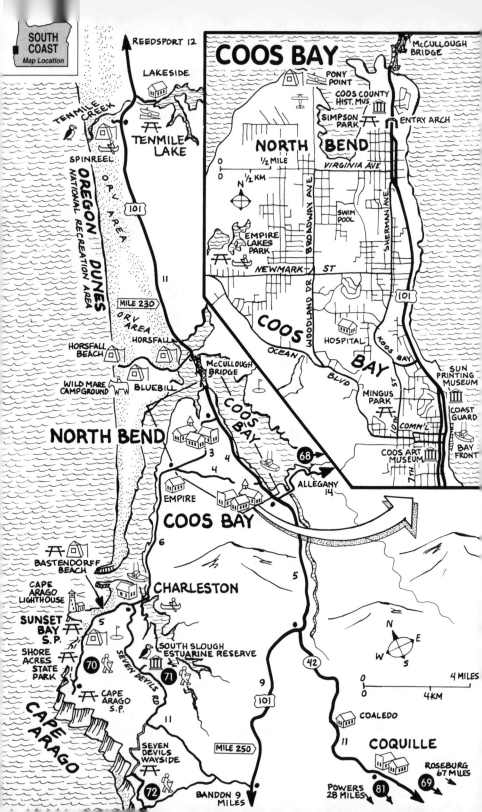

Tugboats on Coos Bay's waterfront.

COOS BAY

Although Coos Bay and North Bend grew side by side in Oregon's "Bay Area," the coast's largest metropolitan center, the 2 timber towns refused to merge in a 1943 election, and have remained rivals ever since. Maps of walking tours through each town's historic district are available in their respective visitor centers along Highway 101. To the north of the Bay Area, sand dunes line the coast. To the south, waves crash against the rocky cliffs of Cape Arago. And inland are the forests that supply the logs stacked on the bay's docks.

Coos Bay Waterfront

Tugboats, yachts, and huge ocean-going freighters tie up at the deep-water port alongside downtown Coos Bay. Inspect the ships by strolling the boardwalk opposite the visitor center at Highway 101 and Commercial Avenue. The Coast Guard patrol boat *Orcas* docks at the north end of the boardwalk. When the ship's not at sea, it'is open to visitors weekdays 3-6 and weekends 10-4.

Coos Art Museum

A fine permanent print collection makes this the most highly regarded art museum on the Oregon Coast. Hours are 11-5 Tue-Fri and 1-4 on weekends.

Marshfield Sun Printing Museum

The city of Coos Bay spent its first 70 years known as Marshfield. From 1891 to 1944 the town's news appeared weekly in the 4-page *Marshfield Sun*. The newspaper's ancient printing press, typecases, and equipment remain in working order in this museum, open Tue-Sat 1-4 throughout summer, at Coos Bay's Front Street and Highway 101, north of the visitor center 8 blocks.

North Bend

This town was founded by the Simpsons—a dynasty of shipbuilders and timber barons whose posh seaside summer estate has been preserved as Shore Acres State Park. During the Depression, North Bend was reduced to paying its public employees with myrtlewood. Prosperity began to return in 1936 with the construction of the graceful, mile-long McCullough Bridge, largest of the Oregon Coast spans designed by luminary Oregon highway engineer Conde B. McCullough. In the same year, North Bend built a steel entry arch across Highway 101. The tacky gateway is still a source of civic pride, though burned-out neon lights sometimes reduce its message to "No end."

Coos County Historical Museum

Beside North Bend's entry arch, the historic artifacts and displays in this museum are open 10-4 Tue-Sat. Behind the museum is Simpson Park, with a picnic area and playground.

Pony Point Park

This bayfront park in North Bend has 5 prmitive campsites, a boat ramp, and a large RV parking lot. It's becoming popular with birders and windsurfers.

Empire Lakes Park

The 2 lakes in this relatively undisturbed, 120-acre forest park off Newmark Street in Coos Bay are ideal for canoeing. Gravel paths explore the shores.

Tenmile Lake

Largest of the sinuous lakes in the forest behind the Oregon Dunes, Tenmile Lake can be accessed near the town of Lakeside at a county park with a boat ramp, all-accessible fishing dock, and picnic area. The best canoeing and bird-watching, however, are on Tenmile Creek, which meanders 5 miles from the lake to the sea. Put in at Sprinreel Campground (an off-road vehicle staging area). Because ORVs are banned from the estuary and the dunes to the north, this area is tops for trailless hiking too (see also Hike #67).

Horsfall campgrounds

Dune buggies rule the southern end of the Oregon Dunes National Recreation Area. All campgrounds here are ORV staging areas—except Wild Mare, a 12-site equestrian campground with corrals. Horsfall and Horsfall Beach campgrounds resemble parking lots, with sites marked off on the pavement. Forested Bluebill Campground abuts Bluebill Lake, a lakeless meadow and springtime bird-watching site circled by a 1-mile hiking trail.

Charleston

Just inside Coos Bay's ocean jetties, this fishing village has a large marina, a boat ramp, whale watching tour boats, and a Coast Guard station.

Bastendorff Beach County Park

Next door to Sunset Bay, this mile-long beach extends to Coos Bay's south jetty, a good strolling goal for those who enjoy watching waves, ship traffic, birds, fishermen, and sunsets. The park's year-round, 55-site campground takes no reservations. A picnic area and playground are nearby.

Sunset Bay State Park

Perhaps the state's best ocean swimming beach is sheltered within Sunset Bay's scenic, cliff-rimmed cove beside this state park's large picnic area. Low tide exposes tidepools on sandstone reefs at the base of cliffs on either side of the cove (the north side is best), but take care when climbing the rocks, and do not touch or walk on tidepool animals. Across the road is a popular, 138-site, year-round campground (summer reservations accepted). See Hike #70.

Shore Acres State Park

North Bend timber baron Louis Simpson bought this dramatic seaside estate as a 1906 Christmas surprise for his wife. Today Simpson's mansion is gone, but a state park preserves the formal English garden, Japanese garden, and rose garden. Rhododendrons and azaleas of 22 varieties bloom March through June. Nearby, a glass-walled observation building overlooks the shore's cliffs, where waves pound reefs of tilted sandstone strata. Visit in winter to watch the most impressive storm waves and see the gardens' 135,000-light holiday display. A day-use parking fee is charged mid-May through September. See Hike #70.

Cape Arago State Park

Bring binoculars and a picnic basket to this rugged bluff at road's end west of Charleston. The binoculars will help you spot the seals and sea lions barking on the scenic rock reefs of Shell Island, a quarter mile to sea. Take the picnic basket down the 0.3-mile North Cove Trail, which passes tables amid windswept trees on a panoramic ridge. The cove's tidepools and sandy beach are off-limits March 1 to July 1 to protect seal pups. A similar trail from the cape down to smaller, less visited, and perhaps more scenic South Cove is open year round. South Cove's tidepooling is among the best in Oregon. Confusingly, the Cape Arago Lighthouse is not on Cape Arago, but rather is 3 miles north on Point Gregory, and is not open to the public. View it from Bastendorff Beach or the trail at Sunset Bay. See Hike #70.

South Slough Estuarine Reserve

A first-rate interpretive center explains the importance of the tidal salt marshes that snake into the forested hills along this arm of Coos Bay. To find the center (open daily 8:30-4:30), drive Seven Devils Road south of Charleston—a scenic option to Highway 101 between Coos Bay and Bandon (see Hike #71).

Better yet, launch a canoe at Charleston, ride the incoming tide 4 miles up the sinuous slough, and return on the ebb tide. Maps, tips, and tide tables are available at the interpretive center.

The 1936 Conde McCullough Bridge across Coos Bay.

Silver Falls.

68   Golden and Silver Falls

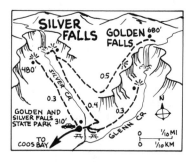

Easy (to top of Golden Falls)
1.8 miles round-trip
370 feet elevation gain

Moderate (all trails)
3 miles round-trip
570 feet elevation gain

A pair of nearly 200-foot-tall waterfalls plummet into this remote Coast Range canyon amid huge myrtlewood trees and 6-foot-thick Douglas firs. Golden Falls was not named for its color, but rather for Dr. C. B. Golden, first Grand Chancellor of the Oregon Knights of Pythias.

At the south edge of Coos Bay, turn east off Highway 101, following "Allegany" signs for 13.5 miles through a number of intersections. From the store at Allegany, follow state park signs 9.4 miles to road's end at a small picnic area. The final 5 miles of this route are one-lane gravel unsuited for motorhomes.

From the parking area, a trail crosses Silver Creek on a footbridge and then forks. The right-hand fork leads through a grove of massive myrtlewood trees 0.3 mile to trail's end at a viewpoint of Golden Falls.

For better views, take the left-hand fork. This path climbs past old-growth Douglas fir with rhododendrons, ferns, and evergreen huckleberries. After 0.4 mile, a left-hand spur leads to the base of Silver Falls. The 160-foot fall spills from a bulbous cliff like long white hair, but thins in late summer to a ribbon.

The main trail continues uphill, following the narrow route of a precarious, long-abandoned road along sheer, unrailed cliffs to the top of 200-foot Golden Falls. Don't allow unattended children near this dizzying viewpoint. A brushy path upstream soon peters out. If you want to hike more, return to your car, cross the parking area, and take a 0.3-mile path up through the woods to a viewpoint with a different perspective of Silver Falls.

69   Doerner Fir

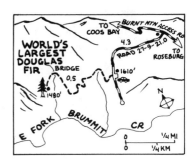

Easy
1 mile round-trip
130 feet elevation gain

When a 1962 windstorm felled Oregon's Clatsop Fir, then the world's largest known Douglas fir, Washington Governor Rosellini telegraphed Oregon Governor Hatfield to announce the title had shifted by default to a tree in Washington. Rosellini added, "I always suspected that the Clatsop Fir couldn't stand up to a rigorous measurement of its supposed greatness."

Hatfield fired back a reply. "Surely there is a tree somewhere in Oregon of equal or greater stature. As soon as this tree is found you will be notified."

Twenty-nine years later, a sleuth in this remote Coast Range canyon found that prize—a 329-foot behemoth between 500 and 700 years old. Its 12-foot-thick trunk rises limbless for 10 stories before vanishing into a stratospheric crown. Originally the tree was named the Brummit Fir after the nearby creek, but in 1993 a departing BLM executive renamed it the Doerner Fir after a friend.

The trail to the fir is short and easy. The drive here, however, is long and complicated. From Interstate 5, drive south of Roseburg 3 miles to Winston Exit 119, drive 3.2 miles to Winston, and turn right on Highway 42 toward Coquille for 8.9 miles. Just before the village of Tenmile, turn right on County Road 5 for 4.4 miles to a T-junction. Then turn left on the Coos Bay Wagon Road for 1.5 miles, turn right onto (possibly unmarked) 1-lane, paved Burnt Mountain Access Road for 7.1 miles, fork left (avoiding the Burnt Ridge Road) for 4.6 more narrow, paved miles, and turn left onto gravel Road 27-9-21.0 for 4.3 miles to a pullout on the left, opposite a small trail sign.

If you're coming from Coos Bay, take Highway 101 south 5 miles and veer left on Highway 42 toward Roseburg 11 miles. Opposite a log pond just before Coquille, turn left on West Central Boulevard for a mile, turn left toward Fairview 8.1 miles to a 4-way junction, turn right for 3.7 miles, turn left onto 1-lane, paved Middle Creek Road for 6.3 miles to a fork, and veer left toward the Park Creek Recreation Site for another 6.6 miles. Then turn uphill to the right on narrow, paved Burnt Mountain Tie Road for 4.4 twisty miles to a T-junction by a water hole, turn left following a "Burnt Ridge Road" pointer for 4.6 miles, and turn right on gravel Road 27-9-21.0 for 4.3 miles to the trailhead.

After the drive, the hike is a piece of cake. Pink rhododendrons bloom in this rainforest in June. As in any proper old-growth forest, large fallen trees have cleared openings where daylight can reach struggling smaller plants—in this case, moss-draped vine maple, hemlock saplings, sword ferns, and salmonberry.

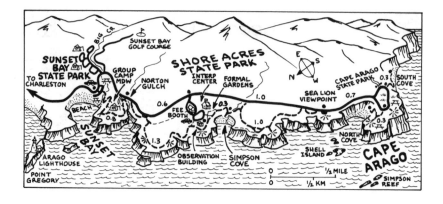

70   Shore Acres

Easy (to sea lion viewpoint)
2.6 miles round-trip
200 feet elevation gain

Difficult (entire trail)
6.8 miles round-trip
300 feet elevation gain

Breakers crash against the tilted sandstone cliffs of Cape Arago's rugged coast. Sea lions bark from offshore reefs. Wavelets lap the beaches of hidden coves. If this seems an unlikely backdrop for a formal English garden, welcome to the surprises of Shore Acres State Park. It's possible to drive to many of the attractions here, and tips for car travelers are detailed on pages 158-159. But to explore this unusual coastline thoroughly, you'll need to hike at least a portion of the 3.4-mile trail between Sunset Bay and Cape Arago.

To find the park from Highway 101 in Coos Bay, follow signs 9 miles to Charleston, and then continue straight 4 miles. A mile past Sunset Bay State Park, turn right into the Shore Acres entrance, pass a fee booth (from mid-May through September there's a day-use charge here), and park by the oceanfront lawns at the far end of the parking area. Dogs are not allowed in Shore Acres.

First walk to the observation building overlooking the sea cliffs. The waves below are slowly leveling the yellow sandstone's tilted strata, creating weirdly stepped reefs in the process. The plateau you're standing on was similarly leveled by waves thousands of years ago before the coastline here rose.

Turn left along the cliff edge. Left-hand forks of this trail lead to the fabulous formal gardens—worth at least an hour's wanderings—but for the longer hike, keep right and follow a paved path 0.3 mile down to the beach at Simpson Cove, a broad triangle of sand embraced by sheer ochre cliffs. You could easily spend most of a day here, too. To hike on, however, hop the cove's inlet creek, take an unpaved path up a forested gully 300 yards, and turn right at a T-shaped trail junction. After the trail enters a salal meadow, spurs to the right lead to breathtaking, cliff-edge viewpoints. In another half mile the path hits the paved road. Walk right 60 yards to find another 0.1-mile section of trail through a tunnel of coastal spruce before the path definitively ends at an Oregon Coast Trail post, 100 feet before a parking pullout. The barking you hear here comes from sea lions on Shell Island, the largest island a quarter mile to sea. Gray harbor seals typically lounge on the rocky reefs closer to shore. Unless you've planned for a shuttle car to meet you here, return as you came.

For a longer hike, start at Sunset Bay instead. When you're driving here from Charleston, pull into the Sunset Bay picnic area on the right and park by the restrooms at the far end of the parking areas. Cross a footbridge to the right of the restrooms, follow the creek to the right 100 yards to the last picnic table before the beach and turn left on a trail up the forested hillside.

For the next 0.8 mile, group campers from an adjacent meadow have created a confusion of paths. Keep to the right, following the rim of a flat blufftop, and you'll reach the paved road at the group camp's entrance. Turn right along the road 200 yards and climb a stile over a guardrail to the right. The path parallels the highway 300 more yards before angling into the woods on the long-abandoned entry road to the original Simpson mansion, built in 1906. Just 60 yards into the forest, however, turn right on an unmarked trail. This path passes a dozen cliff-edge viewpoints before leading to the Shore Acres observation building—the start of the hike described above.

Shore Acres shoreline.   Opposite: Japanese garden at Shore Acres.

71   South Slough Estuary

Easy (to South Slough pilings)
2-mile loop
300 feet elevation gain

The city of Coos Bay was once called Marshfield, but the name no longer fits. Ninety percent of the bay's original marsh fields have been destroyed—diked, drained, or filled for development. Now wildlife biologists are understanding the importance of these lost tidal wetlands. When freshwater salmon smolts migrate to sea, for example, they need to linger in estuaries to gradually adjust to saltwater. Clams, herons, raccoons, and hundreds of other species rely on the rich life of the mudflats once derided as worthless sloughs.

The nation's first Estuarine Research Reserve was established here in 1974 on 7 square miles of abandoned farmland and cut-over forest bordering Coos Bay's South Slough. Today, scores of similar reserves nationwide are watching the reclamation experiments undertaken here to see if wildlife will again flourish when estuary dikes are breached and upland forests allowed to regrow.

Displays in a modern interpretive center help explain the research, but a network of easy trails nearby allows you to investigate the reserve first hand.

From Highway 101 in Coos Bay, follow signs 9 miles west to Charleston. A few hundred yards beyond that harbor town, turn left on Seven Devils Road. After 4.3 miles, turn left onto the South Slough Reserve entrance road for 0.2 mile and pull into the interpretive center's parking area on the left. Take a look at the center's displays before driving another 0.3 mile down the entrance road to the gravel parking area for the Hidden Creek Trail.

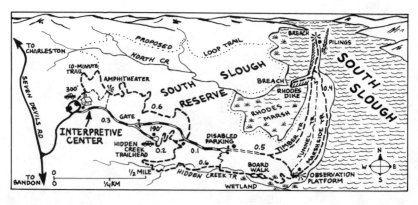

Pilings and breached dike along South Slough.   Opposite: Trail amid skunk cabbage.

The path switchbacks down through a 1980 clearcut regrowing with alder, hemlock, and Port Orford cedar. Among the dense brush are 3 kinds of edible berries in late summer: tough-skinned blue salal, tiny red huckleberry, and pointy-leaved evergreen huckleberry. Turn right at all junctions and you'll follow a small creek down to a meandering boardwalk through an alder bog full of the huge, boat-shaped leaves of skunk cabbage. In spring, the gigantic yellow blooms of these plants intentionally give off a decaying stench to attract the flies required to pollinate them.

After 0.8 mile the path forks at an observation platform amidst big Sitka spruce and rhododendrons, with a view across the estuary's salt marsh. Continue to keep right, following signs 0.4 mile to the "Sloughside Pilings," remnants of a railroad line used to dump logs into the slough for transport by raft to the sawmills at Coos Bay. The trail ends at the tip of a breached dike where tidewaters now flood through, converting pastureland back to marsh.

To make a loop, turn around and return straight on the Timber Trail 0.5 mile to a gated parking area for hikers with disabilities. Walk up the gravel road another 200 yards to a trail crossing. The shortest route back to your car is to the left, but if you'd like a longer loop hike, turn right, climb for 0.6 mile to the interpretive center, and return 0.3 mile down the road to your car.

Bandon's beach.

BANDON

Wildfires spreading through gorse—a thorny, yellow-flowered weed—burned nearly all of downtown Bandon in 1914 and 1936. Surprisingly, Bandon's rebuilt Old Town is one of the most charming on the coast. North of town is a sandy spit along the Coquille River with a lighthouse and a campground in Bullards Beach State Park. To the south, bird-covered islands and needle-shaped sea stacks line the ocean beaches.

Old Town Bandon

Once local shipbuilders helped give this port the largest fleet between San Francisco and Astoria. Riverboats docked here from the Coquille River hinterland. Ocean steamers crossed the treacherous river bar regularly. Then 2 devastating fires and the completion of Highway 101 broke Bandon's commercial power. But now recreation, arts, and retirees are fueling new growth. Archways beside Highway 101 span the entrances to Old Town, a 3-block collection of art galleries, boutiques, eateries, charter boat offices, and craft shops—all wedged beside a river marina with docks, piers, and a boat launch. See Hike #74.

Bullards Beach State Park

In a forest behind overgrown dunes, this park's year-round, 192-site campground is sheltered from the beach's north winds (see Hike #73). Horse trails through the old dunes converge on an 8-site equestrian camp. Picnic lawns are a stone's throw from the Coquille River and a popular boat ramp. Next door to the park, a sternwheel riverboat serving as a bed & breakfast docks beside the Coquille River Bridge and tours the river each morning when guests awake.

Coquille River Lighthouse

At the far south end of Bullards Beach State Park, this picturesque lighthouse was built in 1896, rammed by a schooner in 1906, replaced by an automated beacon in 1939, and restored in 1978 after years of neglect. Nostalgia buffs added a small solar-powered light in 1991. Although you can't climb the tower, the first-floor room is open 7am-8pm in summer (otherwise 8-5). See Hike #73.

Seven Devils Wayside

The Seven Devils are a series of steep coastal ridges that bedeviled early road builders. One of the gorse-covered canyons between ridges holds this picnic area beside Merchants Beach (see Hike #72). The beach would be secluded, but vehicles are allowed onto it from the wayside.

Bandon Marsh Wildlife Refuge

Shorebirds, geese, ducks, and osprey visit this rich, hard-to-access 289-acre salt marsh off Bandon's Riverside Drive. Use binoculars from Hike #73.

Cranberry bogs

Bandon's claim to be cranberry capital of the world is backed by 800 acres of cranberry bogs, the rectangular marshes visible along Highway 101. In fall the bogs are flooded so the bright red berries float for harvest. Most of the local berries are sold through the Ocean Spray Cooperative to color juice drinks.

Bandon Cheese Factory

A riverboat once brought farm milk down the Coquille River to cheesemakers in Bandon. The town's 1936 fire destroyed the original factory. Today an observation window and a video in the new building on Highway 101 show visitors how cheddar and jack cheeses are made. Hours are 8-5:30 daily.

Face Rock Wayside

The best view of Bandon's craggy islands is at this blufftop picnic area on Bandon's Beach Loop Drive. Coquille tribal legends explain why the largest island resembles the uplifted face of a stony Indian princess, while a cluster of small pointy islands look like a cat and her kittens (see Hike #74).

Coquille River Museum

A 1939 Coast Guard building at the west end of Bandon's Old Town bayfront now houses the Bandon Historical Society's varied collections—including Indian artifacts and photos of Bandon's devastating fires. Open Tue-Sat noon-4.

New River

Created by early 19th-century ranchers to drain coastal pasture, this lazy river parallels the beach for 8 miles from Floras Lake (see Hike #75) to Fourmile Creek, isolating the state's most secluded beach and a choice birdwatching site. Drive Highway 101 to milepost 283, turn west on Croft Road 1.5 miles, fork right onto a gravel road into BLM's day-use area for 0.7 mile to a T-junction, and turn right to the grassy riverbank. Canoeists can explore the placid river from here, but winds are often high. Hikers must boat across to the ocean beach, where they can head south 7 miles to Floras Lake or north a mile to the generally unfordable mouth of Fourmile Creek.

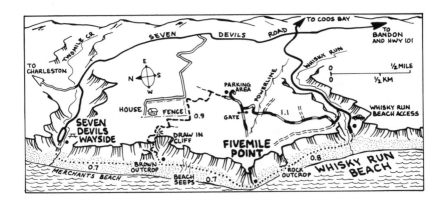

72   Whisky Run Beach

Easy (to Fivemile Point)
1.6 miles round-trip
No elevation gain

Moderate (to road)
3.5-mile loop
300 feet elevation gain

Right: Mussels at Fivemile Point.

A gold rush hit this secluded beach in 1853 when prospectors found sparkling flakes in a layer of black sand. The wide-open boomtown of Randolph sprang up along Whisky Run's creek, but 2 years later the gold was gone and the village was moved lock, stock, and barrel to the Coquille River, 4 miles away.

In the early 1980s energy crisis, a power company built a giant windmill above the beach on Fivemile Point, but the winds were so strong they broke the mill's blades before producing much electricity. The tower was later replaced by more practical smaller windmills with slender blades.

If you're driving here from the south, take Highway 101 north of Bandon 5 miles, turn left on Randolph Road (which becomes Seven Devils Road) for 3 miles, and turn left on paved Whisky Run Road to its end at a parking area by the beach. If you're driving here from Coos Bay, take Highway 101 south 14 miles. Between mileposts 252 and 253, turn right on West Beaver Hill Road at a sign for South Slough Sanctuary. After 1.6 miles turn left at a sign for Whisky Run Beach and follow this road straight 3.8 miles to its end.

The Whisky Run canyon is blanketed with gorse, a spiny shrub that blooms yellow in May. In its native England, gorse forms hedges that corral livestock. Here it spreads with abandon and twice fueled fires that burned Bandon.

The short path to the beach is also passable for 4-wheel-drive vehicles, but you'll leave most of them behind when you cross the creek and hike along the beach to the right. In 0.8 mile you'll round the tip of Fivemile Point—a good goal for a hike with kids. At high tide you may have to scramble along the headland to get by. Low tides expose rocks and ledges with tidepool animals. Sea birds perch on scenic pinnacles in the surf. Sea lions squirm on reefs offshore.

If you're continuing on the longer loop, hike 0.7 mile past Fivemile Point to the start of a beachside forest, 200 yards beyond some beach seeps and 200 yards before a brown outcrop shoulders onto the beach. Where the forest begins, look closely for a "Coast Trail" sign on a post. The path here tunnels up through windswept Sitka spruce and salal to a bench at a blufftop viewpoint surrounded by gorse. In another 0.2 mile the path turns right, following a horse pasture's fenceline 0.3 mile to the bend of a dirt road. Keep right here and also at the next T-shaped trail junction to reach a large gravel road at the start of an immense plain of gorse. A little-used trailhead parking area is to the left. But turn right to complete the loop, follow the road 100 yards downhill, turn left at a road junction, and then stick to the main gravel road a mile back to your car.

73   Bullards Beach

Easy (lighthouse exploration)
1.4 miles round-trip
No elevation gain

Moderate (from beach parking)
5-mile loop
No elevation gain

Just across the Coquille River from Bandon are a picturesque lighthouse, a hikable jetty, and an estuary beach great for birdwatching. To explore the area, drive Highway 101 north of Bandon 3 miles (or south of Coos Bay 21 miles), turn west at a Bullards Beach State Park sign and drive straight past the campground entrance and picnic areas for 1.4 miles to a T-shaped junction.

If you'd like to hike a 5-mile loop around the Bullards Beach peninsula, turn right to a beach parking area and walk left along the wide beach 1.7 miles to the lighthouse. If you'd rather shorten this hike (advisable if it's windy or if you've brought kids), simply turn left at the T-junction and drive to the lighthouse.

The youngest of the Oregon Coast's principal lights, this 47-foot tower was built on a Coquille River island in 1896. When ships continued to founder here (one actually rammed the lighthouse in 1906), the Army built jetties by blasting apart Bandon's Tupper Rock, a site held sacred by the Coquille Indian tribe. Since then sand has collected behind the jetty, connecting the lighthouse's former island to Bullards Beach. In 1990 the site of Tupper Rock was returned to the Coquilles, who built a retirement home there.

Coquille River Lighthouse.   Opposite: Gorse.

After inspecting the lighthouse (the door is open from 7am to 8pm in summer, otherwise from 8am to 5pm), walk 0.3 mile out to the North Jetty's tip, where waves crash against mussel-encrusted boulders. Watch here for sea birds—black cormorants, black-and-white murres, and enormous, diving brown pelicans.

Then return to the lighthouse and continue straight on a sandy car track atop the riverside jetty. Keep straight on this jeep road 0.4 mile to its end at a beach with a view across the river to Bandon's docks. This is a good turnaround point for hikers with kids. If you're doing the 5-mile loop, however, continue 1.9 miles along the river's soft beach to the end of sand at the park's entrance road. Then follow the road shoulder left 0.4 mile to the beach parking area.

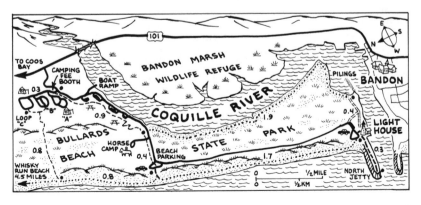

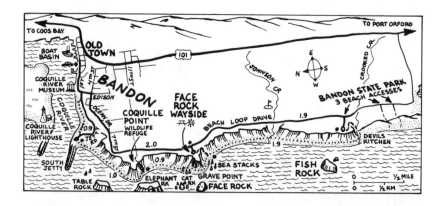

74   **Bandon Sea Stacks**

Easy (to Coquille Point)
3.3-mile loop
100 feet elevation gain

Moderate (to Face Rock Wayside)
4.8-mile loop
100 feet elevation gain

Difficult (to Devils Kitchen)
8.6-mile loop
150 feet elevation gain

This hike begins in Bandon's Old Town, follows the beach past rock "needles" in the surf, and then returns along city streets atop the seashore cliffs. To start, turn off Highway 101 through an archway proclaiming "Welcome to Old Town Bandon," drive a block to the riverfront, and turn left a block to a big parking area beside the boat basin.

First explore Old Town a bit by strolling around the 3 main blocks of gift shops, boutiques, and galleries. Then set off toward the ocean, following First Street along the riverfront. This street curves left at the Coquille River Museum. Shortly afterward turn right on Jetty Road, a narrow street that once was the town's boardwalk to the beach. Because Jetty Road has no sidewalk, it can be more pleasant to climb over some boulders to the right (after the Lighhouse Bed & Breakfast) and follow the river beach most of the way to Jetty Road's end at the South Jetty.

The jetty was built in 1906 to stem a rash of shipwrecks on the Coquille River bar. When the *Oliver Olson* rammed the jetty so hard in 1953 that the ship couldn't be pulled free, the South Jetty was extended by building right over the ship's hull. Now sailors complain the uneven lengths of the river's two jetties make the bar more treacherous than ever.

From the jetty, turn left along the ocean beach. To sea, Table Rock's flat top swarms with seagulls, cormorants, and murres. Bring binoculars to spot the red-beaked puffins that arrive in April. They nest in tunnels up to 30 feet long that they dig in the sides of the island's dirt top. To protect easily frightened seabirds, climbing and tidepooling are banned on all Bandon's islands and sea stacks—even those easily accessible at low tide.

After a mile on the beach you'll cross a sandy gap between Coquille Point and Elephant Rock, a huge island shaped like a big-eared elephant with sea caves for eyes. For the short loop, climb a staircase on the far side of Coquille Point to Beach Loop Drive and follow this street left 1 mile, ignoring the street's frequent name changes. Finally turn left on Edison Street to return to your car.

For the longer loops, however, continue 0.9 mile along the beach to a collection of weird, pointy sea stacks at the tip of Grave Point. The cluster of small islands visible from here are Cat and Kittens Rocks. Face Rock is the large island resembling an uplifted face. According to a Coquille tribal legend, the face belongs to Ewauna, daughter of Chief Siskiyou, who had traveled here to a great potlatch feast in his honor. Ewauna had never seen the ocean before, so one night she sneaked to the beach for a moonlight swim. In the water she was grabbed by the evil ocean spirit Seatka. But she refused to look into his eyes, knowing that this was how he controlled his victims. Instead she fixed her stare on the North Star, and defiantly gazes there even today.

For the moderate loop hike, climb a staircase just beyond Grave Point to the picnic area at Face Rock Wayside, and from there follow Beach Loop Road left to Old Town as described above. For the longest recommended loop hike, however, continue 1.9 miles farther along the beach to the Devils Kitchen, a sandy cove sheltered from the wind by a cliff. Walk inland to the back of the cove, cross a creek on a log, and go left up a trail into the trees to a picnic area. Then walk out to Beach Loop Drive and turn left along it 3.9 miles to Old Town.

Sea stacks from Face Rock Wayside.   Opposite: Bandon's waterfront.

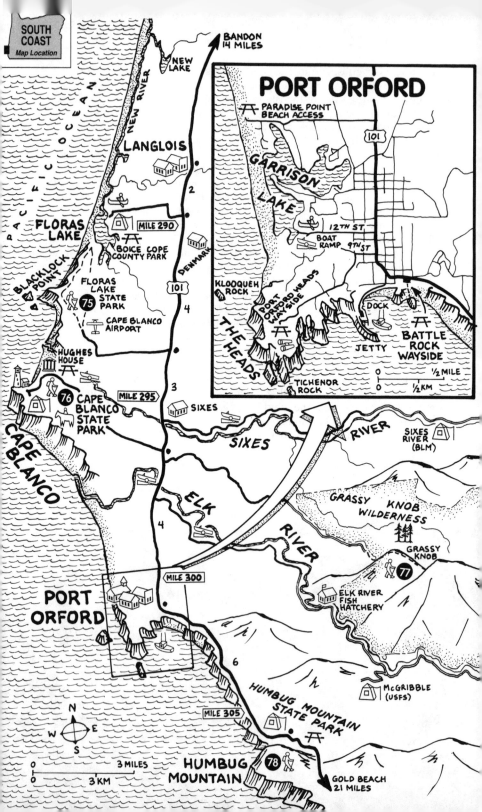

Battle Rock on Port Orford's waterfront.

PORT ORFORD

Westernmost city in the lower 48 states, Port Orford overlooks a sheltered cove with a natural ocean harbor that has attracted settlers since 1851.

Cape Blanco State Park

Cape Blanco's plateau juts more than a mile to sea. A picturesque 1870 lighthouse at the cape's tip is open for tours Thur-Mon 10-5 from May through October. A nearby 58-site campground is open year round (see Hike #76). Also in the park are a horse camp, a boat ramp, and the Hughes House, a gorgeously restored 1898 Victorian ranch house that's open from May to September, 10-5 Thur-Mon (Sun hours are 12-5).

Floras Lake

When developers in 1910 promised to make this lake a seaport by cutting a canal through the dunes to the ocean, the boomtown of Lakeport drew 400 eager settlers. The town vanished when surveys proved the lake is higher than the ocean, so that a canal would only drain it. Today, reliable winds make this sandy lake the Oregon Coast's most popular windsurfing center for beginners. Boice Cope County Park offers a beach, boat launch, and 30 campsites. Turn west off Highway 101 onto Floras Lake Road 2 miles south of Langlois.

Battle Rock

Park along Highway 101 at the south edge of downtown to walk out to a viewpoint atop Battle Rock, a small, forested island on Port Orford's beach. In 1851, nine white settlers were driven to this rock for 15 days, where they killed dozens of Indians with cannon fire. When the white men ran low on ammunition they fled through 80 miles of wilderness to an outpost on the Umpqua River.

Port Orford harbor

Each afternoon a harbor crane hoists the Port Orford fishing fleet, boat by boat, from the ocean for storage atop a dock for the night. Skin divers in wet suits often prowl the underwater reefs nearby.

Port Orford Heads Wayside

A 0.3-mile walkway leads from a picnic area by a decommissioned 1939 Coast Guard barracks to a breathtaking clifftop viewpoint on Port Orford's headland. Turn west off Highway 101 on 9th Street.

Garrison Lake

Within Port Orford's city limits, this forest-rimmed, many-armed lake is best explored by canoe from the boat ramp west of Highway 101 on 12th Street. Lush aquatic weeds hinder swimming or power boating.

Elk River

A visitable salmon fish hatchery is a popular goal for a 7.5-mile drive up the scenic Elk River Road, which joins Highway 101 north of Port Orford 3 miles. Experienced kayakers run the difficult whitewater chutes and emerald green pools of the 6 river miles above the hatchery.

Humbug Mountain State Park

A short path from this park's 108-site, year-round campground leads under a Highway 101 bridge to a pocket beach at the foot of Humbug Mountain's ocean cliffs. See Hike #78.

Blacklock Point.   Opposite: Windsurfer on Floras Lake.

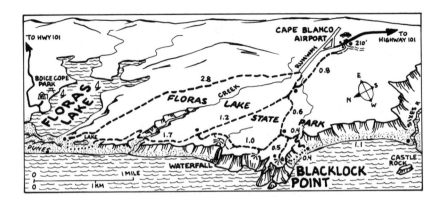

75   Blacklock Point

Moderate (to Blacklock Point)
4.1-mile loop
200 feet elevation gain

Moderate (to waterfall)
5.7-mile loop
250 feet elevation gain

Difficult (to Floras Lake)
9-mile loop
450 feet elevation gain

This little-known headland north of Cape Blanco overlooks scores of craggy islands, a waterfall, and 2 of the most beautiful and secluded beaches in Oregon. Wear boots, because the trail here follows muddy, abandoned roads.

Seven miles north of Port Orford, between mileposts 293 and 294, turn west off Highway 101 at an "Airport" pointer and follow paved County Road 160 for 2.8 miles to a parking area at the gated airport entrance. The trail begins to the left of the gate as a barricaded dirt road paralleling the runway through dense shore pine woods. Expect pink rhododendron blooms in spring, blue iris in early summer, and the tough but edible blue berries of salal and evergreen huckleberry in late summer. After 0.8 mile hop a creek and then keep left at an unmarked junction. The trail's next 3 junctions are marked with Coast Trail posts. If you follow the "Blacklock Point" arrows on these posts for 1.1 miles you'll fork twice to the left and once to the right before emerging at a meadow on the headland's tip. Islands with sea birds and tidepools surround the cape.

To explore the beach on a short loop, scramble to the left (toward Cape Blanco's winking lighthouse) down a meadowed slope to a beach strewn with driftwood logs and whale-sized boulders. Beyond the last boulder 100 yards, look for a driftwood pole that marks where the Oregon Coast Trail climbs up from the beach into spruce woods, just before a grassy draw. Follow this path up 0.4 mile to return to the second junction with a trail post.

If you're ready to head back, turn right. For the longer loops, follow the "Floras Lake" pointer left. This path parallels the bluff edge, with confusing left-hand spurs and loops that lead to viewpoints—including one at the lip of a 150-foot waterfall. After 1 mile reach a T-junction marked by another post.

For a 2-mile return route to your car, turn right. To tackle the longest loop, turn left. After 0.6 mile this trail dips to the beach at a sandy cove, then continues along the bluff edge 0.8 mile before ending at a pond amidst beachgrass. Be careful not to frighten endangered snow plovers nesting in the beach's dry sand here. Head for a large bare dirt opening behind the beach's foredune, 200 yards beyond the end of the pond. This rise has a view of Floras Lake, dotted with windsurfers, but it's also the start of a 2.8-mile return trail through the woods to the airport. When you reach the paved runway, keep right to find a path veering back into the woods. After 300 yards, turn left on the trail to your car.

76   Cape Blanco   

Easy (exploration near lighthouse)
1 mile round-trip
100 feet elevation gain

Moderate (north beach tour)
4-mile loop
250 feet elevation gain

Difficult (loop to south beach)
7-mile loop
500 feet elevation gain

Oregon's westernmost point was named *Cabo Blanco* ("White Cape") on a disastrous 1602 Spanish sea exploration. Most of the crew died of scurvy, and no white men returned for 173 years. A lighthouse built here in 1870 still flashes its white beam to sea. Park trails offer views of the windswept light and its picturesque headland.

Drive 4 miles north of Port Orford on Highway 101 and turn west at a Cape Blanco State Park sign for 4 miles to a fork. If you've only time for a quick hike, veer uphill to the left and continue a mile to the last parking area before the lighthouse gate. A post in the lower, gravel parking area on the right marks the Oregon Coast Trail. This path descends through a meadow of wind-matted salal bushes and white yarrow for 0.3 mile to the cape's windy north beach. After exploring the driftwood (and the marine life exposed on rocks at low tide), return to your car, follow the road left 100 yards, and turn right at another Coast Trail post. Along this path 0.2 mile is a meadow viewpoint and picnic table overlooking the cape's other beach and the islands of Orford Reef.

For longer hikes, it's best to start at the Sixes River boat ramp. To find it from Highway 101, drive 4 miles on the park's entrance road and fork to the right. This route passes Hughes House, an elegantly restored 1898 Victorian mansion that's open May to September from 10am to 5pm Thursday through Saturday and noon to 5pm Sunday. Continue to road's end at a picnic area and boat ramp.

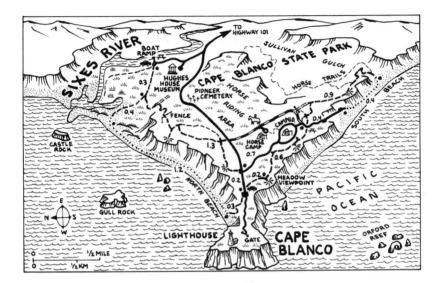

Beyond a gate, 2 mowed paths cross a pasture. Take the left-hand trail for 0.3 mile, and then fork to the right for 0.4 mile to the beach. Walk left along the beach 1.2 miles toward the lighthouse. A stone's throw before the beach runs out of sand, look for a trail up a meadowed slope to the left. Climb this path 0.3 mile to the lighthouse road parking lot described above.

For the moderate loop, turn left along the road 0.2 mile. At a trail post opposite the campground entrance, take a mowed path left across a meadow. Then keep left at all junctions for the next 1.3 miles, passing cliff-edge viewpoints and brushy fields popular with deer before descending to the meadow by your car.

If you'd prefer a longer loop route back from the lighthouse road's parking area, follow the road left 100 yards, turn right at a Coast Trail post, and keep right on this path 0.8 mile to another paved road. Cross the road and climb a mowed path a few feet to an X-shaped junction in a meadow. Turn right and keep right at all junctions for 0.9 mile to reach the south beach. Turn right along the beach 0.4 mile, hike up the paved road 1.1 mile straight through the entire campground to the lighthouse road, and cross the road to a path mowed through the meadow. Keep left at junctions along this path to reach your car in 1.6 miles.

Cape Blanco Lighthouse.   Opposite: Cape Blanco.

77   Grassy Knob

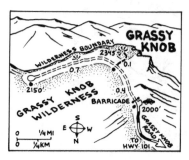

Easy
2.4 miles round-trip
400 feet elevation gain

In the final months of the battle to pass an Oregon Wilderness Bill in 1984, this jungly mountain overlooking Cape Blanco was still an uncertain candidate for preservation. The forest here has rare Port Orford cedars and critical watershed for the salmon runs of the Elk River, but few people knew of Grassy Knob. There was only one trail—a path to a former fire lookout site. Then, hoping to disqualify the area for preservation, a Forest Service supervisor with an anti-wilderness bias ordered a 30-foot-wide gravel logging road built on top of the trail. Congress was so angry that they designated Grassy Knob an official Wilderness Area after all. Today the abandoned road has regrown with trees and wildflowers, providing a surprisingly pleasant hiking route.

Drive Highway 101 north of Port Orford 4 miles (or south of the Cape Blanco turnoff a quarter mile). Turn east on Grassy Knob Road for 3.9 paved miles and an additional 3.8 miles of one-lane gravel, to a barricade and parking area. Then walk up the old road, now full of young Douglas fir and hemlock. Blue lupine and purple iris bloom profusely here in summer. After 0.4 mile a rock arrow in the road points to a trail on the right that climbs 100 yards through a patch of lupine to Grassy Knob's grassless summit. On the western horizon, note Port Orford and the islands of Orford Reef. To the south, distant Humbug Mountain (Hike #78) rises against the sea.

When a fire tower stood here during World War II, the lookouts were startled one morning to see a Japanese airplane buzz the mountain and drop a bomb into the forest. Nobuo Fujita, the pilot of a submarine's scouting plane, was attempting to retaliate for the U.S. bombing raid on Tokyo by using an incendiary bomb to start a forest fire. Although the bomb didn't go off (and was never found), the lookouts frantically radioed to warn of the attack—possibly the vanguard of a vast invasion. When the Army Air Corps heard that Grassy Knob was located "south of North Bend" they mistakenly scrambled fighters to the high desert city of Bend. Meanwhile, Fujita landed his plane on pontoons, bolted it to the submarine's deck, and made his escape. The only other site in the continental U.S. bombed in the war was Wheeler Ridge (Hike #95).

After absorbing the view, continue 0.7 mile along the overgrown ridgetop road to its end at a 2-acre gravel turnaround. Once intended as a base from which to log the impenetrable old-growth forests on either hand, this plain of young trees and flowers has become an unofficial monument to the difficult task of preserving wildness.

78 Humbug Mountain

Moderate
5.5-mile loop
710 feet elevation gain

*Right: Humbug Mountain
from Port Orford's dock.*

When an army of settlers landed in Port Orford in 1851 with hopes of cutting a trail inland to the new Rogue River gold mines, Captain William Tichenor assured them the task would be easy. They would only need to climb this imposing coastal peak to see the gold mine country on the far side, he claimed. After a scouting party labored through ancient forests to the summit, however, they named the mountain Tichenor's Humbug, because all they saw on the far side was more ocean. Today, of course, the ocean vistas and ancient forests are precisely why this loop hike is so attractive.

Drive Highway 101 south of Port Orford 6 miles (or north of Gold Beach 21 miles) and park at a large brown "Humbug Mountain Trail Parking" sign a quarter mile north of the state park's campground entrance. (If you're staying at the campground you can find this trailhead by taking a footbridge across the creek and a tunnel under the highway.)

The trail starts in a glen of huge maple and myrtlewood trees, with sword ferns and black-stalked maidenhair ferns. The well-graded path soon climbs into an old-growth forest of Douglas firs, some 6 feet thick. After a mile the trail forks at the start of the loop. The shorter, slightly steeper North Trail to the right passes the hike's best viewpoint (looking north to Redfish Rocks, Port Orford, and Cape Blanco). Where the routes finally rejoin, take a short uphill spur to the small, steep summit meadow of grass and bracken fern, and the hike's only view south to the Gold Beach coast. Return via the trail's other fork.

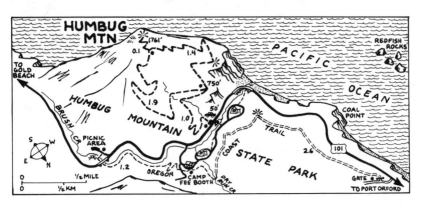

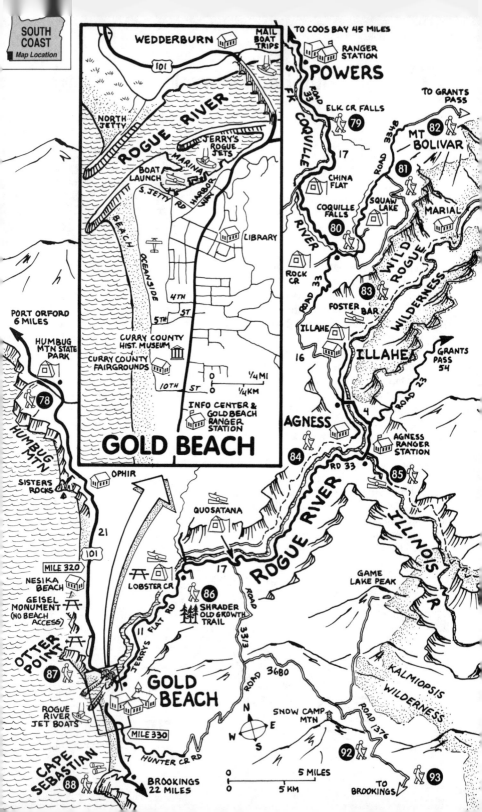

Kayakers in the Wild Rogue Wilderness.

GOLD BEACH

Miners sluiced Gold Beach's sand in the 1850s for gold flakes washed from the Klamath Mountains by the Rogue River. Today the Rogue is prized for different treasures—whitewater, wilderness, and wildlife.

Rogue River

At times the irascible Rogue River is a string of sunny green pools, lazily drifting past salmon-fishing black bears and circling osprey. But the river can also be misty mayhem, boiling through Mule Creek Canyon's Coffeepot or raging over the giant pinball course of Blossom Bar Rapid's boulders. The best views are from trails (Hikes #83 and 84) or from boats (see below), but there's plenty of scenery along the 35-mile paved road from the Gold Beach bridge to the hamlet of Agness. Three campgrounds along the way (Lobster Creek, Quosatana, and Illahe), offer river beaches with nearby boat ramps.

Jet boat trips

In 1895, mail boats began braving the Rogue River's rapids to supply isolated settlers. Today this tradition has evolved into rival fleets of 50-seat jet boats whisking tourists into the Rogue's wilderness. Loudspeakers announce herons, seals, and deer. Stops at rustic lodges allow passengers to buy buffet meals. The 64- to 104-mile tours cost about $30 to $80 and leave Gold Beach at about 8am and 2:30pm from May 1 to October 31. For reservations and details call 1-800-525-2161. Rogue River Mail Boats dock upstream from the north end of Gold Beach's bridge, while their rivals, Jerry's Rogue Jets, dock downstream from the bridge's south end, beside a free museum of Rogue River memorabilia.

Rafting the Rogue

The wildest 40-mile stretch of the Rogue River is so popular with kayakers and rafters during the peak season (May 15 to October 15) that the Forest Service holds a lottery to issue 10,000 permits from 90,000 applications. Boaters launch at Grave Creek (15 miles west of Wolf Creek exit 76 on Interstate 5), float about 3 days, and take out at Foster Bar in Illahe. For applications, write the Rand Visitor Center, 14335 Galice Highway, Merlin, OR 97532, or call (503) 479-3735. No permits are required in the off season, but the river level and weather can be iffy. Commercially guided trips cost at least $500.

Maidenhair ferns.

79   Elk Creek Falls

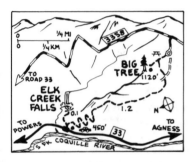

Easy (to falls)
0.2 miles round-trip
No elevation gain

Moderate (to Big Tree)
2.4 miles round-trip
800 feet elevation gain

A slender waterfall and the world's largest Port Orford cedar are the goals of these 2 short trails in the mountains along the South Fork Coquille River.

To drive here from the north, follow Highway 42 part of the way between Coos Bay and Roseburg. At a junction 3 miles east of Myrtle Point, turn south 17 miles to Powers and continue toward Agness 6.9 paved miles to the signed Elk Creek Falls pullout on the left. If you're coming here from the Highway 101 bridge at Gold Beach, take Jerrys Flat Road 32 miles to the Rogue River bridge near Agness and continue straight on Road 33 toward Powers for 25.6 miles. (including 4 miles of gravel) to the trailhead between mileposts 57 and 58.

At the trailhead, the path forks. To the left, a level trail ends in 150 yards at a grotto beside Elk Creek Falls' 60-foot cascade.

If you're headed for Big Tree, take the trail's right-hand fork, lined with delicate maidenhair fern. This path switchbacks up a steepish ridge where 15-foot rhododendrons bloom pink in June. After a mile, turn right on a grassy, abandoned road 100 yards. Then turn left on the trail's continuation. Huge, mossy, bigleaf maples and 8-foot-thick Douglas firs tower above the path. At a junction in a picnic area, turn left to Big Tree, a 239-foot-tall, 12-foot-thick cedar.

Port Orford cedars are often planted in towns as landscape shrubs, but they are threatened in their small native range, here in Southwest Oregon. Because the cedars resemble the nearly extinct hinoki cypress prized in Japan, loggers can sell a single tree for $10,000. In addition, a root rot fungus spread by dirt on muddy tires is wiping out the species in each infected watershed.

It's also possible to drive to the Big Tree picnic area. From the Road 33 trailhead, drive 0.7 mile toward Powers and turn right on Road 3358 for 4 miles.

80   Coquille River Falls

Easy
1 mile round-trip
400 feet elevation loss

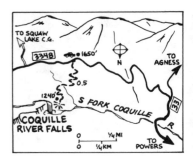

The South Fork Coquille River splits in two and thunders over a 100-foot cliff deep in the forested canyon of this research natural area.

To drive here from the north, follow Highway 42 part of the way between Coos Bay and Roseburg. At a junction 3 miles east of Myrtle Point, turn south 17 miles to Powers, continue another 17 paved miles toward Agness, and fork left on paved, 1-lane Road 3348 (toward Squaw Lake Campground) for 1.5 miles to the signed pullout on the left. If you're coming here from the Highway 101 bridge at Gold Beach, take Jerrys Flat Road 32 miles to the Rogue River bridge near Agness, continue straight on Road 33 toward Powers 15.6 miles (including 4 miles of gravel), and turn right on Road 3348 for 1.5 miles.

The trail switchbacks downhill for half a mile through an old-growth forest of Douglas fir and red cedar. The forest floor has sword ferns, shamrock-leaved oxalis, and Oregon grape. The path ends at a viewpoint of the big waterfall, but little Drowned Out Creek also splashes past the trail in a series of mossy 10-foot cascades. The exposed bedrock here is very slick, so use care if you insist on venturing onward 50 feet to a second viewpoint, or if you dare to scramble to the pools and chutes at the base of Coquille River Falls.

Coquille River Falls.

81 Hanging Rock

Moderate
4 miles round-trip
1200 feet elevation gain
Open mid-April through November

The view from this house-sized boulder is breathtaking even if you don't dare stand on the overhanging lip, a dizzying 3600 feet above the Rogue River. The hike here is best in June, when acres of rhododendron blooms along the Panther Ridge Trail are joined by yellow iris, white beargrass, and delicate fawn lilies.

If you're driving from the north, take Highway 42 (between Coos Bay and Roseburg) to a a junction 3 miles east of Myrtle Point. Turn south 17 miles to Powers, continue another 17 paved miles toward Agness, and fork left on paved, 1-lane Road 3348 toward Glendale for 8.7 miles. Opposite the primitive Buck Creek Campsite, turn right on gravel Road 5520 for 1.2 miles. Then turn left on steep Road 230 for 0.8 mile to a gravel trailhead pullout on the right.

If you're coming here from Gold Beach, take Jerrys Flat Road 32 miles up the Rogue River to the bridge near Agness, continue straight on Road 33 toward Powers 15.6 miles (including 4 miles of gravel), turn right on Road 3348 for 8.7 miles, turn right on gravel Road 5520 for 1.2 miles, and turn left on Road 230.

The Panther Ridge Trail climbs a slope where sparse old-growth Douglas firs leave light enough for rhododendron, salal, manzanita, and chinkapin to thrive. Note the O-shaped ceramic insulators 20 feet up trailside trees, remnants of a phone line that once connected fire lookout towers. After a mile the trail rounds Buck Point's knoll and drops to a campsite where huge cedar trees and tiny lady-slipper orchids surround a spring at the head of Buck Creek.

Next the path switchbacks up a dry ridge where beargrass and 6-petaled fawn

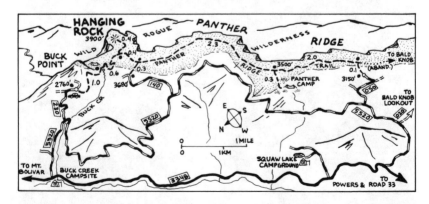

Hanging Rock.   Opposite: Rhododendron.

lilies bloom in June. Turn left at a T-shaped junction for 0.4 mile to reach Hanging Rock's stupendous cliffs. Directly below, the tips of great fir trees bristle up from the Wild Rogue Wilderness. The Devils Backbone, a craggy ridge, seems to dive down through the forests toward a crash landing at Paradise Bar.

Other Hiking Options
   Two other Panther Ridge trailheads provide alternative routes to Hanging Rock. A shorter, 1.1-mile route begins on Road 140 (see map). A longer, 5.2-mile route from the end of Road 050 accesses a spur to Panther Camp's meadow.

82   Mount Bolivar

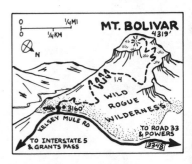

Moderate
2.8-mile loop
1160 feet elevation gain
Open May to mid-November

   Subalpine rock gardens and groves of old-growth trees line the path to Mt. Bolivar's lofty summit, where a 360-degree view encompasses the Rogue River's watershed from the Cascades to the California Siskiyous. Venezuela donated a bronze plaque for the summit because the peak honors Simon Bolivar (1783-1830), the Venezuelan-born liberator of Colombia and Peru.
   The hike is a jewel, despite the long drive required either from Highway 101

or Interstate 5. To find the trailhead from I-5, drive 22 miles north of Grants Pass (or 44 miles south of Roseburg) to Glendale exit 80, and head west 2.9 miles into Glendale. Opposite a small gas station, turn right on Brown Street (which becomes Reuben Road). After 12.3 miles turn left at a large brown signboard on the left. Follow a series of "Oregon Coast" signs another 13 miles to a 6-way junction at Anuktuvuk Saddle. Continue straight on paved Road 32-8-31 for 3.3 miles to the trailhead spur on the left. No parking permit or fee is required.

If you're coming from Highway 101 south of Coos Bay, take Highway 42 past Myrtle Point 3 miles, turn south through Powers 34 miles toward Agness, and turn left onto one-lane Road 3348, following Glendale signs 18.7 paved miles to the trailhead on the right (0.9 mile after entering BLM land). If you're coming from Gold Beach, take Jerrys Flat Road 32 miles up the Rogue River to the bridge near Agness, continue straight on Road 33 toward Powers for 15.6 miles, and turn right on Road 3348, following Glendale signs 18.7 paved miles to the trailhead on the right, 0.9 mile after entering BLM land.

The trail switchbacks a mile up a hot brushy slope with views and June rhododendron blooms. Then the path ducks into a cool forest of big Douglas fir, with lots of 6-petaled fawn lilies in May. Contorted yew trees form an understory. Then the trail climbs through a gorgeous rock garden of red Indian paintbrush, purple larkspur, and yellow stonecrop to the summit's former fire lookout site, now marked by foundation piers and a plaque.

View west from Mt. Bolivar.   Opposite: The Coffeepot from the Rogue River Trail.

83   Rogue River Trail

Difficult (to Flora Dell Falls)
8.6 miles round-trip
600 feet elevation gain

Very Difficult (to Marial)
15 miles one way
950 feet elevation gain

Very Difficult (to Grave Creek)
40 miles one way
2800 feet elevation gain

At Inspiration Point, the trail through the Rogue River's wilderness canyon has been blasted out of sheer basalt cliffs. Hundreds of feet below, kayaks and rafts drift through green-pooled chasms toward the roar of Blossom Bar's whitewater. In other places the river trail ducks into forested side canyons with waterfalls. Sometimes the path emerges at grassy river bars with ancient ranch cabins and gnarled oaks. Hikers always share this wilderness gorge with the plentiful wildlife drawn by the river—kingfishers, black bears, deer, and eagles.

If backpacking the entire 40-mile path from Illahe to Grave Creek sounds daunting, consider an 8.6-mile day hike as far as Flora Dell Falls. If you don't mind shuttling a car on long, gravel roads you can hike one-way on the 15-mile segment between Illahe and Marial. The most comfortable way to rough it, however, is to hike lodge-to-lodge, spending nights in rustic trailside inns.

Hikers may want to avoid mid-winter, when cold rains are the rule. It's also best to skip August, when the rocky, exposed slopes often shimmer with 100-degree heat. Poison oak is common, so learn to recognize its shiny triple leaflets. Backpackers should bring a lightweight stove, because campfires within 400 feet of the river are only allowed if they're packed up in firepans without a trace. Because black bears have become accustomed to raiding poorly cached food at night, campers must hang food bags at least 10 feet high and 5

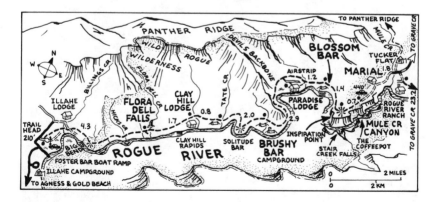

feet from a tree trunk. Don't bring bicycles or horses, but do bring the wilderness map and trail guide available at ranger stations in Gold Beach.

The river's name comes from the Takelma and Tututni Indians, whom the early French trappers called *coquins* (rogues). When gold attracted white interlopers, the tribes retaliated in 1855 by massacring settlers. The Army pursued the Indians to this remote canyon, where the soldiers were besieged by a superior force of well-armed warriors. The Army's trenches are still visible above the trail at Illahe's Big Bend Pasture. Relief troops from the east turned back when Indians rolled rocks on them from the steep slopes above Solitude Bar. When soldiers from Gold Beach arrived, however, nearly 1200 Indians were taken captive and forcibly moved 150 miles north to the Siletz Reservation.

To find the trailhead, turn off Highway 101 at the south end of the Gold Beach bridge and follow Jerrys Flat Road (which becomes Road 33) up the Rogue River for 32 miles. Just after crossing a river bridge, fork to the right at a sign for Illahe and follow a one-lane, paved road 3.5 miles to the trailhead spur on the right.

From the trail register, the path skirts Big Bend Pasture for half a mile through the woods, crosses some fields and a dirt road, and then contours along a wooded slope above the river. In its first 4.3 miles, the path bridges 5 streams (Billings, Buster, Dans, Hicks, and Flea creeks) before reaching Flora Dell Creek. Here a 20-foot waterfall showers into a swimmable pool beside the trail. Fifty yards before the creek, a side trail descends to a bedrock bank of the deep, green river, a good place to eat lunch while watching drift boats and jet boats pass. Beware of lush poison oak along the side trail to the river.

For a day hike, turn back here. If you're planning an overnight trip, continue upriver. In 1.7 miles you'll pass Clay Hill Lodge. A room for 2 here runs about $160, but includes meals. Book well in advance at 1-800-525-2161. For a backpacking campsite, either continue 0.8 mile to Tate Creek or hike an additional 2

Flora Dell Falls.

Blossom Bar Rapids.

miles through Solitude Bar's scenic gorge to Brushy Bar, a forested plain with a large, official campground.

Beyond Brushy Bar 2.9 miles, take a side path to the right across a grassy airstrip to Paradise Lodge. Drop-in hikers are welcome at the bar and buffet restaurant here. Book in advance if you want an overnight room (rates and phone number are the same as for Clay Hill Lodge). Paradise Lodge is a scheduled stop for Gold Beach jet boats from May through October. In winter, overnight guests can arrange to be ferried from Foster Bar at Illahe.

From Paradise Lodge, hike upriver 1.2 miles to Blossom Bar Creek, with campsites and a swimmable creek pool. Across a brushy lava flat to the right is the river's most treacherous rapids and the limit of jet boat traffic.

The trail climbs gradually for 1.4 miles to Inspiration Point, opposite Stair Creek's dramatic waterfall, and then traces the edge of Mule Creek Canyon, a gorge so narrow that boaters sometimes bridge sideways or spin helplessly in a cylindrical maelstrom called The Coffeepot. Half a mile beyond is the Marial trailhead. To shuttle a car here from Illahe, take Road 33 toward Powers for 15.6 miles, turn right on Road 3348, (following Glendale signs) for 22 miles to a 6-way junction, veer right at a Marial pointer for 18.3 miles to the Rogue River Ranch museum turnoff, and continue straight 1.8 rough miles to road's end.

If you're hiking onward past Marial, walk the road 1.8 miles and turn right into the Rogue River Ranch 200 yards, where the trail resumes. The final 23.2 miles to Grave Creek (not shown on map) are not officially Wilderness, but are plenty wild. There are no jet boats here, and no trailside lodges catering to hikers. The path climbs along the canyon slope, seldom nearing the river itself. Measured from the Marial road, the trail's highlights are author Zane Grey's cabin at Winkle Bar (5.5 miles), the Kelsey Creek campsite (7.6 miles), Meadow Creek's campsite (9.4 miles), the Russian Creek campsite (17.2 miles), Tyee Rapids (18.2 miles), Big Slide Camp (19.3 miles), the Whisky Creek Cabin museum (19.7 miles), Rainie Falls (21.2 miles), and Grave Creek (23.2 miles). To shuttle a car to Grave Creek, take Road 33 from the Illahe junction 2 miles west toward Gold Beach, turn left on paved Road 23 for 31 miles to Galice, and turn left for 8 miles.

84 Lower Rogue River

Moderate (to Painted Rock Creek)
6.2 miles round-trip
500 feet elevation gain

Difficult (entire trail)
12.6 miles one way
750 feet elevation gain

Far less crowded than the famous wilderness portion of the Rogue River Trail (Hike #83), this path traces a milder portion of the rugged river canyon. The trail contours along a forested slope above the river, dipping to a gravelly beach at Big Eddy and climbing to a clifftop viewpoint at Copper Canyon. Along the way the path bridges a dozen side creeks and passes half a dozen private cabins.

The most interesting day hike begins at the trail's eastern end in Agness. To drive there from the Highway 101 bridge in Gold Beach, turn inland on Jerrys Flat Road for 32 miles. After crossing a river bridge, turn left at a sign for Agness. Follow this paved, one-lane road 3 miles to the Agness Store and turn right on Cougar Lane for 0.2 mile. Immediately after a school, park on the right in the Agness Community Library's gravel lot. Then walk straight on the gravel road (where there is no parking), follow trail signs 200 yards to a pair of gates by a mobile home, go through the gates, and climb a steep road 150 yards to find the start of the actual trail on the right.

After this somewhat confusing start, the trail sets out through big Douglas firs and tanoaks with glimpses down to river riffles. Large gray squirrels shake their bushy silver tails at passing hikers. At the one-mile mark the trail forks. The larger, left-hand path descends to a gravel bar beside Big Eddy, where the Rogue swirls at a tight bend. This is the trail's only convenient river access, so stop awhile. Then take the trail's right-hand fork half a mile through tanoak

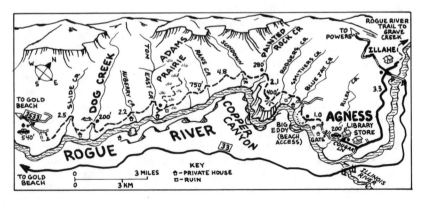

Lower Rogue River from Copper Canyon.   Opposite: Tanoak acorn.

woods to a road. The path jogs 80 yards left on the road across Blue Jay Creek, climbs 0.4 mile to Smithers Creek, and then forks to the right for 0.2 mile to Morris Rodgers Creek. This lovely creek is, alas, on private land, so continue up the trail to the craggy viewpoint on the cliffs above Copper Canyon. A natural rock garden here includes tiny purple penstemon, red Indian paintbrush, and blue, 6-petaled brodiaea lilies.

Day hikers could turn back here, but it's tempting to continue half a mile to the cool, mossy glen of cascading Painted Rock Creek. The creek is named for colored clay Indian pictographs painted on a rock overhanging the river at the creek's mouth. When you return to your car, check for ticks around your collar and cuffs. If you find any, unscrew them until they let go.

If you're backpacking or have arranged a car shuttle you can continue along the well-maintained river trail 9.5 miles to the western trailhead. To find this trailhead by car, drive 11.3 miles east of Gold Beach on Jerrys Flat Road. Just beyond Lobster Campground, turn left on Road 3310 across a scenic one-lane bridge. Then turn right onto gravel Road 3533 and follow "Lower Rogue River Trail" signs for 5.7 miles.

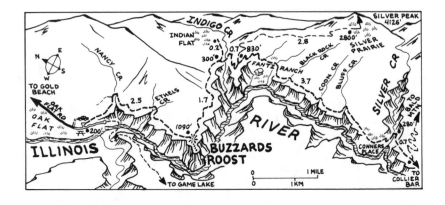

85   Illinois River

Moderate (to Buzzards Roost)
5 miles round-trip
900 feet elevation gain

Difficult (to Indian Flat)
9.8 miles round-trip
1700 feet elevation gain

Very Difficult (to Silver Creek)
17.2 miles round-trip
2900 feet elevation gain

The Illinois River is even wilder than its famous neighbor, the Rogue. In fact, the canyon here is so rugged that the 27-mile Illinois River Trail never actually reaches the riverbank. Instead the path traverses up to a viewpoint atop the cliffs of Buzzards Roost, dips deeply into the canyons of several side creeks, and finally climbs over 3747-foot Bald Mountain. Backpacking the entire 27 miles to the Briggs Creek Trailhead (not shown on map) is a serious adventure, but day hikers can get a good sample with trips to Buzzards Roost, Indian Flat, or Silver Creek.

From the Highway 101 bridge in Gold Beach, take Jerrys Flat Road up the Rogue River 28 miles. On the far side of the Illinois River Bridge, turn right on Oak Flat Road for 3 miles. A few hundred yards beyond the end of pavement, park in a gravel lot on the left.

The trail starts at a register box and ambles through a park-like Douglas fir forest with a few tanoaks and canyon live oaks. Poison oak bushes masquerade here as tree seedlings. Climb to a crossing of Nancy Creek at the 0.8-mile mark, cross Ethels Creek at the 1.6-mile mark, and continue up 0.9 mile to the forested saddle at Buzzards Roost. To get a panoramic view here you have to scramble (cautiously!) 100 feet up the rocky crest of a precipitous ridge.

If you have energy for a longer hike, continue on the main trail 1.7 miles downhill to a fork. To the left is Indian Flat's oasis-like meadow beside Indigo Creek. (The far end of the meadow is private property.) To the right, the main trail crosses Indigo Creek on a scenic footbridge, another possible turnaround point.

If you're headed for Silver Creek, cross the bridge and switchback up 0.7 mile to a ridgetop junction. Avoid the rarely used Silver Peak Trail to the left, which heads steeply up the ridge to distant viewpoints in high, bracken meadows. Instead continue on the main trail, descending to Fantz Ranch, a grassy bench recently acquired by the U.S. Forest Service in a land trade. There are nice campsites beside a creek here.

Beyond Fantz Ranch the trail traverses a canyon slope 3 miles before dropping to Silver Creek's dramatic bedrock chasm. Camping is impossible in this gorge, and if a long-planned bridge is not yet built, crossing the swift, narrow creek requires a daring leap.

When you return from your hike, check for ticks around your collar and cuffs. If you find any, unscrew them until they let go.

Other Hiking Options

To backpack the remainder of the 27-mile Illinois River Trail, continue past Silver Creek 0.7 mile, fork left and switchback up 3200 feet in 4 grueling miles. The trail then ambles past small bracken meadows on the crest of Bald Mountain's ridge for 3.7 miles before gradually descending 10 miles to the Briggs Creek Trailhead at the end of Road 4103. This final portion is not shown on the map and should only be undertaken with the Forest Service's topographic Kalmiopsis Wilderness map. The difficult 94-mile car shuttle to the Briggs Creek Trailhead (via Galice, Grants Pass, and Selma) calls for a map of the Siskiyou National Forest.

Illinois River trailhead.   Opposite: Madrone branches.

86   Shrader Old Growth Trail

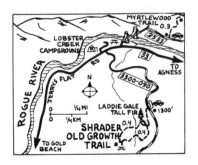

Easy (Schrader Old Growth Trail)
0.8-mile loop
100 feet elevation gain

Easy (Myrtlewood Trail)
0.6-mile round-trip
300 feet elevation gain

This nature trail explores a stately glen of giant trees, including the 220-foot-tall, 10-foot-thick Laddie Gale Douglas fir. If the 0.8-mile loop seems short, add an encore—a nearby 0.3-mile path to the world's largest myrtlewood tree.

From the Highway 101 bridge in Gold Beach, turn toward Agness on Jerrys Flat Road for 11.2 miles. Just beyond the Lobster Creek Campground, turn right at a sign for the Frances Shrader Memorial Trail and follow steep, one-lane Road 3300-090 for 2.1 miles to a parking lot on the left. In June, 20-foot rhododendrons surround the lot with blooms.

The packed gravel path that begins across the road leads past benches and a picnic table beside the grove's mossy creek. A brochure available at the trailhead explains how the old-growth forest's complex ecosystem includes minute fungi, hollow snags, brushy streams, and blowdown openings. The Laddie Gale fir at loop's end is named for the basketball star who led the University of Oregon's legendary "Tall Firs" team to a national championship in 1939.

If you'd like to try the Myrtlewood Trail, drive back to Jerrys Flat Road (Road 33) and turn right for 0.1 mile. Following Lower Rogue River Trail signs, turn left on Road 3310 across a scenic one-lane bridge and then turn right on Road 3533 for a mile. The steep, 0.3-mile trail that begins here switchbacks up to the massive myrtlewood tree, beside a picnic table and a lovely creek.

Myrtlewood twig with fruit.

View south from Otter Point.

87   Otter Point

Easy (from Old Coast Hwy)
2.8 miles round-trip
100 feet elevation gain

Easy (from turnaround)
0.4 miles round-trip
No elevation gain

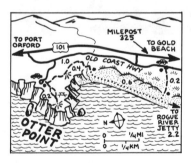

No signs on Highway 101 alert travelers to this scenic, wave-pounded head-land north of Gold Beach. As a result, few people have discovered the state park trails that descend to a secluded beach nestled against the little cape.

Drive Highway 101 north of Gold Beach 3 miles. Near milepost 325, at a sign marked "To Old Coast Road," drive west one block to a T-shaped junction and turn left for 0.2 mile to a small gravel pullout on the ocean side of the road. The pullout is marked only by a Coast Trail post.

Park here and follow a slot-like path through the salal and wild azaleas to a broad beach. Head to the right along the beach 0.6 mile toward Otter Point. A rare pink form of sand verbena blooms in summer near the beach's end.

Look for a Coast Trail post beside a creek 400 yards before the beach ends. A trail here climbs 0.4 mile through alders and coastal shrubbery to a trail junction near a parking area atop Otter Point. Turn left 0.2 mile to trail's end at a meadow on the headland's tip. Summer wildflowers here include blue iris, red Indian paintbrush, and white wild strawberries.

Notice that the cape's exposed rock strata are turned on edge like sliced bread. These layers began as mud deposited 150 million years ago on the seafloor 500 miles south of here. When faults slid the Pacific Ocean plate north, the compacted mudstone scraped off onto the continent and tilted sideways. On the horizon are other reminders of that colossal collision—Cape Sebastian to the south (Hike #88) and Humbug Mountain to the north (Hike #78).

If you're short on time, trim the hike by parking on top of Otter Point. To find this trailhead, turn off Highway 101 at milepost 325, drive a block to the Old Coast Road, turn right for 0.6 mile, and turn left at a state park sign.

88   Cape Sebastian

Moderate (to beach)
3.8 miles round-trip
700 feet elevation loss

Difficult (from Myers Creek Pullout)
5.8 miles round-trip
700 feet elevation gain

An often-overlooked state park road leads to a spectacular viewpoint in the windswept meadows atop this huge coastal cliff. From there, a 1.9-mile path switchbacks down through spruce woods to one of Oregon's most-photographed beaches—a scene framed with craggy islands and sea stacks.

Drive Highway 101 south of Gold Beach 7 miles (or north of Brookings 22 miles). Near milepost 335, turn at a "Cape Sebastian Viewpoint" state park sign and follow a very steep paved road 0.6 mile to the viewpoint at road's end. Strong winds here have mowed Sitka spruce trees to a waist-high mat. To the north, the shore stretches past Gold Beach to Humbug Mountain (Hike #78). To the south, grassy-topped Hunters Island and countless smaller sea stacks shelter the beach at Hunters Cove.

Take the paved path across the cape's meadow to an even better viewpoint. Pavement ends when the path continues, following a ridge. The trail then switchbacks downhill at a good grade for a mile to a rocky shore fringed with shore pine, evergreen huckleberry, and a few 3-leaved poison oak plants. Black, crook-necked cormorants dry their wings atop the wave-sculpted rocks here. Sea palms bend with the waves' spray.

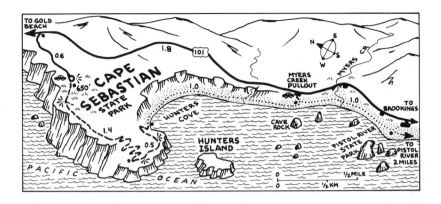

The trail levels for a scenic half-mile tour of the rocky shoreline. Then the trail descends to the bouldery start of Hunters Cove's beach. Sea otter hunters once sought refuge from storms here. But by 1911, the hunters had driven their cute, fur-bearing prey to extinction in Oregon.

In summer, blue lupine blooms along the beach. It's possible to walk the beach 4 miles to the mouth of the Pistol River, but be sure to leave energy for the return climb to your car.

Other Hiking Options

If you'd rather end your hike with a downhill grade, start at the bottom of Cape Sebastian instead. Drive Highway 101 south of the Cape Sebastian turnoff 1.8 miles (or north of the Myers Creek Bridge 0.4 mile) to an unmarked viewpoint pullout. Take the beach trail that starts at a gap in the guardrail, walk right a mile to the beach's north end, and continue across boulders 200 yards to find the Cape Sebastian trail.

Sea stacks at Pistol River State Park .   Opposite: Cape Sebastian from Myers Creek.

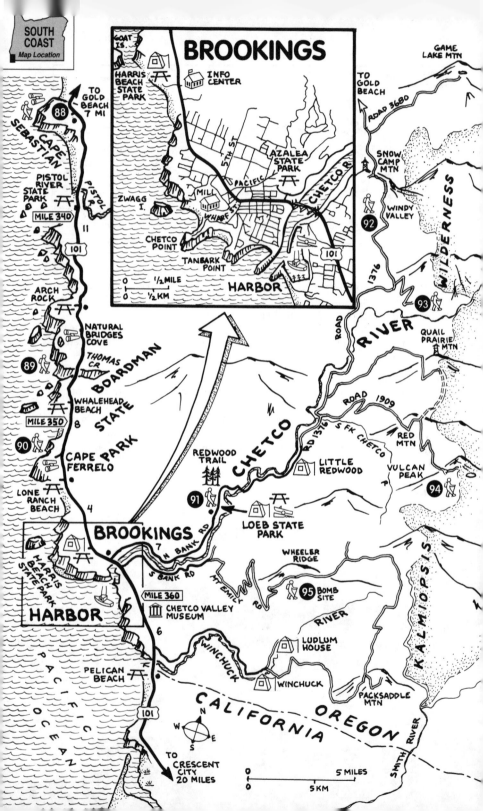

The beach at Harbor, just south of Brookings.

BROOKINGS

Known as Oregon's "banana belt," the Brookings coast has the state's balmiest climate, with average temperatures between 50° F and 70° F year-round. Boardman State Park preserves 13 miles of picturesque coves, capes, and islands along Highway 101. Inland, the 281-square-mile Kalmiopsis Wilderness drapes the rugged Klamath Mountains.

Brookings/ Harbor

Platted in 1908 as a lumber company town, Brookings has evolved into a major retirement destination. Attracted by the scenery and mild climate, retirees now account for over half the population. Across the Chetco River in the adjacent city of Harbor is the local port, with a large marina, docks, charter boats, a jetty, and a scenic beach.

Pistol River State Park

Hundreds of sea stacks and craggy islands shelter the beach at the mouth of the Pistol River, 23 miles north of Brookings. Parking areas along Highway 101 access the picturesque beach and grassy dunes (see Hike #88).

Samuel H. Boardman State Park

Plan to stop often when driving Highway 101 through this long, narrow coastal park. From north to south, top roadside attractions are Arch Rock Picnic Area (on a grassy bluff surrounded by views), Natural Bridges Cove (a viewpoint of churning sea caves), the 345-foot-tall Thomas Creek Bridge (Oregon's highest), Whalehead Beach Picnic Area (a lovely beach with a whale-shaped island that sometimes spouts surf), Cape Ferrelo (a viewpoint on a grassy headland), and Lone Ranch Beach Picnic Area (at the foot of Cape Ferrelo). For maps and recommended trails, see Hikes #89 and #90.

Harris Beach State Park

This popular beachside park just north of Brookings overlooks Goat Island and countless offshore rocks that serve as habitat for seabirds and sea lions. The 156-site, year-round campground accepts summer reservations. A 0.2-mile path from the camp fee booth climbs to a viewpoint atop Harris Butte.

Azalea Park

Wild western azaleas (*Rhododendron occidentale*) fill this park with fragrant white blooms in time for Brookings' Azalea Festival, held here each Memorial Day weekend. Follow signs from the north end of the Chetco River Bridge.

Chetco Valley Museum

The world's largest Monterey cypress grows outside this restored 1857 stagecoach stop and trading post, just off Highway 101, south of Brookings 2 miles. The museum's collection of pioneer and Indian artifacts is open Wed-Sun noon-5 in summer; otherwise Thu-Sun noon-4.

Loeb State Park

Along the Chetco River, surrounded by groves of huge myrtlewood trees and redwoods, this all-year park offers a 53-site campground and a picnic area beside a gravelly river bar. See Hike #91.

Western azaleas in Azalea Park.   *Opposite: China Beach headland at low tide.*

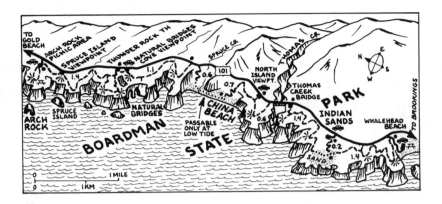

89 Boardman Park North

Easy (4 viewpoint walks)
2.8 miles round-trip
600 feet elevation gain

Easy (Whalehead Bch to Thomas Cr)
2.8 miles one way
500 feet elevation gain

Moderate (Thomas Cr to Arch Rock)
4.4 miles one way
700 feet elevation gain

Boardman State Park's coast is a spectacular parade of islands, coves, and capes. Both Highway 101 and the Oregon Coast Trail trace the 12.6-mile length of the narrow park. Because the two routes touch every mile or so, it's easy to divide the trail into smaller day hikes or to shuttle a car between trailheads for one-way hiking. Below are recommendations for the northern half of the park; Hike #90 describes the park's southern half.

If you only have time for a quick tour, the best bet is to stop at 4 different trailheads for short hikes to viewpoints. The northernmost of these stops is the Arch Rock Picnic Area, between mileposts 344 and 345. Park here and stroll the paved, 0.2-mile path around the rim of the picnic area's bluff. Waves crash against seabird-dotted islands on all sides of the cape.

Next drive south 1.2 miles to a pullout near milepost 346 marked "Natural Bridges Cove Viewpoint." Trails leave from both the left- and right-hand edges of this parking area. First take the left-hand trail 100 feet to a viewpoint of the cove below, where the sea boils through 2 archways into a collapsed former cave. Then return to the car and take the right-hand trail along the cove's rim to discover a 0.7-mile loop with more views. This route crosses the Thunder Cove Viewpoint pullout, continues into the woods, and then forks to the left. The path switchbacks downhill, passes several cliff-edge viewpoints, and finally switchbacks back up the hill to a T-shaped junction. Turn right to return to your car.

Oregon Coast Trail north of Indian Sands.   *Opposite: Kelp on Whalehead Beach.*

For the third of the 4 short viewpoint hikes, drive south another 1.5 miles to a pullout with a guardrail and a small sign, "North Island Viewpoint." Take the trail to a junction in the woods and turn right. This path rounds a hill and descends 0.7 mile to beautiful, secluded China Beach.

After prowling China Beach, return to your car and drive Highway 101 south another mile to Indian Sands Viewpoint. From the left side of the parking lot's entrance, a 0.2-mile trail descends through forest to an unusual area of sand dunes perched above a rocky shore. It's a good place to explore or to let kids play in the sand before heading back.

If you'd prefer a longer, more connected hike, try the 2.8-mile trail between Whalehead Beach and Thomas Creek Bridge. Drive Highway 101 to the Whalehead Beach Picnic Area turnoff, south of milepost 349. Only drive 100 feet down the picnic area entrance road before parking beside a big trail sign on the right.

The path begins at a Coast Trail post. After 0.2 mile, the trail forks to the right in a headland meadow with breathtaking views south to Cape Ferrelo. At the 0.5-mile mark, the path briefly parallels the highway guardrail before following posts across a meadow to the woods. After 1.4 miles you'll enter the trailless dunes of Indian Sands. Continue straight and slightly downhill, following posts along the forest edge 0.3 mile to the trail's continuation. After skirting 4 scenic coves (and briefly following the highway guardrail again), the trail ends at a big parking lot at the south end of Oregon's tallest bridge, the 345-foot-tall Highway 101 span across Thomas Creek's gorge.

The remaining 4.4-mile trail section between Thomas Creek and Arch Rock is also suitable as a day hike. The best place to park is 0.2 mile north of Thomas Creek Bridge at a pullout marked "North Island Viewpoint." Take the trail into the woods, turn right, descend 0.7 mile to China Beach, and turn right. Unless it's high tide, you'll be able to round a small headland on the sand. Beyond it, look for a Coast Trail post marking the steep trail back up to the highway. Then turn left along the highway shoulder 0.1 mile to find a trail post marking the path's continuation. The final 2.5 miles pass several viewpoints and 3 highway pullouts before reaching the Arch Rock Picnic Area's entrance road.

90   Boardman Park South

Easy (3 viewpoint walks)
2 miles round-trip
100 feet elevation gain

Easy (Lone Ranch to Cape Ferrelo)
2.4 miles round-trip
300 feet elevation gain

Moderate (Lone Ranch to Whalehead)
5.1 miles one way
600 feet elevation gain

Although it's possible to backpack the entire 12.6-mile length of Boardman State Park's spectacular coast, most hikers take advantage of the trail's frequent junctions with Highway 101 to plan shorter day trips. Below are suggestions for hikes in the park's southern half. (The northern half is described in Hike #89.)

Even if you're just passing through, squeeze in time for a collection of 3 short viewpoint walks. First turn off Highway 101 near milepost 352 at the Cape Ferrelo Viewpoint. From the parking area, walk 0.5 mile out through grassy wildflower meadows to the cape's panoramic tip. Then return to your car, drive 3 miles north, and take the Whalehead Beach turnoff down to a picnic area beside a gorgeous, secluded beach. Whalehead Island won its name because waves send a spout-like plume of sea spray above its rocky "head" when the tide is just right. Hop across Whalehead Creek and explore the beach as far as

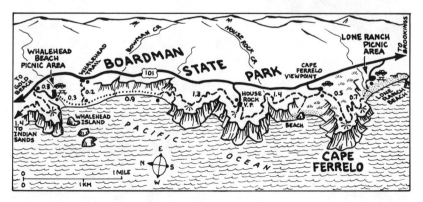

you like. Then return to your car , drive 0.3 mile back uphill to the highway junction, and park by a trail sign on the left. Take this path 0.2 mile out along a meadowy cape to a breathtaking viewpoint overlooking Whalehead Island.

If you have time for a more connected hike, climb Cape Ferrelo from Lone Ranch Beach. Start by driving to the Lone Ranch Beach Picnic Area, halfway between mileposts 352 and 353. Take the concrete path down to the beach, cross Lone Ranch Creek on driftwood, and walk to the right until the beach's sand ends. Continue on boulders a few hundred feet to a trail post on a grassy bluff. The path that starts here makes 3 long switchbacks up through the wildflower meadows to the cape's tip. Continue inland 0.5 mile to the Cape Ferrelo Viewpoint parking area. For an easy hike, turn back here.

If you'd prefer a longer, 5.1-mile hike—and if you've had the foresight to shuttle a car ahead to the Whalehead Beach Picnic Area—continue north on a trail that angles down from the Cape Ferrelo parking area. A left-hand spur of this path descends to a pocket beach. The main path climbs through woods, approaches the highway at House Rock Creek, crosses the parking lot at House Rock Viewpoint, and descends past viewpoints to scenic Whalehead Beach, where a 1.2-mile walk along the sand brings you to the picnic area parking lot.

Whalehead Beach from the cape above the picnic area.

The Chetco River from the Riverview Trail at Loeb State Park.

91   Redwood Nature Trail

Easy
2.6-mile loop
400 feet elevation gain

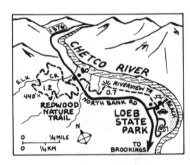

Although redwoods are better known from California, 12-foot-thick *Sequoia sempervirens* giants also thrive along the Chetco River. A nature trail loop through this grove connects with the Riverview Trail through Loeb State Park.

From the Highway 101 bridge in Brookings, turn inland on North Bank Road for 7.3 miles and turn right into Loeb State Park to a trailhead parking area. The Riverview Trail starts on the left by a box with nature trail guides. Huge, gnarled myrtlewood trees form a canopy over a forest floor carpeted with shamrock-leaved oxalis and sword ferns. The parkland here was donated to the state for preservation in 1948 by a group called Save the Myrtlewoods.

The path crosses a picnic area and follows the bank of the broad, gravelly Chetco River. Foot-long moss fringes hang from bigleaf maple branches above the trail. Delicate, black-stalked maidenhair ferns wave beside the path. After 0.7 mile the path ends at the road. Cross to the Redwood Nature Trail parking area, follow the trail up along a creek, and turn left on the 1.2-mile loop route. The path climbs for 0.6 mile through ever grander redwoods. Then the trail descends and crosses a mossy, bouldery creek twice before completing the loop. Turn left and return along the Riverview Trail to your car.

Windy Valley

Moderate
4.4 miles round-trip
500 feet elevation gain
Open May through November

Nowhere in Oregon are you likely to find such an astonishing variety of wildflowers and trees along such an easy trail as at Windy Valley, high in the Klamath Mountains. Jumbled together here are odd knobcone pines, insect-eating pitcher plants, rare Port Orford cedars, and masses of wild azaleas. The valley itself is a meadowed Eden, bordered by a sparkling mountain stream.

The long drive here over gravel roads keeps the area uncrowded. From the Highway 101 bridge in Brookings, take North Bank Road inland 8 miles and continue straight on one-lane Road 1376 another 8 miles to a T-junction after the South Fork Chetco Bridge. Turn left (following "Snow Camp Lookout" signs) and continue on twisty, gravel Road 1376 for another 13 miles to the trailhead on the left, 0.2 mile after milepost 21.

An alternative driving route from Gold Beach route is only open June 1 to September 30. Take Highway 101 south of Gold Beach 1 mile, turn left on Hunter Creek Road (which becomes gravel, 1-lane Road 3680). Stick to Road 3680, following Snow Camp Lookout signs 24.6 miles, and then turn right on Road 1376 toward Brookings for 7 miles.

The trail to Windy Valley sets out among long-needled Jeffrey pines. In June, expect white beargrass plumes, blue iris, red Indian paintbrush, and creamy wild azalea blooms. After 0.4 mile, pass the remains of a collapsed shelter, hop across Cedar Creek, and climb 100 yards to a switchback where green orchids and carnivorous pitcher plants line the trail. The cobra-shaped pitcher plants (*Darlingtonia californica*) lure insects into their hairy throats with a honey aroma, then dissolve the bugs to make a nitrogen-rich fertilizer. In early summer, look for the plants' weird brown blooms.

Next the trail crosses a brushland where trees have been dwarfed by an outcropping of red, nutrient-poor peridotite. Look here for fuzzy cat's ear lilies and stalks of white death camas. Then the trailside rocks shift to the bluish hue of serpentine. Look here for knobcone pines, resembling cone-bearing flagpoles.

The trail forks at the 1.7-mile mark. To the left is Windy Creek, where a calf-deep, icy ford will stop most hikers. Instead take the right-hand fork toward Windy Valley. This path skirts a tiny meadow, ducks through a grove of huge, old-growth Douglas fir, and crosses Windy Creek on a fallen log. On the far shore is Windy Valley, a long, park-like meadow with buttercups and violets. The trail ends here, but walk 0.3 mile to the far end of the meadow, where the log foundations of a dugout cabin overlook a pool and small waterfall. This is

Windy Valley.   Opposite: Insect-eating pitcher plants.

a good turnaround point, but explorers can cross the creek on slippery logs and continue upstream through the woods 0.3 mile to a fork in Windy Creek.

Other Hiking Options

What Windy Valley lacks is a viewpoint, but 2 panoramas are nearby. As you hike back toward your car, notice a rocky knoll straight ahead. Just before the trail switchbacks down to Cedar Creek, plow through 200 feet of tangly brush and scramble another 200 feet to the knoll's summit for a view that stretches from the ocean at Crescent City to the Kalmiopsis Wilderness. For a gentler viewpoint path, return to your car and drive 5.4 miles up Road 1376 (only open June through September here) to a sign for Snow Camp Lookout at a gated spur road on the left. Walk this track 0.4 mile to the tower and a 360-degree view. The restored 16-by-16 lookout, complete with double bed, woodstove, and fire finder table, can be reserved for overnight rental by calling the Chetco Ranger District at (503) 469-2196. A rocky 2.3-mile trail descends from the lookout to the Windy Creek ford.

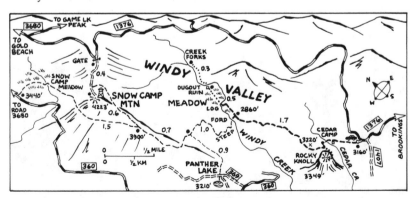

93 Tincup Trail

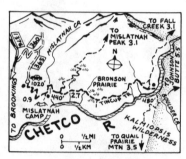

Difficult
7.2 miles round-trip
1450 feet elevation gain

The Chetco River roars out of the Kalmiopsis Wilderness through one of the most remote forested canyons in Southern Oregon. The Tincup Trail follows an old prospectors' route along this canyon's slope to a river bar surrounded by boulders, whitewater, and a craggy horizon of old-growth firs.

From the Highway 101 bridge in Brookings, take North Bank Road inland 8 miles and continue straight on one-lane Road 1376 another 8 miles to a T-junction just beyond the South Fork Chetco Bridge. Turn left and continue on gravel Road 1376 another 10 miles. At milepost 18, fork right onto Road 360 and keep right for 3 rough, twisty miles to the Tincup Trailhead at a turnaround.

The path drops 580 feet in its first 0.9 mile, descending through a Douglas fir forest mixed with sun-tolerant tanoak, madrone, and myrtle. At the bottom of the hill, the trail passes privately owned Mislatnah Camp (a grassy flat), continues to a 90-foot bridge over cold, rushing Mislatnah Creek, and sets off on a 2.7-mile traverse along the canyon slope to Boulder Creek. Along the way you'll pass rarely used side trails (sometimes blocked by blowdown trees) to Mislatnah Peak's lookout site, the Bronson Cabin site, and Fall Creek.

Finally the trail descends to the Chetco River's wave-sculpted boulders and hidden, black sand beaches. A pungent, sweet smell fills the air. Butterflies of many colors flit by. Water ouzels zip above the clear green river. Bring the Forest Service's Kalmiopsis Wilderness map if you intend to explore farther, but be warned that the trails on the far shore of this bridgeless, 6-foot-deep river can only be reached in late summer, when it may be possible to ford 0.2 mile upriver.

Chetco River at Boulder Creek.   Opposite: Kalmiopsis leachiana *near Salamander Lake.*

94   Vulcan Lake

Moderate (to Vulcan Peak)
2.6 miles round-trip
900 feet elevation gain
Open May through November

Moderate (to Vulcan Lake)
3.7-mile loop
650 feet elevation gain

Difficult (to Salamander Lake)
8.2 miles round-trip
1050 feet elevation gain

Stark red ridges, shimmering green lakes, and the strange plants of the Klamath Mountains highlight this remote but popular area. Pick up a topographic Kalmiopsis Wilderness map at a Forest Service station, and remember that winter snows usually close the trails here until May.

From the Highway 101 bridge in Brookings, take North Bank Road 8 miles and continue straight on one-lane Road 1376 another 8 miles to a T-junction just beyond the South Fork Chetco Bridge. Unless there's a temporary detour posted here for a longer, alternate route, turn right on gravel Road 1909 for 13.3 increasingly rough miles (keeping right when in doubt) to a fork where signs point left for Vulcan Lake and right for Vulcan Peak. Here you face a decision.

If you have time for a side trip—or if your goal is a viewpoint—turn right and park at the Vulcan Peak trailhead. From here you can walk up the Chetco Divide Trail's abandoned roadbed 0.2 mile and fork left onto a well-graded path that climbs gradually 1.1 mile across an open, brushy slope to the rocky crest of Vulcan Peak. Anchor bolts and melted glass remain from the old lookout tower. A map-like view of the Kalmiopsis Wilderness spreads to the east, while the ocean glints to the west and the snowy Siskiyous rise to the south.

If your goal is Vulcan Lake, drive left at the road fork for 1.7 rough miles to a trailhead at road's end. (The road's final 1.7 miles may only be open June through September.) This trail also begins as an abandoned mining road, but

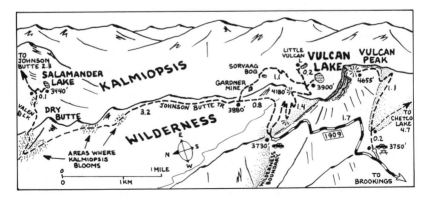

Vulcan Lake and Vulcan Peak.

after 50 yards turn right on a path that switchbacks up through snowbrush and wind-twisted Jeffrey pine. After a mile, reach a rocky pass with sweeping views. The trail then angles down 0.4 mile to Vulcan Lake, a magical place where red bedrock curves into deep green water. During the Ice Age this basin was a cirque—the birthplace of a glacier—and the immense weight of moving ice shaped the rounded, scratched bedrock. Only a few pines and cedars have gained a foothold. If you're backpacking, bring a stove and build no campfire.

To find another lake nearby, backtrack 200 yards from Vulcan Lake to a rock cairn, turn right, and keep to the right on a faint downhill path. After 0.2 mile you'll reach Little Vulcan Lake's shore, ringed with carnivorous pitcher plants, the baseball-bat-shaped bog plants that trap insects for fertilizer.

Then walk back to the rock cairn near Vulcan Lake. The quickest way to your car is to return as you came, but if you'd like to try a loop route, walk 50 steps toward Little Vulcan Lake and turn left at a cairn in a wet spot. From here, a series of these rock piles marks a faint, level path. Follow this rocky trail 0.6 mile to Sorvaag Bog, a brushy pond. Walk to the right of the pond, cross its outlet creek, and continue straight to an old bulldozed road. Follow this track left for 0.5 mile—passing the Gardner Mine's tunnel entrance along the way—to a T-shaped junction with the Johnson Butte Trail. Your car is 0.8 mile to the left.

The difficult hike to Salamander Lake can either be added as a long side trip to the loop described above or as a separate trip. Hike this route in early June to see the pink blossoms of *Kalmiopsis leachiana*, an extremely rare, azalea-like shrub almost entirely confined to a few isolated patches within this wilderness.

Start at the Vulcan Lake Trailhead but keep left, following the Johnson Butte Trail's abandoned bulldozer road through sparse, brushy woods. The road peters out after 2.6 miles , and a view-packed trail continues along the crest of a rocky ridge. Look here for struggling *Kalmiopsis* shrubs, reduced to a mat by winter's snowstorms and summer's baking sun. In a saddle at the 4-mile mark, a side trail to the right leads 0.1 mile steeply down to Salamander Lake, a shallow, brush-rimmed lake full of yellow-blooming lilypads.

95 Wheeler Ridge Bomb Site

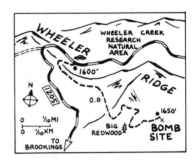

Easy
1.6 miles round-trip
100 feet elevation gain

Below: Trail sign showing WW II submarine-launched seaplane.

In the darkest hours of World War II, after Pearl Harbor and the retaliatory night bombing of Tokyo, a Japanese submarine surfaced off the Southern Oregon coast. Sailors unbolted an airplane from the sub's wave-swept deck, attached a pair of wings, loaded 2 incendiary bombs, and launched the aircraft by catapult. With his family's 400-year-old samurai sword strapped to the seat to give him courage, pilot Nobuo Fujita flew inland, determined to undermine the U.S. war effort by starting a forest fire.

It was September 9, 1942. Fire lookouts spotted an unknown plane over Wheeler Ridge and scrambled through the dense redwood forest. They found a cluster of shattered trees and easily put out a few small, smoldering fires. The only other bomb dropped by aircraft on the mainland U.S. in World War II fell on Grassy Knob (see Hike #77) and did not explode.

Fifty years later, Nubuo Fujita returned to the Wheeler Ridge bomb site, this time as an ambassador for peace. He had already presented his ancient samurai sword to the city of Brookings as a token of reconciliation. Now he hiked a short path across the ridge to plant a redwood seedling where his bomb had fallen.

To find the trail, turn off Highway 101 at the south end of Brookings' bridge, take South Bank Road inland 5 miles, fork right onto gravel Mt. Emily Road, and follow "Bombsite Trail" signs for 13 twisty, uphill miles to the trailhead sign.

Parking is easiest at a pullout 0.2 mile before the trailhead. The trail winds through a surprisingly varied forest where rhododendrons and tanoaks mingle with pines, 6-foot-thick Douglas firs, and redwoods up to 12 feet in diameter. The path ends at the bomb site's display board and Fujita's courageous seedling.

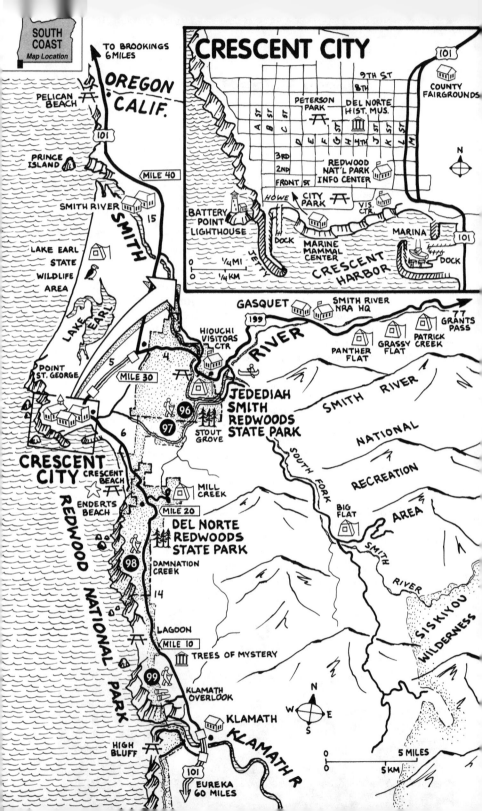

The Battery Point Lighthouse in Crescent City.

CRESCENT CITY

Behind the beaches of California's redwood coast, 15-foot-thick trunks vanish upward into the fog, like ancient pillars mooring the clouds to the rugged shore.

Redwood National Park

The area's most famous redwood preserve, Redwood National Park, hugs 50 miles of coastline south of Crescent City. Surprisingly, much of the park bears the scars of previous logging. The national park itself is only a couple decades old, purchased from timber companies in a wave of national outrage over the clearcutting of the 1960s. The best redwood groves are tucked away in California state parks set aside in the 1920s. Today these preserves are surrounded by the long, narrow national park like Christmas presents stuffed in a tube sock. Visit the National Park headquarters on 2nd Street in Crescent City for maps and information about all of the redwood coast's parks.

Jedediah Smith Redwoods State Park

If you're arriving from Interstate 5 via Grants Pass, a good first stop in redwood country is the Hiouchi Visitors Center on Highway 199, east of Crescent City 9 miles. This information center offers displays, books, and rangers with advice. The rangers usually advise that you visit the Stout Grove, a 44-acre stand of behemoth redwoods beside the Smith River (see Hike #96). From June through September (river levels permitting), a temporary plank footbridge spans the green Smith River to connect the grove with the park's popular, 107-site campground on Highway 199. Campsite reservations are strongly recommended between May 21 and September 5, and can be placed up to 8 weeks in advance by calling MISTIX at 1-800-444-PARK.

Del Norte Coast Redwoods State Park

This large state park covers the rugged, foggy coast south of Crescent City. The park's 145-site Mill Creek Campground is 3 miles inland in a second-growth redwood forest. For reservations, call 1-800-444-PARK. In summer, you're only likely to find unreserved sites available if you arrive before noon.

Battery Point Lighthouse

Hit hard by the double whammy of logging cutbacks and declining fish runs, Crescent City is now marked by empty storefronts. But don't pass by this rustic harbor town. Turn off Highway 101 at a "Visitors Info" pointer near the south end of town and drive the length of Front Street to a viewpoint of Battery Point Lighthouse. The tower is on an island a hundred yards offshore, but you can walk out to it when the tide is low. A museum inside is open Wed-Sun 10-4, tide permitting. Also at the end of Front Street are an explorable jetty and dock.

Del Norte County Museum

This Crescent City museum at 6th and H streets features a 5000-pound lighthouse lens and displays of pioneer, Tolowa, and Yurok artifacts. It's open 10-4 Mon-Fri from May through September.

Marine Mammal Rehabilitation Center

Volunteers nurse injured seals and seal lions back to health at this center on Crescent City's waterfront. Beside a city park on Front Street, the center is free and open to the public. Feeding times are most fun. Call (707) 465-MAML for hours or to report marine mammals in distress. The center warns visitors not to approach seal pups found on the beach, because they are most likely resting while mother hunts for food, and human contact could scare the mother away.

Crescent City harbor

Crescent City's waterfront, at the southern edge of town, was nearly demolished by a 1964 storm, but has been rebuilt with a Citizens Dock, a boat ramp, and a commercial harbor full of fishing and charter boats.

Smith River National Recreation Area

California's largest undammed river churns through the forested canyonlands of this remote recreation area. A historic 1930s ranger station in Gasquet houses a visitor center. Kayaks, canoes, and rafts can run 3 of the wild river's forks. The most popular hiking trails climb to the alpine meadows of the Siskiyou Wilderness. The area's 4 campgrounds are less expensive, smaller, and less developed than those in the redwood state parks to the west.

Lake Earl State Wildlife Area

Grassy dunes and marshy lakes south of the Smith River's mouth are protected for wildlife habitat in this new California state park. Fees for a primitive, walk-in campground among the overgrown dunes can be paid at Jedediah Smith or Mill Creek campgrounds.

Crescent Beach

Just 2 miles south of Crescent City on Enderts Beach Road, a picnic area and national park interpretive center flank this popular beach. For the area's best tidepooling, drive another 2 miles to road's end and hike a steep 0.6-mile path down to Enderts Beach.

Coastal Trail

The Coastal Trail extends 44 miles through the redwood empire from Enderts Beach south to Orick. The Klamath River interrupts the trail, forcing long-distance hikers to detour inland on roads to the Highway 101 bridge. Elsewhere, much of the trail simply follows abandoned sections of Highway 101, and is used primarily by bicyclists. Hike #99 describes a scenic, unpaved portion of the path between Lagoon Picnic Area and the Klamath Overlook.

Trees of Mystery

Skip this tourist trap's pathetic nature trail loop, but don't miss the astonishing and absolutely free museum of Native American artifacts at the back of the gift shop—among the best exhibits of its kind on the West Coast. It's on Highway 101, south of Crescent City 16 miles.

Klamath River

This wild river's lower canyon is part of the Hoopa Valley Indian Reservation. Tribespeople here keep alive the culture of the once powerful Yuroks, who built plank houses and carved huge sea-going canoes out of redwoods. A nature loop trail at Lagoon Picnic Area describes the tribe's traditions (see Hike #99). For a sweeping view of the Klamath River's mouth, turn off Highway 101 north of Klamath 3 miles and take Requa Road to the Klamath Overlook. The town of Klamath was swept away by a 1964 flood, but has been rebuilt with RV parks and a dock for jet boat tours up the wild river.

The Smith River from the Hiouchi Trail (Hike #96).

96 Stout Grove

Easy
0.5-mile loop
No elevation gain

Moderate (via Hiouchi Trail)
4.1 miles round-trip
100 feet elevation gain

Towering above the green Smith River, the 44-acre Stout Grove was preserved by the Save-the-Redwoods League in 1929. Since then the grove has become the centerpiece of California's 9600-acre Jedediah Smith Redwoods State Park.

Both the park and the river are named for Jedediah Strong Smith, the legendary mountain man who led the first party of white men overland from St. Louis to California in 1826. Because California's Mexican government did not welcome Americans, his crew of fur trappers trekked north through the redwood country to the mouth of Oregon's Umpqua River. Native Americans killed 15 of the group there, but Smith and 3 others escaped to Fort Vancouver. Three years later, at age 33, Smith was killed by Comanches while riding to Santa Fe. By then the tales and journals of his exploits had left his name emblazoned across the West.

The redwoods here remain from Smith's day, but the trails are better. A good orientation point is the Hiouchi Visitors Center on Highway 199, east of Crescent City 9 miles (or south of Grants Pass 77 miles).

For the quickest route to Stout Grove, drive Highway 199 east from the visitors center 2.1 miles, turn right on South Fork Road for 0.5 mile to a T-junction, and turn right on a one-lane road that becomes gravel Howland Hill Road. After 1.5 miles you'll pass a pullout marked "Stout Grove Trail." The path that starts here follows the riverbank 0.5 mile before reaching the actual grove—a nice route,

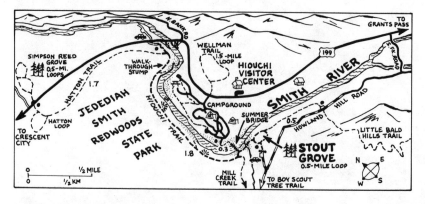

The Stout Grove.   Opposite: Summer footbridge over the Smith River.

but most hikers skip it. Instead drive another 0.8 mile along Howland Hill Road and turn right to a parking lot that's just a 150-yard walk from Stout Grove's half-mile-long loop trail. Part way around the loop look for a fork that leads down 100 yards to a gravelly beach beside the Smith River. In July and August, temporary plank footbridges cross Mill Creek and the river to site #55 of the popular campground on the far shore.

For a more substantial hiking route to Stout Grove, try the Hiouchi Trail. From the Hiouchi Visitors Center, drive Highway 199 west a mile to the far end of the Smith River Bridge, beside milepost 4.20. A post here marks the Hiouchi Trail, which follows the Smith River bank through a mixed forest of redwoods, Douglas fir, hemlock, and tanoak. Watch out for poison oak, growing both as a triple-leafletted bush and as a vine on tree trunks. The trail ducks through a 14-foot-thick redwood stump and passes viewpoints of river rapids. Just before reaching Mill Creek, take a left-hand spur to a river beach. Then cross the beach's temporary footbridge across Mill Creek to the Stout Grove loop trail. When the bridge is removed in winter, cross Mill Creek at an easy, knee-deep ford.

Other Hiking Options

Jedediah Smith State Park has 5 other short loop trails through redwood groves. The most popular are the 2 connected half-mile loops through the Simpson Reed and Peterson groves, at milepost 2.9 of Highway 199. Across the road is the 0.2-mile Hatton Loop—a possible beginning point for a longer trek to Stout Grove. The 1.5-mile Wellman Trail loops over a ridge opposite the campground entrance. Finally, an 0.6-mile self-guided nature loop begins at the campground's picnic area.

97   Boy Scout Tree

Moderate (to Boy Scout Tree)
4.8 miles round-trip
500 feet elevation gain

Moderate (to Fern Falls)
5.8 miles round-trip
600 feet elevation gain

While crowds throng to the big redwoods in Stout Grove (Hike #96), few hikers discover the even larger trees in this rainforest just a few miles away. A well-graded trail leads 2.4 miles to the 20-foot-thick Boy Scout Tree. An extra half mile walk takes you to lacy little Fern Falls.

From the Hiouchi Visitors Center (9 miles east of Crescent City or 77 miles south of Grants Pass), take Highway 199 east 2.1 miles, turn right on South Fork Road for 0.5 mile to a T-junction, and turn right on a road that eventually becomes gravel Howland Hill Road. Follow this narrow road 2.3 miles to the Stout Grove turnoff and continue straight another 2.2 miles to a small, railed pullout on the right for the Boy Scout Tree Trail.

The path sets off through a great, ferny rainforest where redwoods tower above delicate white spring wildflowers—stalks of wild lily-of-the-valley, shamrock-leaved oxalis, and big, triple-leaved trillium. Next the trail climbs a broad ridge amidst 2 kinds of tall huckleberry bushes. Evergreen huckleberry

The Boy Scout Tree.   *Opposite: Redwood needles and cone.*

plants have pointy, serrated leaves, while red huckleberries have tiny round leaves. After cresting a broad pass and traversing down through more redwood groves, you'll reach a junction at the 2.4-mile mark. To the right, a spur switchbacks up 100 yards to the colossal Boy Scout Tree. To the left, the trail continues 0.5 mile through Jordan Creek's mossy jungle of alder, maple, and Sitka spruce to Fern Fall's modest, 20-foot fan.

Other Hiking Options

For an easy 1.9-mile loop from the same trailhead, walk 0.2 mile west on Howland Hill Road to a very small pullout for the Nickerson Ranch Trail. Take this path through redwoods 0.6 mile, turn left on the lovely Mill Creek Trail 0.8 mile, and walk left on Howland Hill Road to your car to complete the loop.

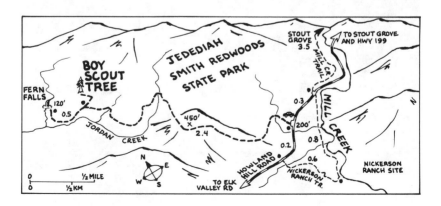

98 Damnation Creek

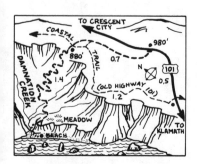

Moderate
4.2 miles round-trip
1000 feet elevation gain

Massive redwoods line the trail down to the rocky beach at the mouth of Damnation Creek. The beach is in a wonderfully remote cove. Cliffs rise from the sea on either hand. Cormorants pose on white-stained rocks offshore. Green sea anemones line seaweedy tidepools. The only damnable part of the hike is that you have to gain a thousand feet of elevation to get back to your car.

To find the trailhead, drive 10 miles south of Crescent City into Del Norte Coast Redwoods State Park. Stop at a small, obscure pullout at the 16.0 mile marker of Highway 101. From the trailhead sign, take a wide path up to the right through a grand redwood forest. Among the big trees, look for white trilliums in April, pink rhododendrons in May, and blue evergreen huckleberries in August.

Footbridge on the Damnation Creek Trail.

Beach at the mouth of Damnation Creek.

After 0.7 mile the path crosses the Coastal Trail, an abandoned stretch of old Highway 101 now used primarily as a paved bike route. This junction is a good turnaround point for hikers with children, because the Damnation Creek Trail now narrows and dives downhill in a series of switchbacks. Along the way the forest shifts from redwoods to Sitka spruce and Douglas fir, with decorative thimbleberry bushes and maidenhair ferns. Finally the path crosses 2 side creeks on massive footbridges and enters a beachfront meadow. In summer this brushy garden blooms with big white cow parsnip, feathery white yarrow, purple iris, and a host of other coastal wildflowers.

If you continue straight, you'll cross an arch to a cliff-edge overlook of the beach. If you veer right in the meadow you'll find a scrambly path that descends across the driftwood of the creek's mouth to the beach itself. Normally the bouldery beach extends about 300 yards in either direction, but it disappears altogether ar very high tides. Low tides reveal pools with sea anemones and black turban snails. On the horizon to the north are Sister Rocks and the cliffs of Midway Point. To the south are the onshore Footsteps Rocks and distant False Klamath Rock.

99   Hidden Beach

Easy (to Hidden Beach)
2.4-mile loop
100 feet elevation gain

Moderate (shuttle to Klamath Overlook)
4.1 miles one-way
700 feet elevation gain

The prettiest part of Redwood National Park's 44-mile Coastal Trail has no redwoods at all. Instead it traverses meadowed headlands and windswept Sitka spruce forests overlooking a dramatic, island-dotted shore. For an easy walk amidst this scenery, make your goal Hidden Beach, a sandy cove with a ship-sized rock anchored in the surf. For a longer, one-way hike, shuttle a car ahead to the trail's end and walk to a viewpoint above the Klamath River's mouth.

Start by driving Highway 101 to the Lagoon Creek Picnic Area at milepost 11.70, south of Crescent City 14 miles. Park at the far right-hand end of the picnic area. The trail that begins here skirts a lagoon full of yellow pond lilies. This long slough is actually an old Klamath River channel, abandoned when the river found a shortcut through the sea cliffs 4 miles to the south. False Klamath Rock, a landmark island offshore, won its name because early sailors were sometimes fooled by this old, silted-up river entrance.

After 100 yards turn left on the Coastal Trail and cross a footbridge to the start of the Yurok Loop nature trail. A box here has trail brochures describing the culture of the local Native Americans—whose tribe still flourishes along the lower Klamath River. Using the trunks of fallen redwoods, the Yuroks built plank houses and carved huge sea-going canoes that made them one of California's most powerful tribes. They sailed to offshore rocks to hunt mussels and sea lions. They called False Klamath Rock *olrgr* ("digging place") because of the edible brodiaea wildflower bulbs there. A smaller rock near shore was known as *prgris-o-tsiguk*, "where bald eagle rests."

Following Coastal Trail pointers, traverse a meadow with views up and down the coast. Small white yarrow, big white cow parsnip, and daisy-like wild chrysanthemum bloom amongst the bracken ferns. After 0.6 mile the trail forks. To the left is the return route for the Yurok Loop, but don't take it yet. Instead veer right for another 0.6 mile on the Coastal Trail and take a right-hand spur to Hidden Beach. This secluded, sandy, quarter-mile-long cove is perfect for a picnic. If you've brought kids, they'll find plenty of driftwood and boulders to climb around on. Low tide exposes marine life among the rocks.

For an easy hike, return from Hidden Beach 0.6 mile and turn right to complete the Yurok Loop back to your car. If you'd prefer a longer hike, continue south on the Coastal Trail past Hidden Beach. This route climbs along bluffs above the

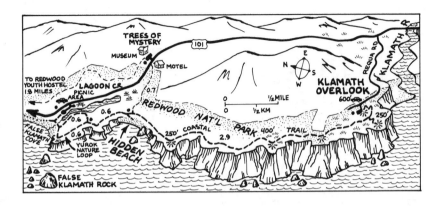

rocky shore, passing increasingly dramatic viewpoints. Beyond Hidden Beach 2.7 miles, a spur to the right descends 0.1 mile through steep meadows to a cliff-edge viewpoint above the 3 sea stacks guarding the Klamath River's mouth. The main trail switchbacks up 0.2 mile to its end at a parking lot with a similarly dramatic view. To shuttle a car to this trailhead, drive Highway 101 south of Lagoon Creek Picnic Area 3.7 miles to a Klamath Overlook pointer and turn right on Requa Road for 2.4 miles.

Hidden Beach from the Coastal Trail.   Opposite: Pond lilies in lagoon.

Burls on redwood trunk along Miners Ridge Trail (Hike #100).

REDWOODS

The world's tallest trees grow in this portion of the redwood coast. A network of trails and roads helps visitors explore the parklands. Elk and bear are common.

Redwood National Park
Discovery of the world's tallest trees in a bend of Redwood Creek in the 1960s led to the creation of this national park. By that time, nearly all old-growth redwoods outside of state parks had already been logged. To protect the remaining tall trees, most of Redwood Creek's valley was added to the park, logging roads were painstakingly removed, and eroding slopes were replanted. Note that pets are banned on national park trails.

Redwood Information Center
If you're coming from the south, make this visitor center on Highway 101 near Orick your first stop. In addition to maps, exhibits, and advice, the center features a nature trail boardwalk through coastal wetlands.

Tall Trees Grove
Only hikers can visit this grove to see the world's tallest tree (367.8 feet) and the third and fifth runners-up. A moderate, 1.3-mile trail to the big trees starts at the end of a 7-mile gravel spur off paved Bald Hills Road. A free permit,

available at the Redwood Information Center near Orick, is required to take a private car on the trailhead road. Only 35 permits are issued each day, starting at 9am. The permits are usually gone by 10am. Spots on the national park's 7-person shuttle bus to the trailhead are snapped up even quicker.

Redwood Creek Trail

A more rugged hiking route to the Tall Trees Grove follows the 8.2-mile Redwood Creek Trail. To find the trailhead, drive Highway 101 north of Orick a mile, turn right on the Bald Hills Road for 0.5 mile, and turn right for 0.5 mile. In summer, 2 temporary footbridges across Redwood Creek make the trip an easy backpack, but in other seasons the route is all but blocked by dangerous creek fords.

Lady Bird Johnson Grove

The paved Bald Hills Road from Orick climbs to this ridgetop grove of big redwoods, with a picnic area and a 1.3-mile loop trail. Lady Bird Johnson used her position as first lady to press for creation of Redwood National Park. She dedicated the park here in 1968.

Prairie Creek Redwoods State Park

Surrounded by the national park and bypassed by Highway 101's new freeway, this state park has the best redwood forests, the most hiking trails, and the only developed public campgrounds in the area. When driving north from Orick (or south from Klamath), be sure to take the Drury Scenic Parkway, a lovely portion of old Highway 101 through the state park's redwoods. The parkway crosses Elk Prairie, a meadow that usually does have a herd of genuine Roosevelt elk. Pullouts north of Elk Prairie allow travelers to see the Corkscrew Tree and Big Tree, a 307-foot giant circled by easy walking paths.

Elk Prairie Campground

In Prairie Creek Redwoods State Park 6 miles north of Orick, this mile-long meadow is bordered by a visitor center, a picnic area, and a 75-site campground. Campsite reservations, critical in summer, can be placed up to 8 weeks in advance through MISTIX (1-800-444-PARK). Stop at the visitor center here to see the displays, get free advice, and pick up a 25¢ map to the park's trails— many of which begin at the center's front door (see Hike #100).

Coastal Drive

Redwoods, viewpoints, and a World War II radar station camouflaged as a farmhouse highlight this 8-mile loop road from the northern end of the Elk Prairie Parkway to Highway 101 at the Klamath River. Portions are unpaved.

Gold Bluffs Beach

Prospectors flocked to this remote beach in 1851 when grains of gold were discovered in the sand. Today, elk, redwoods, and the quiet beach are the big draws. Prairie Creek Redwoods State Park provides a 25-site campground in the beachside grass here; reservations aren't taken. Drive 3 miles north of Orick on Highway 101 and turn left on Davison Road (trailers prohibited). Beyond the campground, the road ends at Fern Canyon Picnic Area, beside a misty grotto where Home Creek winds between green cliffs (see Hike #100).

Humboldt Lagoons

The long beach south of Orick has dammed 3 large lagoons. These lakes fill with rainwater and spill across the narrow beach several times each year. Redwood National Park allows primitive camping along the beach of the northernmost lake, Freshwater Lagoon. The best canoeing is in Stone Lagoon, within Humboldt Lagoons State Park, Six primitive campsites on Stone Lagoon's southwest shore are accessible only by boat. A county park at the south end of Big Lagoon has a boat ramp, beach access, and a 26-site campground.

Patricks Point State Park

The popular park on this headland features a 124-site campground, a reconstructed Native American village of Yurok redwood plank houses, a blufftop picnic area, 3 areas of tidepools, and an agate-strewn beach.

Roosevelt elk at Gold Bluffs Beach.

100 Prairie Creek Redwoods 🥾 🏕️ 🌲

Easy (around Elk Prairie)
3-mile loop
No feet elevation gain

Moderate (to Clintonia Trail)
6.2-mile loop
500 feet elevation gain

Difficult (to Fern Canyon)
10.9-mile loop
800 feet elevation gain

These loops through California's Prairie Creek Redwoods State Park explore some of the grandest remaining redwood forests. The easiest route circles a meadow where you're almost certain to see elk. The moderate loop follows trails blazed by gold rush miners. The longest loop continues to the ocean beach and Fern Canyon, a jungly grotto walled by cliffs.

All 3 hikes begin at the Elk Prairie Visitor Center. To find it, drive Highway 101 to the Drury Scenic Parkway. If you're coming from the south, the turnoff is 5 miles past Orick (or 46 miles north of Eureka). If you're coming from the north, the turnoff is 5 miles past Klamath (or 25 miles south of Crescent City). Take the parkway to milepost 127, turn west at the Elk Prairie entrance booth (a day-use fee is charged), and park at the visitor center.

First go into the visitor center to pick up a topographic trail map for a 25¢ donation. Then walk across the parking lot to a big signboard marking the trail. Dogs and bicycles are banned. The path crosses Prairie Creek on an 80-foot bridge and promptly launches into a forest of 15-foot-thick redwoods. Some trunks have been hollowed by fire; one such cavern was equipped with a ceiling and door by a homeless family in the 1930s. Growing in the shade of the redwood giants are sword ferns, shamrock-leaved oxalis, and huckleberries.

If you're interested in the short, 3-mile loop (a nice trip with kids), keep left

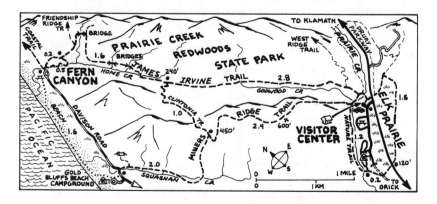

Fallen redwood across the Miners Ridge Trail.   Opposite: Bridge on James Irvine Trail.

at all junctions for 1.2 miles, following Nature Trail pointers to bridge at post #24. Straight ahead is a shortcut back through the campground, but for the 3-mile loop, turn right on the Elk Prairie Trail across a field where Roosevelt elk often graze. Don't approach these antlered, half-ton animals. The path crosses the paved road and skirts the prairie through redwoods for another mile. Then turn left at a T-junction to return to your car.

For the longer loops, start out the same but only follow the Nature Trail 0.2 mile from the visitor center. At post #6, turn right onto the James Irvine Trail. Follow this wide path up a valley where skunk cabbage bloom yellow in spring.

Thousands of men stormed over this trail in the spring of 1851 to build a boomtown tent city at the mouth of Home Creek, where 5 wandering prospectors had discovered gold the previous fall. The bonanza faded when miners realized the gold dust was so powdery it could only be separated from the beach's fine sand with expensive machinery.

If you're wearing down by the 2.8-mile mark, return to your car on a moderate loop by turning left on the small, uphill Clintonia Trail for a mile and then turning left on the Miners Ridge Trail back to the Nature Trail.

If you have energy for the longer loop, however, continue straight on the James Irvine Trail another 1.6 miles, crossing 4 creeks on footbridges. Then turn left at a Fern Canyon Trail pointer and descend into this charming grotto. The path hops Home Creek half a dozen times before the gorge suddenly opens onto a beachside picnic area. Walk left along the gravel entrance road 100 yards, head cross-country through grass to the beach, and stroll along the ocean.

After 1.2 miles, angle inland toward the tents of Gold Bluff Beach Campground. Cross the campground to the main gravel road and walk briefly left to a gated road on the right marked "Miners Ridge Trail." This route soon becomes a path, climbs a ridge, and follows the crest through magnificent redwood groves to the Nature Trail. Then turn left to complete the loop.

All-Accessible Trails of the Oregon Coast & Coast Range

People with limited physical abilities need not miss the fun of exploring new trails. Here are 42 paths accessible to everyone. If you're in a wheelchair, remember to bring binoculars—a handy way to get close-up views of tidepools, waves, wildflowers, and wildlife. The Coast also has 21 public campgrounds that offer one or more all-accessible campsites. Most campgrounds in coastal state parks have accessible yurts, restrooms, and campsites with paved or brick surfaces, extended picnic tables, and elevated fire rings. Before setting out for a state park, call 800-452-5687 to check site availability or to place reservations.

NORTH COAST & Coast Range

101. North Head Lighthouse. Gravel 0.3-mi path to lighthouse in blufftop meadow. See Hike #2.

102. Lewis & Clark Interpretive Center. Explore an artillery bunker along the 300-yd tr to this accessible museum and coast vista (see Hike #3).

103. Fort Stevens Park. The entire bicycle path network described in Hike #5 is barrier-free. So are 6 campsites and a 100-yd tr to a birdwatching blind from Clatsop Spit's parking lot D (Hike #4).

104. Fort Clatsop National Memorial. Visit a replica of Lewis and Clark's fort on 0.3 mi of trails at this barrier-free museum (see p 23).

105. Seaside Promenade. This concrete, 1.6-mi beachfront promenade (Hike #6) ends at an all-accessible restroom at 12th St.

106. Ecola Park. Viewpoints on the paved 0.2-mi picnic area paths around the rim of Ecola Point are perfect for photography (see Hike #7).

107. Banks-Vernonia Railroad. The 1.5-mi and 5.3-mi segments of this abandoned railroad grade described in Hike #12 are all-accessible, but challenging.

108. Nehalem Bay Park. Traverse woods, grassy dunes, and bayshore on this park's paved, 1.5-mi bike path loop. A boat dock and 3 campsites are also barrier-free (see Hike #15).

109. Cape Meares Lighthouse. Paved 0.4-mi loop passes dramatic viewpoints of ocean cliffs and lighthouse (see Hike #17).

110. Hagg Lake. Motorized elevator descends from end of paved, 100-yd tr to floating fishing dock at W end of Hagg Lake's dam. Also, the lakeshore tr from Boat Ramp A is paved 100 yds to a viewpoint (see Hike #20).

111. Cape Lookout Park. From day-use parking area, go S on 0.4-mi Nature Tr loop, or go N on 0.2-mi loop through wooded picnic area beside beach (see Hike #22). The park has 2 all-accessible campsites nearby.

112. Hebo Lake. Gravel and boardwalk 0.5-mi loop around shallow lake passes 4 fishing docks and an all-accessible campsite (see Hike #25).

CENTRAL COAST & Coast Range

113. Drift Creek Falls. The packed gravel, 1.5-mi tr to this waterfall will open when bridge at end is built, perhaps by June, 1995 (Hike #34).

114. Yaquina Head Tidepools. Dramatic cove of tidepools (a converted sea-level quarry) is accessed by 0.6 mi of wheelchair-friendly concrete paths (see Hike #37 map).

115. Oregon Coast Aquarium. Completely accessible Newport museum has trails through outdoor bird, seal, otter exhibits (see p 89).

116. Yaquina Bay Estuary. Signs describe estuarine ecology along 0.7-mi paved bayfront path from Hatfield Marine Sci Ctr (see Hike #38).

117. Ona Beach Park. Paved 0.3-mi loop circles picnic lawns, forest to 180-ft footbridge (see Hike #39).

118. Marys Peak. Park at Observation Pt and go around gate to reach graveled 0.6-mi tr to peak's summit (Hike #42). Nearby 6-site campground is also accessible.

119. Finley Wildlife Refuge. Gravel 1.2-mi Woodpecker Loop to viewpt platform on oak knoll is open all year, but 2.9-mi Mill Hill Loop is only accessible in dry weather (Hike #44).

120. Yachats. Dramatic gravel path along scenic lava shore from Smelt Sands Wayside is accessible for 0.7 mi, almost to beach (Hike #46).

121. Cape Perpetua. Start at all-accessible visitor center, take paved 0.8-mi loop to tidepools and Cooks Chasm. 1-mi gravel path to Giant Spruce also has no barriers (Hike #47).

122. Holman Vista. 200-ft path to viewpt deck overlooks Sutton Cr, coastal dunes. (see Hike #52).

123. Darlingtonia Wayside. 100-yd boardwalk from forested picnic area leads to bog with insect-eating pitcher plants (see p 123).

124. Coast Horse Trails. Trail network through Cape Mountain's forests is designed to let disabled equestrians park, mount, and ride. Wheelchairs can't use trails, but

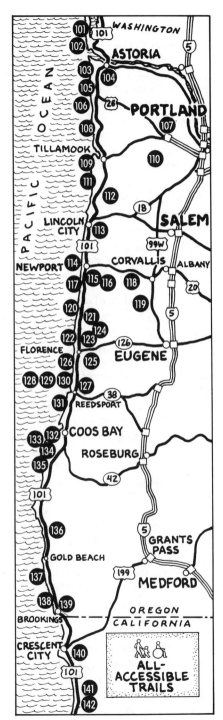

Horse Cr Trailhead has accessible campsites (Hike #53).

125. Sweet Creek Falls. Packed gravel makes the first 200 yds of Hike #58 accessible–a woodsy route from Homestead Trailhead to Split Falls.

126. Honeyman Park. From the Sand Dunes Picnic Area, either take a 0.4-mi paved loop around Lily Lake (partly on a road, or a beautiful, paved path along Cleawox Lake's shore 0.6 mi (see Hike #59).

127. Umpqua Discovery Center. All-accessible interpretive center features 200-yd boardwalk along Reedsport's riverfront docks (see p 137).

128. Taylor Lake Dunes. Packed gravel tr leads through rhodies, woods 0.1 mi to lakeside deck, then climbs 0.4 to dunes overlook platform (see Hike #62).

129. Oregon Dunes Overlook. 50-yard boardwalk ramp to viewpoint of coastal dunes (see Hike #63). Volunteer naturalist on hand daily 10-3 in summer.

130. Tahkenitch Creek. First 200 yards of Hike #64 is accessible, packed gravel tr to scenic 80-foot bridge over lazy coastal creek.

131. Lake Marie. Park at Umpqua Lighthouse State Park's picnic beach, take paved tr to left along shore 0.3 mi. Remainder of 1-mi loop around lake is challenging (Hike #66).

SOUTH COAST & Klamaths

132. Empire Lakes Park. Coos Bay city park off Newmark St has 1.2 miles of gravel and paved paths along forested lakeshores (see p 153).

133. Shore Acres Park. Waves crash onto scenic, tilted cliffs below this park's observation bldg. Paved tr follows cliff rim 0.3 mi (see Hike #70). Don't miss gravel paths in adjacent formal gardens with azaleas, roses.

134. South Slough Estuary. Stop at this nature reserve's interesting interp ctr, get key to gate, drive 0.6 mi to disabled parking, take woodsy 1.3-mi loop tr to shore of Coos Bay estuary (see Hike #70).

135. Bullards Beach Park. 1.3-mi paved bike path from campground fee booth crosses picnic areas, forest, to parking area at beach's foredune (Hike #73). Park has 2 accessible campsites nearby.

136. Humbug Mountain Park. Old piece of Hwy 101 forms 2.6-mi segment of Oregon Coast Tr from campground fee booth through coastal woods to ocean viewpoint (see Hike #78 map). Nearby are 2 accessible campsites.

137. Cape Sebastian. First 300 yards of Hike #88 are paved, through mdw to sweeping coastal viewpoint.

138. Boardman Park. Stop at Arch Cape for 0.2-mi paved viewpoint tr around picnic area, then drive south 1.2 mi to Natural Bridges Cove Viewpoint for a 100-ft tr to overlook of sea caves (see Hike #89).

139. Azalea Park. Wild azaleas bloom in May along level pathways of this forested Brookings park (see p 198).

140. Stout Grove. Unpaved but well-packed 0.5-mi loop tours Jedediah Smith State Park's grandest redwood grove (Hike #96).

141. Lost Man Creek. Redwoods line a road-cum-trail along this cr, 3 mi N of Orick (see map, p 222). Wheelchair-accessible for 1 mi to 3rd bridge.

142. Lady Bird Johnson Grove. Famous ridgetop redwood grove with all-accessible 1.3-mi loop tr, picnic area (see p 224).

More Hikes of the Oregon Coast & Coast Range

Adventurous hikers can explore lots of additional paths in Oregon's coastal country. Many of the trails listed below are rough or unmarked, and descriptions are brief, so be sure to bring appropriate maps. Unless noted, mileages given are one-way, not round-trip. For more information, check with the trail's administrative agency, abbreviated (A)–Alsea Ranger Dist, (AS)–Audubon Soc, (CS)–California State Parks, (C)–Chetco Ranger Dist, (F)–Finley Wildlife Refuge, (M)–Mapleton Ranger Dist, (OF)–Oregon Dept of Forestry, (OD)–Oregon Dunes Nat'l Rec Area, (OS)–Oregon State Parks, (OSU)–OSU Research Forest, (P)–Powers Ranger Dist, (R)–Redwood Nat'l Park, (W)–Waldport Ranger Dist, (WR)–Willapa Wildlife Refuge. Phone numbers for agencies are on page 13.

NORTH COAST & Coast Range

143. Long Island Cedar Grove. 0.8-mi loop amid old-growth cedar rainforest on island in Willapa Bay (map, p 14). From Willapa Refuge HQ (12 mi N of Ilwaco on Hwy 101) paddle a boat to island, walk rd 2.5 mi to tr. (WR)

144. Scarboro Hill. Start at museum in Washington's Fort Columbia State Park (see p 16), climb 0.5-mi tr uphill through rhododendrons (bloom April) to views across Columbia R to Astoria, Saddle Mtn. Gain 600 ft. (Washinton SP)

145. Columbian White-Tailed Deer Refuge. Once thought extinct, deer species survives in only 4 locations, including diked Columbia riverbank fields, marshes. Drive 2 mi W of Cathlamet, Washington (or 29 mi W of Longview) on Hwy 4, turn L on Steamboat Slough Rd 0.3 mi, park on R just beyond refuge HQ. Walk gated Center Rd 2.8 mi (expect swans, geese, ducks), turn L for 3.3 mi on Steamboat Slough Rd along Columbia R dike to return to car. (WR)

146. Wilson River Wagon Route. Mostly supplanted by a logging rd, this 1893 route is hikable (or bikable) for 6 mi from Hwy 6 at the Elk Cr CG turnoff (see Hike #18) along S Fk Rd to University Falls tr jct (see Hike #19). (OF)

147. Hebo Plantation Trail. 0.7-mi loop through Doug fir woods replanted in 1912. Drive as to Mt. Hebo (Hike #25), but stop at hiker-symbol sign 0.9 mi before Hebo L. (Hebo Ranger Dist)

CENTRAL COAST & Coast Range

148. Calloway Creek. New nature tr near Corvallis loops 3.3 mi through experimental Doug fir plantations, crosses cr (see Hike #43 map). Drive into Peavy Arboretum, keep R for 0.2 mi to Additional Parking lot. Start on Intensive Management Tr, keep L. (OSU)

149. McDonald Forest Old Growth. Drive 4 mi N of Corvallis on Hwy 99W, turn L on Lewisburg Ave 1.5 mi, turn R on Sulphur Spgs Rd 1.5 mi to Lewisburg Saddle. Hike gated Rd 580 on right for 0.3 mi, turn L onto 0.5-mi Old Growth Tr loop, turn R on Rd 580 for 0.8 mi to return to car. (OSU)

150. Dan's Trail to Dimple Hill. Near Corvallis, 2.5-mi tr crosses fields, follows Jackson Cr, climbs through woods to view of Willamette Valley, Cascades, Marys Pk. Drive 2 mi N of Corvallis on 10th St (which becomes Highland Dr), turn L on Lester Ave 0.8 mi to its end at Chip Ross Park. Walk old farm rd 0.5 to McDonald Forest, continue 2 mi on tr to logging rd at summit. (OSU)

151. McCullough Peak. Hike 4.2 mi on mtn bike trails, gated rds through McDonald Forest to vista. Drive 5 mi W of Corvallis on Harrison Blvd (which becomes Oak Cr Dr) to gate blocking the rd. Hike L on Homestead Tr 0.4 mi, keep R on log rds 0.7 mi, jog L 100 ft on Rd 6020, continue uphill on Extendo Tr 1 mi, turn left on Rd 680, and keep left at all rd jcts (except avoid Rd 770) for 2.1 mi to find summit viewpt at end of Rd 1790. (OSU)

152. Alsea River Run. Rough 1-mi riverbank tr through maples, blackberries. Drive Hwy 34 E of Waldport 17 mi (or W of Corvallis 47 mi), cross river at Mike Bauer boat ramp, keep L for 1.5 mi to parking lot at switchback. (A)

153. Cabell Marsh. Just E of Finley Wildlife Refuge HQ (see Hike #44) walk gated rd 0.8 mi along diked marsh. Turn L along 0.8-mi Muddy Cr Tr for return loop. Or turn R for 2.1 mi to Pigeon Bu. Only open 5/1-10/31. (F)

154. Pigeon Butte. Grassy oak knoll with Willamette Valley views is 1.7 mi up gated old rds. Drive Hwy 99W to milepost 96 (S of Corvallis 13 mi), turn W on Bruce Rd 1 mi to hiker symbol sign. Only open 5/1-10/31. (F)

155. Tenmile Creek Audubon Preserve. Explore homestead mdw, old-growth spruce in new preserve between coast wildernesses. Trails planned. Drive 19 mi N of Florence on Hwy 101, turn R 4 mi on Rd 56 (map, p 110). (AS)

156. Rock Creek. Rough 0.5-mi tr through coastal rainforest to creekside homestead mdw in Wilderness. Wade to continue upstream without tr. Start at far end of Rock Cr CG, 16 mi N of Florence off Hwy 101 (map, p 110). (W)

157. Alder Lake. 0.5-mi tr circles forest lake at N end of Alder Dune CG (see Hike #52). At S end of CG, sand slide descends into Dune Lake. (M)

158. Threemile Lake South. Woodsy 0.6-mi tr leads to fork: go left 0.2 mi to open dunes and campsite (0.5 mi from ocean), or go right 0.2 mi to beach at tip of long lake. Drive 4 mi N of Reedsport on Hwy 101, turn L on Sparrow Park Rd 3.4 mi to small sign on R (map, p 138). (OD)

159. Umpqua Spit. Circle spit on 13.1-mi loop. Drive 4 mi N of Reedsport on Hwy 101, turn L on Sparrow Park Rd 4 mi to its end, walk 100 yds to beach (vehicles allowed on beach), hike left 5.7 mi to Umpqua R jetty, continue L through grassy dunes along river 4.8 mi, cut L across spit 1.3 mi on dune buggy track, turn R along beach 1.3 mi to car. (OD)

160. Tenmile Creek Dunes. Secluded, scenic portion of Oregon Dunes (no vehicles), ideal for birdwatching. Park at Spinreel CG picnic area, N of Coos Bay 11 mi (see map p 152), wade across cr, follow cr 2.6 mi through dunes to beach. As always in dunes, avoid snowy plover habitat in driftwood zone. (OD)

161. Bluebill Lake. Forested 1-mi loop around lakeless meadow (good birding in spring) passes Bluebill CG, crosses boardwalks. Drive 1 mi N of Coos Bay's Hwy 101 bridge, turn L toward Horsfall Bch 2.7 mi. (OD)

SOUTH COAST & Klamaths

162. New River Beach. Oregon's most remote beach extends 8 mi from Fourmile Cr (unusual botany, birding) to Floras Lake SP (see Hike #75). Best access is by boat across lazy New River (see p 164). (Coos Bay BLM)

163. Humbug Mountain Coast Trail. Park at Humbug Mtn Park's day-use area near Hwy 101's milepost 308, take tr over footbridge, under hwy, and along

Brush Cr 1.2 mi to CG fee booth. Continue on paved, abandoned section of old Hwy 101 past ocean vistas 2.6 mi. See Hike #78. (OS)

164. Barklow Mountain. Hike 0.6 mi through woods to former lookout site; take 0.4-mi spur to collapsed shelter. From Powers, drive 11.5 mi S on Rd 33, turn R on gravel Rd 3353 for 11 mi, turn R on Rd 220 for 1.5 mi to its end. (P)

165. Johnson Creek Trail. Yellow iris, 7-ft-thick Doug fir line misnamed tr above Sucker Cr. From Powers, drive 11.5 mi S on Rd 33, turn R for 3.1 mi on Rd 3353, turn L on Rd 5591 for 1.4 mi. Tr promptly crosses creek (slippery 20-ft wade), then gains 1200 ft in 2.4 mi to abrupt end at spur 260 of Rd 3353. (P)

166. Azalea Lake. Wild azaleas bloom in May at brush-rimmed lake. Tr gains 640 ft in 0.8 mi, then circles lake 0.4 mi. Drive Rd 33 south of Powers 34.1 mi (or N of Agness bridge 15.3 mi), turn W on Rd 3347 past Rock Cr CG 1 mi. (P)

167. Game Lake. Tr from primitive CG at this remote lake climbs 500 ft in 0.8 mi to lookout site atop Game Lk Pk. From same trailhd, steep, rocky Tr #1174 descends 3500 ft in 6 mi to treacherous Illinois R ford at Collier Bar (see Hike #85). Drive 1 mi S of Gold Beach, turn L for 27.4 mi on Hunter Cr Rd (which becomes Rd 3680), veer R on Rd 400 for 5.5 mi. (Gold Beach Ranger Dist)

168. Chetco Gorge. Wade Chetco R (only possible in summer) to access easy 1.7-mi riverbank tr. From Brookings, take N Bank Rd (#1376) 16 mi to T-jct. Turn L for 0.6 mi, then turn L on Rd 170 to trailhd. (C)

169. Upper Chetco River. Tr #1102 crosses Kalmiopsis Wilderness 17.1 mi, scales rocky ridges, meets Chetco River 3 times. From Brookings take N Bank Rd (#1376) 16 mi to T-jct, follow signs 10 mi to Quail Prairie Lookout, continue 0.3 mi to tr. (C)

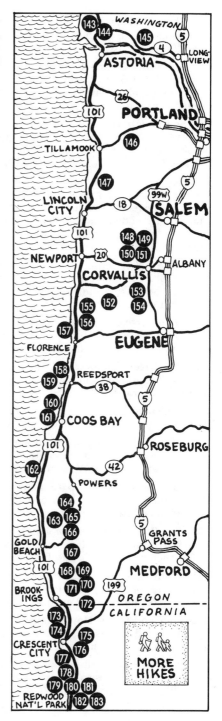

170. Chetco Divide. Park as for Vulcan Pk (Hike #94), follow rocky Tr #1210 along ridge 4.7 mi to brushy Chetco L, continue 2.3 mi to lookout site. Gains 1300 ft, loses 500. (C)   🏞❄

171. South Fork Chetco River. Start on Chetco Divide Tr (Hike #170) for 1.5 mi, turn R on Tr #1105 and descend either 2400 ft in 2.5 mi to Cottonwood Camp or 2700 ft in 3.2 mi to Navy Monument (1944 plane crash site). Both forks reach campsites near remote river. (C)   🏞❄

172. Sourdough Trail. Pitcher plants, odd Klamath flora line 3.9-mi tr from Packsaddle Mtn to bridgeless N Fk Smith River. Loses 1300 ft elevation. From Brookings, drive S for 5 mi on Hwy 101, turn L on Winchuck Rd 8 mi, turn R on gravel Rd 1107 for 10 mi, turn R on Rd 220 for 1 mi. (C)   🏞🌿

173. Yontocket. Explore Smith R Spit, remote beach, site of Indian village along closed roads through grassy dunes in Lake Earl State Wildlife Area. Drive Hwy 101 N of Crescent City 6 mi, turn L on Elk Valley Rd 1 mi, turn R on Lk Earl Dr 2 mi, turn L on Lower Lk Rd 6 mi, turn L on Pala Rd 1 mi to gate. Walk past gate 1 mi to village site. Turn R on old rds to Smith R (0.6 mi) and beach (0.8 mi). Mouth of Smith R is 2.5 mi beyond. (CS)   🏞🦅

174. Dead Lake. From Crescent City, take Hwy 101 N 1 mi, fork L onto Northcrest Dr 1.5 mi, turn L on Old Mill Rd 1.8 mi, turn L on Sand Hill Rd 0.6 mi to its end. Hike tr through overgrown dunes 0.3 mi to jct. Either turn L for 0.5 mi to Dead L or turn R for 0.8 to ocean beach. (CS)   🏞

175. Craigs Creek. Tr along S Fk Smith R leads 7.4 mi to mouth of Craigs Cr. Drive Hwy 199 E of Hiouchi 2 mi (or E of Crescent City 11 mi), turn R on S Fk Rd 0.4 mi. (Smith River Nat'l Rec Area, 707- 457-3131)   🌿🏞

176. Mill Creek Campground. In Del Norte Redwoods SP, trails loop 2 mi around CG through young redwoods, along creek. Hobbs Wall Tr climbs 2 mi from CG toward Hwy 101. (CS)   🏞

177. Footsteps Rock. Easy 0.5 mi path to vista at rock outcrop above beach. Park at Hwy 101 pullout, S of Crescent City 13 mi at milepost 13.42. (R)   🏞

178. Flint Ridge. Pretty 4.5-mi section of Coastal Tr amid redwoods crosses 900-ft ridge near Klamath R mouth. At S side of Hwy 101 Klamath R bridge, take Klamath Beach Rd W 1.7 mi to jct and trailhd. (R)   🌿🏞

179. Carruthers Cove. Steep 0.8-mi tr from Coastal Dr (see p 224) descends 500 ft to secluded beach with driftwood, dramatic cliffs. Beach to S is hikable at all but high tide; Fern Canyon is 4 mi (see Hike #100). (R, CS)   🏞☆

180. West Ridge. For 6.3-mi or 9-mi loop through redwood groves, start as for Hike #100 (Prairie Cr Redwoods), but after 0.3 mi turn R on W Ridge Tr, gaining 800 ft. Then turn R on Zig Zag Tr #1 or #2 and return via Prairie Cr Tr. (CS)   🌿

181. South Fork Loop. Expect big redwoods on 3.2-mi loop from pullout at milepost 129 of Drury Scenic Parkway. Hike S Fk Tr 0.8 mi (gaining 600 ft), turn L on Rhododendron Tr 1.2 mi, turn L on Brown Cr Tr for 1.2 mi to car. (CS)   🌿

182. Redwood Creek Horse Trails. Open to hikers, 34-mi horse tr network (mostly on old log rds) has 4 loops, extends to Tall Trees Grove. Park at rodeo grounds in Orick (see map, p 222). (R)   🐴🌿🏞

183. Dolason Prairie. All-yr hiking tr to Tall Trees Grove requires no permit and no creek fords, but loses 2800 ft in 7 mi. From Hwy 101 just N of Orick, drive Bald Hills Rd 11 mi (see p 222). Tr descends 4.7 mi to Emerald Ridge Tr. Turn R 1 mi to Tall Trees Tr, descend 1.3 mi to grove. (R)   🌿🏞

Index

Page numbers in *italics* refer to locations on Travel Guide maps.

William L. Sullivan (photo by Paul Neevel)

About the Author

William L. Sullivan is the author of 6 books and numerous articles about Oregon, including a regular outdoor column for *Eugene Weekly*. A fifth-generation Oregonian, he received his English degree at Cornell Univeristy, studied linguistics at Germany's Heidelberg University, and completed an M.A. at the Unviersity of Oregon.

In 1985 he set out to explore Oregon's wilderness on a 1,361-mile solo backpacking trek from the state's westernmost point at Cape Blanco to Oregon's easternmost point at the bottom of Hells Canyon. His journal of that 2-month adventure, published as *Listening for Coyote*, was a finalist for the Oregon Book Award in creative nonfiction in 1988 and topped the *New York Times'* year-end review of travel books.

Sullivan's love for the Oregon Coast dates to childhood explorations from a family beach cabin near Lincoln City. In 1977 he and his wife Janell Sorensen built a log cabin by hand on a remote, roadless stretch of the coastal Siletz River. Together with their children Karen and Ian, they spend summers at the Siletz log cabin and live in Eugene the remainder of each year.